SHARECROPPERS:
the way we really were

Fifth Printing

Printed in the United States

Published by J-Mark
203 North Cone Street
Wilson, N.C. 27893

Library of Congress Catalog Number 84-90379
ISBN 0-9613485-0-X

SHARECROPPERS:
the way we really were

By Roy G. Taylor

To Kay, Marshall,
Jason and Andy

Acknowledgments

Gratitude is expressed to the management and employees of the Wilson Daily Times for their cooperation in preparing these columns for publication.

To Phillip E. Fleming of the Public Relations Department of Carolina Power and Light Company for his efforts in helping to find suitable photographs at the N.C. Department of Archives and History and the University of North Carolina Library at Chapel Hill, and Duke Historic Site.

To Artist Horace Raper and his "Memories of Yesterday" who supplied some of his drawings for reproduction in the book, and a family picture with the mules loose in the yard. Raper is a citizen of Wilson County.

Shapiro Bernstein & Co., Inc. for use of the song lyrics "There'll Be Bluebirds Over the White Cliffs of Dover." Copyright 1941, Shapiro, Bernstein & Co. Inc. Used by permission.

Duke Homestead and Historic Site, Durham, N.C. for the photograph of Golden Grain Smoking Tobacco.

Geraldine Laudati, East Carolina University music librarian, for searching for songs during the World War II era.

The N.C. Department of Archives and History for several pictures in its collection.

Photographic Services Section, University of North Carolina at Chapel Hill.

The Library of Congress for pictures from its collection.

Connie Jernigan, Wilson County Agricultural Extension chairman, for photographs of picking cotton and tobacco on the Wilson market.

Ashley Boyette for the picture on making soap.

Pauline Lancaster for the picture of her father, Mr. Emmett.

Sarah Smith for the picture of her grandmother, Aunt Sene.

Emma Holmes for the picture of her mother, Miss Mag.

Emma Walton for the picture of Dr. Heck.

Jimmy Smith for picture of old barn.

Jimmy Ellis for picture of old house.

Esther Taylor, my sister-in-law, for several pictures from her family album.

Foreword

Take a piece of backer twine 10 miles long. Attach a piece of chalk at the end. Place the other end at Woods Grove Church, Saulston crossroads, or the spot where Hood Swamp School once stood in Wayne County, North Carolina. Draw a circle and you have the area about which I have written. It is of such a small radius it would hardly show on the map.

Remove the backer and cotton in some instances; take this minute area and place it in a thousand different places across rural America, and it would mirror the lifestyles of the general farm population 50 years ago.

Tobacco is King in eastern North Carolina. It is a way of life as well as the greatest source of income for farmers in the East. Its economic impact is so great for the entire state and adds so many million dollars to local, state and national treasuries it cannot be overlooked as a major contribution to the economic well-being of the populace. And we are in the heart of "tobacco country" and tobacco has been a way of life for the farmer for many, many years.

The "endearing" word we used to describe tobacco out in the sticks 50 years ago was "backer." If Scarlett O'Hara had used the word in "Gone With the Wind," she would no doubt have said "bacca." But for poor people who worked with the golden weed throughout the year, it was always "backer."

"SHARECROPPERS: the way we really were," is about a place and a time in our past. It is a part of our history that didn't make the history books. It is at eye level, close up, detailing the everyday lives of very poor people at a critical time in our past.

This is a true story, a recollection of events from yesterday that can never again be a part of rural life. Those days cannot be recreated or duplicated, for it is only memories of a time that holds no resemblance today of a land and a people almost forgotten by time.

"SHARECROPPERS" is a happy story, for it is viewed from the eyes of youth, with the tragic events and hardships forgotten, leaving a beauty and much nostalgia about a slower-paced, more closely-knit society.

The language used is the language we spoke. There has been no attempt to glorify that era or to change our customs to make us appear more favorable than we were. We were sharecroppers and proud to be a part of the life experience. We still take fierce pride in our heritage. We apologize to no one for who we are or how we were. If you were a sharecropper, a tenant farmer or a landowner in those days, it will be easy to identify with poor farmers of that era in eastern North Carolina.

Looking Backward 50 Years

Before radio. Before television. Before commercial airline service. Before antibiotics. Before World War II. Before the atomic bomb. Although it may be hard for many of the young to imagine, there was an America in those prehistoric days and people populated the earth and lived and died just as they have done in the modern age. But it was a different America then.

In writing about our world a half-century ago, it is like an old manuscript, yellowed with age and with fragmented edges that leave deciphering to the imagination. Some pages are missing, causing an abrupt end to a trend of thought. It could be compared to a foggy morning when the mist is so dense there is no visibility in some areas, while in others the sun shines through and brightens the skies.

A look back in time is only memories of events that transpired, some without any consequence even at the time they were a reality; some with a poignance that is indescribable; some tragic, some comical, some trivial, but all part of the human existence.

During these years of a nation-turned-modern-in-turmoil and with daily reminders of the Great Depression era, it might be well to reflect back on those days and take a look at our past in order to see how far we have come. This does not mean trying to analyze the cause-effect theory, but rather a look at how the poor classes, of which most all of us were a part, lived and survived.

As a matter of fact, the Great Depression had little impact on most rural dwellers, since we didn't have anything before the depression and we continued to have home-grown food, home-grown wood and homemade clothes. We had homemade lye soap, home-canned vegetables, fruits and preserves, home-grown peas and beans that were threshed in the fall and were a sizable part of our diet in winter. We had home-grown chickens and when guests came unexpectedly on Sunday, we ran down a hen and made enough chicken pastry to feed the family as well as "company."

The homemade clothes that we boys wore were BVDs made from flour sacks and overalls made from Smith-Douglass white fertilizer bags, boiled in lye water to tone down the bold black lettering of the brand name.

It was a live-at-home society in rural eastern North Carolina in those days. There were no supermarkets, although there were grocery stores like A&P and Pender's even then, but they were a far cry from today. There were no frozen foods, nor refrigerated foods as a matter of fact. Chickens and turkeys, geese and ducks were alive in pens at the stores and food products were displayed prominently outside the stores.

People who lived in area towns had a big edge over the rural community. They had electricity, inside bathrooms and toilets, paved streets and movie theaters although there wasn't sound with the films at first. There was a world of difference in city living and country living in the 1920s and 1930s in North Carolina. But by far the majority of us were out in the "sticks" and far removed from city living. That was before power and telephone lines dotted the rural countryside or before most highways were paved. That was rural America at its poorest.

It is also well to remember that in those days there was no welfare system as we have today. There was the County Home or "poor house" as it was called for those who became unable to work and had nobody to care for them, or when they had been thrown out by non-caring families. And "poor house" was the best way to describe the County Home. In other words, people made their own way and handouts were unheard of. What handouts? Everybody fought for his own survival. And we survived! We didn't starve if we did go cold in winter with our open fireplaces in one room and all the other rooms ice-cold.

By whatever name today's generation may refer to us — Clod-Hopper, Red-Neck, Hillbilly — remember that we are as proud of our heritage as other segments of society today. After all, we were the progenitors of the modern age and however humble may have been our past, we contributed our share to the affluent society of today. After our world changed and we entered an entirely new way of life, we ensured that our children would have the opportunities in life that we didn't even know about before the world became modern.

There will be no attempt to glamorize that era or to whitewash the society that I knew into something different than we actually were. To do that would present a fictitious picture of "poor folks" 50 or more years ago. To some the events about which I write will appear incredible, or actually untruthful. And there will be those who lived during the early part of the century whose lives were not touched to the extent most of we Tar Heels in the eastern region were, but even many of those can associate with their poor "country cousins."

Since beauty is in the eye of the beholder, many senior citizens today can reflect back on those days with nostalgia and see through the maze of years something so beautiful and simplistic about their childhood and youth the drabness of the setting becomes second-place to the beauty that prevailed about us. It all shines through as a brilliant star that helps to light my pathway even today. So I will write about how we were in that remote past.   □

A Typical Day In Tar Heelia

Rock music in stereophonic sound floods the room, interrupting a dream. The sleeper gathers the sheet close around him and quickly slumbers again. Fifteen minutes later a louder alarm awakens him and he rises from his air-conditioned comfort and takes a quick shower, turns the dial to get coffee boiling, puts toast in the toaster, reads the morning paper, dresses and dashes off for another busy day.

His $75,000 home is spacious, almost luxurious in its rural setting along the four-lane highway leading to the city. He will jet to Atlanta for a round of conferences and return home by early evening. His time and his thoughts are taken up with his business ventures. He lives the good life even with the hectic pace. Yet something is missing that he can't quite put his finger on. Life is just a little too fast-paced and when he is reminded of a time in our past when people lived a more simple lifestyle it is hard for him to understand, for he hasn't known that kind of world. That's a good example of today's young business executive.

Go back 50 years.

A rooster crows from a henhouse down the road and almost instantly the sound is like an echo as the crowing is heard all over the community. It is the dawn of another day in eastern North Carolina.

Feeble lights from kerosene lamps begin to appear in houses along the road as the women prepare breakfast for hungry, growing families. A screech owl gives his last call of the night from the woods across the way and a dog barks out in response.

The sun suddenly appears over the trees and the heavy dew sparkles like millions of diamonds. Morning glories in pink and purple stand out on the corn stalks and pea vines where they have grown and twisted as if they are a part of the plants. Corn is turning brown in the fields and tobacco patches, shorn of their leaves, stand bare except for their growth of suckers at the top as they get all the nurture possible from the stalks.

Cotton patches are beginning to turn white, although it is still too early to pick the lint. Most of the bolls must be open before the field hands go in to pluck the cotton from the burrs. Another week or two and cotton picking will begin in earnest.

Tobacco barns, where the activity centered during the curing season, now look forlorn and the bushes that were cut and placed over the looping shelter and racks to provide shade from the sun, are now brown and dried. Hard weeds are replacing the cleared area.

Children begin to appear outside the houses, already beginning their day of play. Boys roll their wheels around the yards and imitate the sounds of automobiles as they pretend they are in an automated world with the discarded wheels from some pieces of machinery and a tobacco stick in which a nail is driven near the end to guide the wheel. This was a major homemade toy of boys 50 years ago. (What would the video game fans think of such a contraption today?)

With a promise of blue skies, women draw water and fill the washpots to do the family laundry. The pots sit on the edge of the woodpile where there is usually a supply of chips from wood cutting. The chips are raked around the pot and dead limbs or other fast-burning wood placed over the chips to get the pot boiling in a hurry. With big families, washing is a back-breaking chore.

There is a wash bench, usually behind the smokehouse, where the tubs sit and where the clothes are scrubbed by hand on old, time-worn washboards that sometimes injure the knuckles, and if they don't the lye water in which the clothes are boiled, will eat away at the hands when getting them out of the "boiling suds."

"Chaney ball" (chinaberry) trees provide shade for the washing area. The abundant balls that grow in bunches like grapes are turning yellow and are beginning to accumulate in the yards. A few bunches of water grass have come up in some yards, and this must be pulled up for a yard must be totally free of grass, and swept every week, usually on Saturday morning and all the trash taken away and burned. It is almost a shame to have an unswept yard over the weekend. (I have never known how those yards remained bare of grass when I realize how much of it grew in the fields we tilled.)

Tobacco has been placed on the grass so it will come in order and allow grading and tying. As many sticks as a family expects to process in a day are placed row after row on the grass to soak up the morning dew. The aroma of cured tobacco is heavy in the air as it lies in piles in the packhouses. In many ways it is unlike the tobacco grown today, for farming in those days was backward at best. Much less fertilizer was used and it showed up in smaller, more peaked leaves with less yield per acre.

Hayfields must soon be cut and the hay raked and stacked and later hauled to the barns to feed the mules through the winter months. The leaves are turning dark in the potato patches and it will be tater-digging time soon.

It is Indian summer and the sky has taken on a deeper blue. In the thickets and on the hillsides, the sassafras bushes are showing the first hint of autumn — just a touch of yellow that will turn into fiery red later.

Wagons and carts move slowly along the roads and occasionally a Model T Ford. A chicken with a late summer brood of multi-colored biddies dashes off the road as the car "speeds" by.

The day moves on and people are absorbed in their everyday tasks. A frothy-mouthed dog meanders down the road aimlessly and someone hollers "Run mad dog!" The sound reverberates across the neighborhood and someone else issues an alert. Children scramble into the house and people watch closely as the animal passes by. If the men decide the animal is rabid, someone puts a shotgun blast into it and it is buried (very carefully).

A cow in estrus lows constantly somewhere in the area. Babies cry and mothers change their diapers and breast-feed them and place them back in their play pens under the trees. A strapping boy with a shotgun on his back and a bird-dog at his side, goes off toward the thickets to hunt for doves. A few people have time to take their fishing poles down to the old mill in hopes of snaring a big catfish for supper, or bream and other species that live in the muddy waters. Some people even eat eels!

The day wanes and women gather the clothes from the long lines and the garden fences. Tobacco graded and tied during the day is placed on sticks and packed down. Boys rush to the barns to shuck corn for the hogs and mules and hay or oats are placed in the mule stalls. Chickens, guineas, ducks and geese with their half-grown goslings come home to roost. The sun sets and darkness falls and families gather around their homemade tables for their evening meal. One typical day in the lives of the poor people of eastern North Carolina half-a-century ago goes down in history. ☐

Oil Cloths, Old Safes, Cooking

W hat is decor? Is it a glossy, multi-colored oilcloth showing bunches of fruit — apples, grapes, bananas, flowers, leaves? Is it an ecru curtain hung at a window with a reed pole as a rod? Is it a calendar with a bird-dog at point that adorns the wall of a room for 12 months? If decor means, as the dictionary says, the decorations in a room, then that was the decor in our homes in the 1930s.

Those long tables filled a good part of the dining room, for many mouths were fed there, and the brightly-colored oilcloths stand out from my childhood. So does the wooden bench with peg legs, made from rough lumber, but smoothed by children who slid on its surface over the years until it became as smooth as if it had been planed except that it appeared to have had a coat of gray shellac that left the rough grain of the wood intact.

Are dishes, knives and forks and glassware decor? Or are they appointments? Whatever, I have never seen any of the patterns I remember in the fine stores where such things are sold. They were a conglomeration of different patterns and sizes, and hardly enough to go around at that. Pint jars and jelly glasses sometimes served as water glasses (that was before iced tea became the craze of poor folks). We never had a spoon or a knife that wouldn't turn green if they were left in food for a while. We were poorer than a church-house mouse.

Knives and forks were almost always made with "horn" inserts on each side of the metal that formed the handle. In remembering, it did look like some animal's horn might have looked, except that it was sort of like a variegated marble with a pattern. The "horn" that adorned the knives was attached to the "silverware" with perhaps three pieces of metal. But at least one side of the "horn" came off and the little metal pieces stuck out.

If there were two safes, the best one was in the dining room and they almost always had glass fronts. But instead of displaying fine china and crystal, they held food. It was the ones in the kitchens that take to the fancy of present-day antique buffs. They were the ones with all the little holes punched in the tin front panels at the factory that allowed air to get inside and prevent flies from taking over the food.

The Majestic wood range was a fixture in most households and children grew up with it. Majestic ranges apparently lasted forever. They were large and heavy and sat flat on the floor. They boasted two warming closets and a reservoir on the side to heat water for dishwashing. They were made of cast iron and the warming closets had doors with enamel finish, usually gray-flecked. They had sizable wood boxes and there was a door at the bottom and a small metal rake to remove the ashes and soot.

It was also something to keep little boys and girls busy toting in wood to fire the stoves.

There was the heavy cast iron pot with four legs that surely came with the range, for if an eye were removed the pot fitted the eye. But don't knock those pots if you haven't eaten from them.

There was the side table in the kitchen and when the dining room oilcloth became so worn that the slick top wore off and the cloth backing showed and became dirty looking, as soon as there was money to buy a new cloth, the one in the dining room was cut down and put on the side table. There was the slop bucket that sat near the stove and where dish water and peelings and other things were discarded and taken to the hogs.

In the pantries were the flour barrels, the bread trays that sat over the flour barrels, the coffee grinders, sacks of dried apples and peaches, strings of hot pepper, and jars of fruits, preserves and jellies.

But whatever was lacking in decor, appointments or adornments in those old places, there was one outstanding feature that can't be duplicated. Those ingenious women were the best cooks that God ever created. They had to cook three meals a day from foods that were mostly grown at home. They were without the simplest conveniences. They had to make do with what they had. There were no multiple choices or last-minute menu changes. But they took the simplest foods and made them so appetizing they are mouth-watering to remember today.

Whatever they cooked they did it well. Was it because they spent a good part of their day in the kitchen and the pots boiled slower, making the cooking process longer? For the 12 o'clock meal, they usually put the pot on to boil by 9 a.m. Those buttermilk biscuits (perhaps 80 at a time in a pan that fitted the oven of the big ranges) were not just edible. They would melt in your mouth! If there was gravy, it had the flavor to go with the color. If there were peas, they had just the right amount of liquid, or liquor, that made them just slightly thickened.

Take any vegetable, any meat, any fruit, and the finished product was the absolute in perfection in the art of cooking. To think about apple jacks and peach jacks made from fruits dried on tin shelters that were brown when cooked rather than the golden, or light colors from the same fruits today, is to remember a taste so delicious there is no way to compare the two. And those jacks, fried to a golden brown in pure lard, were as tender as a baby's skin.

Country ham. Oh boy! If there are those today who think they know what real country ham is and they are not of the older generation, forget it. One pan of "pure" country ham frying would spread its aroma a mile away and I know many remember how hungry it made them when it was an hour or two before eating time. And the gravy from that one pan of ham would flavor all the rice and eggs a family could eat. That gravy was as brown as chocolate and totally indescribable in flavor. I'd love to take a bath in ham gravy right now! I have never known what happened to the formula for country ham, and I know that today's meat processors could make a "killing" if they could only duplicate that taste. But in some things, modern technology just hasn't met the test.

There will never again be fruit pies and dumplings — peach, apple, huckleberry — that compare with those of half-a-century ago. They took worm-damaged peaches and apples and cut away all the ruined fruit and took the small pieces that were good and made pies and dumplings in large, deep pans, maybe 14 inches across, and the crust on top was buttered and the syrup from the cooking fruit oozed outside and when the pies were eaten there was a taste that defies description. Anybody remember?

Let nobody say we were not ingenious in those days. In the kitchen, we had quantity, for it took a lot to fill all those hungry mouths, and quality was the best that man has ever been able to devise. □

Picking Cotton In Eastern North Carolina

Cotton Fields Are White

C otton fields are white and the mornings are chilly. October has arrived and the thickets and lowlands are beginning to show color. Yellow has appeared and pink is showing faintly. No frost yet, but the dew is heavy. Those with Model T's are rising before dawn to go into town to find workers to come to the cotton fields. A little tobacco has been sold and some of the money kept out to pay for cotton picking. With 20 to 30 acres of cotton, help must be brought in to harvest the crop before bad weather sets in.

Since most people in town are even worse off than those in the country, it isn't hard to find cotton pickers. They are up early also and making themselves available when the cars come by for workers.

But preparations have been made before the cotton pickers arrive. Tow sacks have been rounded up and shoulder straps fashioned from fertilizer bags and attached to the sacks with heavy strings and leather attachments cut from old worn-out shoes. These bags must be strong for the pickers cram them full of cotton before they are emptied. Cotton sheets have been made by taking four fertilizer bags and sewing them together. But there are also sheets available in stores and tow bags strictly for holding cotton.

The weigh horse has been checked and if a board is rotten, it is replaced. The weigh horse is an important feature, for the workers' cotton is weighed daily and the pounds transcribed in the little book carried in a hip pocket and all the pounds are added up at the end of the week. The scale is attached to the extension of the weigh horse with hay wire and there are large weights with a handle that weighs the cotton.

By sunrise, the pickers are ready to take to the fields. Quite a few workers cram into those Model T's and on the running boards. And sometimes two trips are made to town if there are a lot of people waiting around for work. Grass has grown waist-high at the end of the rows and most of the foliage is still on the cotton stalks, so workers get wet up to their waists in early morning. However, there is one advantage to this for wet cotton also absorbs moisture, and that early-picked cotton weighs more than after the dew is gone and the cotton becomes fluffy.

It is serious business for the pickers and some are "experts," picking 300 or more pounds a day. It takes two sheets to hold their pickings. At midday they gather around their sheets and eat their sardines and Vienna sausages and "soda crackers."

There were some kinds of soft drinks in those days, but they hadn't become the habit of the day at that time. Plain water from fruit jars was the refreshment for people working in the fields, whether picking cotton or plowing corn. And the younger children had to take that water to the fields. By the time they arrived in the fields a mile or more away from the wells, the water was lukewarm, although it quenched thirst. And children knew that they had to get that water to the fields as quickly as possible.

There is a silhouette that stands out in memory today of sunset in a cotton patch when the sheets are tied and the weigh horse is brought up to the sheets of cotton and weighed. That weigh horse, with a setting sun in the background and the horizon bounded by endless trees and people holding their dinner pails and clothing, would be a photographer's dream today.

Cotton picking went on for two or three weeks, depending on the number of pickers. But that wasn't the end of cotton picking, for there were still green bolls in the fields, and later on, around Thanksgiving, the family had to go out and "scrap" the fields.

Tobacco grading was delayed for the picked cotton had to be taken to the gin and processed into 500-pound bales (or thereabout) and that also involved a lot of work. As to the tobacco grading, it could be done later for markets then were open until around Thanksgiving. Most farmers graded a sizable amount of their tobacco in a room in the house where fires could be built or in packhouses with a flue jutting through a window. All the furniture in a room would be moved out and a regular tobacco room provided. But some people slept in the same room where the tobacco was graded and tied.

The picked cotton had to be loaded on two-horse wagons and the older boys in the family were delegated this chore. Rounds were attached at the top of the wagons and curtains, also made from fertilizer bags, were draped around the wagons and they were driven beside the sheets of cotton and two boys would take hold of the sheet, one on each side, and swing the sheet a time or two and hurl it to the top of the curtain where another youth would grab the sheet, untie it and let the cotton loose in the wagon. This continued until the wagon was filled with the loose lint and it was ready to be taken to the gin.

Along those dirt roads, with goldenrods yellow on each side and dog fennels grown tall and the side ditches in need of scraping, many wagons were en route to the cotton gin. Sometimes there would be a long waiting line and the wagons would pull up to await their turn.

Ginning began early and the chug, chug, chug of the gin's motors could be heard for a mile or more and with each chug round puffs of smoke rose from the exhaust. Once the wagon was in place for ginning the cotton, a long, large suction pipe was placed over the lint and it was taken into the bowels of the gin, the seeds removed, the lint moved on to the baling process, and the finished product winding up on the loading platform and weighed and the weight put on the cotton in black paint. The finished product was then ready to be taken back home.

A few people had shelters for the bales of cotton, but many people dumped them in the yards until the cotton was sold. When several bales were placed in the yards, they became a source of play for the neighborhood boys. A very few had bicycles and they would place strong boards on the ground and run them to the top of the cotton bales, across them and down to the ground again at the end of the row. They'd get up speed and run up the ramp, over the bales of cotton, and down again, doing their Evel Knievel antics even in that unenlightened society.   □

New Clothes For School

S chool had started in the 1930s. The "old folks" had been to town to do their trading for new clothes. This chore had to be done after the first tobacco was sold for there wasn't a penny of money around for anything until then. Sharecroppers had survived by the skin of their teeth through the entire year. With the small amount of money they were able to get from their landlords, they had managed to buy those things that they considered essential to survival — flour, fat back, coffee, snuff and smoking tobacco. The young'uns' clothes were threadbare.

There were two pairs of overalls for every boy, two cotton shirts, two pairs of "union suits" (those heavy cotton ribbed long handles that every boy hated but was required to wear from October until May). There was one pair of brogans and two pairs of socks. There was a heavy wool sweater with the roughest surface I have ever felt. In whatever manner that wool was processed, the finished result was a fiber that would eat away at the human flesh like lye eats away at the hands. There was one bibbed cap of tweed or herringbone weave. And that was it for each boy. Nothing else during the eight-month school year.

Dresses in Indian head, calico or gingham had been made at home for the girls, with long sashes that tied in the back. Two or three dresses were the most each girl had to wear. They had two or three heavy petticoats and bloomers, long black stockings and shoes of solid construction. They also had a new sweater, made of almost as rough wool as the boys.

We were proud of our new attire when we set off for school on a two- to three-mile walk each day. We were resplendent in those overalls of indigo blue, dresses in solid dark colors or plaids; blue, maroon or gray sweaters, and brand new shoes. We had worn faded, tattered clothes for so long our spirits were uplifted with a new wardrobe. But oh, how those shoes hurt! After going barefoot all summer, the feet "spread out" and felt like they were bound in those hard brogans.

But before the end of school in late May, we would hate those clothes with a passion. Growing children may get two or three inches taller in the span of a school year, or it seemed that we did at least, and those overalls, now faded and with knee patches that would be the craze of today's society, came up two or three inches above our shoetops. We had extended the suspenders and dropped the bibs as far as they would go, too. The extension buckle rested at the very end of the suspender and our black stockings showed above the shoetops. The hems of the girls' dresses had been let out and there was the telltale sign where the hem had been.

Those sweaters had caused chapped faces and lips, for children have a way of wiping their noses on the arms of wearing apparel, and in too many cases we used those sweaters as a handkerchief. Brogans had gone through the mill also and were beginning to come apart and some shoe soles flopped when the children walked. Those black ribbed stockings had holes in the heels, and although they were not usually evident above the boys' brogans, girls' heels showed through the holey stockings sometimes.

My earliest recollection of lunch boxes was a reasonably small lard bucket. Maybe they made four-pound buckets in those days. Anyway, most children lugged those lard buckets to school every day. The contents were generally the same except on Monday. If there was anything left from Sunday dinner, the children took that to school. It might be a chicken thigh or wing, or even a back, a slice of cake or an apple jack. Whatever was left was a delicacy because the everyday menu consisted of collards, sweet potatoes, Irish potatoes, or any other vegetable left over from day to day, and sausage in season as well as fat back or white side. That was before the peanut-butter and cracker and Johnny cake days.

Later, children began to have regular lunch pails with two handles that criss-crossed and they came in many colors and honey buckets were used by some children who couldn't afford the lunch boxes. Mine was a honey bucket.

It would be an absolute laugh today to see children of that era as we were in our treks to and from school, with booksacks made from striped ticking that was used for feather beds and bolster covers, the sweaters thrown over our shoulders, the lunch boxes dangling in our hands and shoes tied together after the weather got warm in spring. We would tie the shoe "strings" together and sling the shoes over our shoulders.

When spring came we would walk in groups and some of us would climb a clay hill along the road and slide down, head first on our bellies, time after time until the clay covered our overalls. Then we would stop at the old wooden bridge, drop all our "junk" and go down under the bridge and play in the water, and sometimes somebody would get pushed into the water. Luckily, it wasn't more than about a foot deep.

We whiled away the time so that we could arrive home a little while before sunset, for if we had arrived earlier we would have been sent to the fields to work. We knew that we had to "feed up" and get in stove wood and wood for the fireplace as well as the fat lightwood for use in starting the morning fire, so we tackled those chores before darkness arrived.

But those teachers meant business and there was little foolishness in the school room. We were taught the three "R's" religiously, and maybe that was the secret to our survival. We were taught to pronounce syllables, sound the words and spell them. I can still remember as clearly as if it had been yesterday the word "Con'stan'ti'nople" as if that far-away city would have some meaning in our lives at some time. We were taught to read in the same manner, and English was stressed even then.

We were taught geography and history, and even though we were isolated and bound by our horizon, we knew there was another world out there, although few of us ever dreamed of really seeing any of the places we read about. Little did we know that things would take shape as we matured that would take a great many of us to the far-flung corners of the world.   □

Grading And Tying Tobacco

With cotton-picking almost finished and October nearing an end, tobacco grading is resumed. There will be feverish activity in the grading room in the next week or two for the tobacco has to be gotten to market before the warehouses close around Thanksgiving.

With the children in school, the older children who no longer attend and the "old folks" take to the packhouses and hardly take time out to eat. It's a long and slow process before the tobacco is ready to pack down and get ready for market. First, it has to be taken from the sticks, so one person "takes off" the tobacco and gets it to the graders.

Grading the tobacco is a real chore since there are often five or six grades, ranging from trash, green, red, speckled, "best," and wrappers. The tobacco is graded according to color and quality and since the children are in school, the graded tobacco is taken from the benches when it piles too high and placed in piles so that it can be tied at night after supper.

The tobacco has become dry and brittle as the weather gets colder, and it has to be "sprinkled down" so that it will come in order and become soft to the touch during the grading and tying process. This is accomplished with a "stumpy" broom and a pail of water. But even the broom must be clarified. It isn't any kind of broom bought in a store, but rather one made from broom sage that grows in nearby fields. The tall sage is cut with a scythe in the fall and made into brooms for the house. Enough broom sage is gathered in the hand so that the end used as a handle is about three inches thick and tobacco twine is twisted and wound tightly around the straw and the string worked into the ends of the broom to hold it together. A "stumpy" broom is one that has had so much wear it is no longer considered good enough to sweep the bare floors with.

The broom is dipped into the pail and the water sprinkled over the dry tobacco and it is packed into a pile and left overnight and is ready for grading the next day.

Tobacco tying was a nightly ritual for many people in late October and early November, and sometimes people who were in a hurry to get a barn or two of leaf ready to sell would have "tobacco tyings." They would grade up the tobacco and invite all the young people in the neighborhood to the social event. And you'd better believe those young people wanted to attend any tobacco tying in the area, and they did if they didn't have to tie tobacco at home on those nights. That is if the "old folks" would allow the girls to attend. They watched those girls like hawks and usually sent one of their brothers along as a safeguard.

There were two major incentives for young people to attend tobacco tyings. The first was to get out from under the ever-watchful eyes of their parents and to mingle more freely with the other young people. The second was that there were "treats" after all the tobacco was tied. Parched peanuts were almost always served and that was sort of a standing thing like shelled peanuts are served at most functions today. There were Mary Janes sometimes, or Baby Ruths, or coconut creams, and after RC Cola and Pepsi became popular, the soft drinks would be placed in buckets of ice and served also. It was an inexpensive as well as a quick way to get tobacco ready for the warehouse.

After the tobacco was tied into bundles, the farmers would "stick it up" on hand-smoothed sticks that had been rounded with pocket knives during winter days when there was no outside work to do. Care was taken in "sticking up" tobacco for a good appearance was essential when the weed was placed on the warehouse floor.

When the sticks were filled the tobacco would be smoothed down with the hands, then placed on the floor and pressed with a board to smooth it further. The family ironing board was about the best pressing board available, for ironing boards then were not equipped with legs, but instead one end rested at the top of a ladder-back chair and the other end usually placed on the dining table.

Course after course of tobacco was packed down and sometimes the pile was five or six feet high. After the tobacco was packed down tow bags or curtains used when the green tobacco was trucked from the fields, were placed around the tobacco to hold in the moisture until it was taken to market.

At the warehouse, the tobacco was removed stick by stick and half of the tobacco removed from each end of the stick and placed in four stacks around the warehouse baskets with the tied ends on the outside. Good tobacco was a pretty sight in the warehouse, for it had a starched look and every leaf was in place. But such a process would be totally prohibitive today for the costs of raising a crop of tobacco would soar.

In those days it wasn't a matter of looking forward to money to spend after selling the crop, but rather just hoping to pay out, and that was an impossibility in most cases, for prices were so low there was nothing left, and actually, most sharecroppers were left with debt hanging over their heads as they began another crop year.

One indication of the severity of the economic crunch in those days is a case I know of where a family of five received $12.50 a month to run themselves on through the year, from January until the selling season. That included all the money available to this family for anything during the year, including clothes. (That family was mine.)

Landlords who might have had a few hundred dollars on hand were reluctant to let any money go to the sharecroppers, for they were aware that there was little likelihood of them paying it back. The landlords furnished the house the team and half of the fertilizer and the sharecroppers furnished the labor, paid for half the fertilizer and gave the landlord half of the proceeds from his crops. We called fertilizer "guano" in those days, and in checking Webster I find this a perfectly good word, although we seldom if ever hear the word used today.   ☐

Autumn: Time To Dig Taters

T rees so bright on the ridge they look out of place. Just a green mass in summer, they shine like diamonds in late October. Try to pick out all the colors and you get lost. Which are brighter? The reds, the yellows, the pink-oranges, the golds? Sunshine makes them sparkle. They look like ripe fruit ready to fall to the ground. A little whiff of wind and rain would bring every one to the earth and set them blowing everywhere. Too pretty to be real and too short-lived to satisfy the eye.

Taters must be dug before the ground freezes. Load up the two-horse plow, the guano sacks, the baskets and buckets and take to the tater patch.

Put the plow down to the beam so it'll get under the taters and turn them on top of the ground. Get up everything except the strings and the little tiny ones. Folks'll be turning out their hogs after corn's housed and they'll get all that's left.

Stop the plow and pull the vines off when it gets too clogged up. Good thing frost has blackened them and wilted them a little or they'd be a mess to handle.

Everybody take a row now and wipe off the dirt as you pick up the taters. Don't want to be hauling a passel of dirt around. If there are any long, stringy ends, break them off. And if the plow cuts one real bad, just leave it for the hogs. The older ones will have to tote the buckets for the young'uns when they get heavy, and that don't take long.

And be careful dumping them in the wagon. If they're bruised they'll rot. Just look at that color in the thicket. Ever seen anything any prettier?

Looks like a right good crop of taters. May have to fix three tater hills. No need to raise 'em and let 'em freeze.

Have to go to the woods and cut some pine saplings. It'll take quite a few to do the job. They'll have to be cut in about six-foot pieces. Pine straw will have to be hauled too.

Set the poles up so they'll look like an Indian wigwam, close together at the top and farther apart at the bottom. Fasten the tops and put the poles fairly close together. Got to put a layer of pine straw on the ground to cushion the taters and keep them from freezing. Use rubber roofing at the top to keep out the water.

Cut out for a door and fix it good and solid so it'll be easy for the women folks to get to. These hills will be good to put hens and biddies in if any set and come off in early spring. Taters will all be gone by then.

When it comes to digging taters and things like that, young'uns will just have to stay out of school for a day. But they won't have to be out of school to get the cotton scrappings for school will be out Thursday and Friday for Thanksgiving, and there will be Saturday if they need it. Never paid too much attention to Thanksgiving. Reckon it's because it's so close to Christmas and poor folks can't afford two feasts in a month's time.

But that's not saying we shouldn't pause to give thanks. Thanksgiving is every day with poor folks. Thankful to just be here and making it through another day.

Tired to the bone from digging taters. Hard job. Stooping down gets to the back. Leg muscles get sore. Sore all over as a matter of fact. Dirt's thick under the fingernails.

But riding the wagon along the thicket and the pretty colors everywhere, it brings a sense of peace that's almost unreal. Far back in the fields, it seems to be a world all its own with nothing beyond the trees. Peaceful and lonely. Shouldn't be any loneliness in the midst of all the peace and quiet. But that's not the way of the human mind. Got to have the high spots and the low ones. Something inside just gets restless sometimes. Maybe it's at the prettiest times that the loneliness creeps in, like when it snows. And the Lord knows there's nothing on this earth prettier than snow falling. But loneliness creeps in then, too.

Shouldn't be like that though. Being able to see the autumn leaves and the winter snows would be pure heaven to a blind person. Even that old turkey buzzard circling over the woods over there would be the prettiest sight in the world to them. 'Specially with that blue October sky up there. Prettiest season there is. Spring's pretty with all the green and the flowers and all that. Summer's pretty too, and winter, but something about the fall says it all. The fruit's there, the reward for a year's work, as well as all the other pretty sights like gourds hanging on wire fences and bunches of chrysanthemums growing at the end of the garden rows look out of place with all the brown around them. Some pink, some yellow, some almost blood-red. 'Simmons shine like little oranges on the trees. Citrons looking like watermelons in the fields. Hayfields raked clean with the stacks in neat rows look like something manicured in the midst of the rough landscape.

There's a turtledove! Fly into blue skies, little bird. Fly over the woods and into the wild blue yonder and feed in all the fields. All you've got to worry about is man and his shotgun. Stay out of his way and you'll be around another year when the pea pods pop open and the grain falls to the ground to feed you.

There goes an old "mash" rabbit. Look at him skip and hop. Better be careful, old rabbit, or you might end up on some eating table.

So peaceful. Everything all colored up and pretty. But it'll pass and every leaf will fall and the tall trees will stand out against the sky with their limbs looking lonely in the cold of winter.

Lord, don't let old Gray balk and show herself when we get to that shackly bridge and cause this wagon, all the taters and me to land up in that ditch. If that happens all the beauty of this day will be lost and cuss words will replace the nice thoughts. Careful now Gray, take it easy and go across real slow. Old Zeb will do his part. You just do yours. That's it. We made it!

It's sure pretty in late October.   □

(N.C. Dept. Archives and History)

A Corn Shucking From The Past

Getting Up Corn

A h, those blue skies of fall! Bluer than a bluebird. Bluer than the hydrangeas that grow in some neighborhood yards in summer. Blue skies and cold mornings and warm days, turning cool again at night. The season hasn't quite settled down and it isn't winter but neither is it summer. Ideal would be the better word for there is neither sweating nor freezing. It is the period before the storms of winter set in.

Getting up corn is the last remaining big job to be done for the year. And the time has come. Tobacco has all been sold and the cotton picked. Frosts have already come and soon it will be the onset of real winter. It's now nearing Thanksgiving and the trees have lost their foliage and it is a brown world after the frosts. But the corn breaks easily on a cold, clear morning and the men take to the fields early.

We hadn't even learned the art of taking the mules and wagon with us as we broke the corn, and tossing it into the wagon. Instead, we made heap rows and had to come back and throw the corn into the wagons. And this was a back-breaking chore and stooping down to pick up all the ears pulled muscles and made us sore all over.

If there were four persons breaking corn, it was all thrown into one heap pile and there was a lot of corn to be gathered up and thrown into those wagons.

A covey of birds flies over the field occasionally and a hunter fires a gun somewhere in the marshlands and a little spiral of smoke rises into the atmosphere after the shot. It doesn't require a great deal of concentration to break the ears of corn and the workers can observe the world about them as they throw the ears onto the heap pile.

Somebody's burning leaves across the way and white smoke billows up when leaves are added to the pile. The smell of burnt leaves pervades the air and occasionally little flecks of white ash filter down into the corn field.

In the distance, the old graveyard shows up with all the foliage from the trees gone and the tombstones appearing as gray blobs, some tilted and some still standing erect.

An old 'possum passes by with babies hanging on to her back, heading for the 'simmon tree on the hedgerow. And to think that some folks eat them! Saw a 'coon down by the creek the other day. But a dog ran him off in the bushes and he got out of sight real quick. Pretty little animal with all the markings in his face. A lot prettier than an old gray 'possum with its albino-looking nose and grinning at you when you get close up. Looks almost like an overgrown rat. Wonder what that kind of animal is doing over here? They're like the animals that live in Australia that carry their babies in their pouch. 'Possum must have gotten off at the wrong place when they were put out of the ark.

In a good year, there will be enough corn to last until the next crop is harvested. Corn isn't a commercial crop, not in eastern North Carolina. A farmer tries to grow enough to feed his mules, hogs and chickens and enough to be ground into meal for the family. Corn is shucked and only the best ears used, with the small end slushed off, shelled and taken to the mill for grinding. It takes a lot of meal for corn bread with the big families. There is the shallow griddle for "hoe cakes" to be cooked on top of the stove, but it is better baked in the oven. There are large pans and they either make fairly small cakes and separte them in the pan, or make one large cake and pour grease in the bottom of the pan and after spreading the meal evenly, scoop up grease and rub it over the top, and when the corn bread comes from the oven it is golden brown and crisp and about three-fourths of an inch thick. And nothing is used except meal and water unless salt is added. No eggs, no additive to make the bread rise. Nothing but meal and water.

A crib full of corn makes a farmer feel mightly good. It reassures him that he can go through another year and be able to keep the livestock sleek and fat, and also provide an outlet for those rambunctious boys on rainy days. To have a pack of boys around the house and just loafing around is asking for trouble. They can always be sent to the barn to shuck corn.

The boys always wonder why the "old man" is so anxious to have corn shucked when he never has to feed up anyway. But no matter how much corn is shucked on a rainy day, it doesn't last long. And the shucks are packed into the basket and taken to the cow stable.

Sometimes a farmer will have a "corn-shucking" and neighbors are invited over to participate. Whenever "corn-shuckings" are held, the grain is dumped in the barnyard in front of the barn door so that the ears can be thrown into the crib as they are shucked. And the "corn-shuckings" are held at night, always with a full or growing moon shining down and providing light for the participants. It is an easy way to get the corn shucked and men are always looking for something to do at night rather than just sit by the fire. It gives them a chance to talk about things that men talk about, away from the ears of the women folks.

A few bottles of "white lightning" will be placed among the corn as it is dumped from the wagons or carts, and some of the fellows might get a little boozy at a "corn-shucking" sometimes. Somebody might have a banjo around and play a "hoe-down." Those are more fun nights than work spells.

There is a lot of hollering and "whoopee" at a "corn-shucking," especially after the alcohol begins to take effect, and the dogs in the neighborhood become aroused and bark and bay at the revelry.

When corn is plentiful in the crib, as winter wanes and summer arrives, the pile of grain in the barn goes back halfway of the corn crib, and sometimes nests of baby rats are found — nasty little pink things looking like embryos with black swollen places where the eyes will eventually open — minute and wriggling in their nest of corn shucks. We gather them up by their tails and throw them into the yard and a chicken immediately gobbles them down and looks for more. Big changes over a 50-year span. ☐

Hogs Hanging On The Gallows

It's Hog-Killing Time

T he pork department in every supermarket is filled with cellophane-wrapped, tempting portions of hog meat from ham to liver pudding. All that is required is a sizable amount of money to purchase the tempting variety. Most of the younger generation knows nothing about the many processes required to bring the meat to market. We did it the hard way 50 years ago.

A bright fire lights up the yard and a cold wind howls around the buildings. A thin coating of ice is on the mule troughs and mudholes. The stars are bright but in the east there are signs of the dawning of another day. It's hog-killing time.

Tubs of water that were drawn from the well and poured into the vat the night before are getting hot in preparation for scalding the hogs. Neighbors are coming over to help for there are many chores associated with hog-killing.

Soon after sunrise the men go out to the floored pen where the hogs have been fattened, use their axes, rifles, and butcher knives, knock the boards off the front of the pen, drag the hogs up to the vat, scald two or three at a time in the near-boiling water to loosen the hair, place them on tow sheets and begin scraping off the carcasses. Jar lids make good scrapers. When this is finished the hogs are placed on a tobacco truck and pushed over to the gallows. The backs of the hind legs are slit, exposing the heel string and strong hardwood pegs are placed between the legs and the hogs hung on the gallows. There they are weighed, the entrails, heart, liver and lungs removed, in preparation for cutting out the pork.

The livers are slung across one end of the gallows and somehow a bladder almost always ends up on that gallows too; the sweet breads, melts and long tongue pulled from the intestines and saved for cooking, and the entrails taken in a tub to the hole dug at the back of the yard for "ridding" the chitlins. This is the first big chore for the women. Several of them gather around the hole and take the intestines and each woman holds a portion and when all the intestines are in the hand they are cut so that each woman can "rid" her share of the chitlins.

When this is accomplished the chitlins are turned inside out and placed in tubs of warm water and and washed and washed and washed. Then they are put into another tub to soak. The small intestines are kept separate from the large for they will be used for stuffing the sausage.

Toes and feet are numb from the chilling cold and the workers hover around the wash pots where fires are kept going, for a lot of hot water is required in hog-killings.

After the entrails are removed, the hogs are taken from the gallows and put back on the trucks to be cut out. The feet are cut off and placed in scalding water for cleaning. The head is removed and the carcasses split at the backbone. The tenderloins are pulled from the backbone area. The various pieces of meat are shaped with the butcher knife and the remains placed into tubs for making sausage and lard. This continues until all the hogs have been cut out. The tubs filled with meat are taken into the kitchen for processing.

There is a veritable feast on hog-killing day, for most people haven't had "freshes" in a long time and with large families raising enough meat to last from one hog-killing to another is an impossibility. Fat back has been the source of meat for some time. The sweet breads, melts and long tongue are simmering on the stove, a large pan of sweet potatoes, covered in their juices, are cooling on the table. Lean meat along the backbone of the hog has been pulled off and steaked with sumptuous amounts of brown gravy and rice. Collards have been cooked and corn bread baked in the oven. Biscuits are also a part of the menu. There may be a molasses cake or bread pudding for dessert.

Heat from the wood stove warms the hands and feet of the workers as they stuff themselves on the delicacies. But time is a factor and a lot has to be done, so they soon return to their chores. The men take the meat to the smokehouse, lay it out flat on old oilcloth or tow sheets and dump salt on top of it. The skin side is rubbed well with salt as well as the exposed knuckle ends of the hams and shoulders. After all the meat is salted, more salt is dumped on top of the meat.

The hogs' heads are split in half and the brains removed. The ears, nose and part of the feet will be used in making souse. The brains will be eaten with scrambled eggs. The backbones are salted and placed alongside the meat. (Those were real backbones in those days, with plenty of lean meat left on them.)

In the kitchen, women are busy separating the meat that will be ground into sausage from the fat that will be rendered into lard. Even the skins are dried up and they will be used for making soap later. Some of the women are scraping chitlins that will be used for stuffing sausage. A tub filled with fat meat cut into small blocks is taken outside and dumped in the wash pot for cooking. Wash pots were put to major use 50 years ago for they were the only cooking utensils of sizable dimensions. The wooden lard paddle is taken from the smokehouse and washed thoroughly, for a paddle is required for stirring the fat meat to prevent sticking while it is cooking. Scorched lard would taste and constant stirring is required to prevent this when cooking the meat.

The sausage meat is seasoned in a wooden tub with salt, plenty of sage and red pepper. The secret of good sausage is in the seasoning, and most people have their own recipe to suit individual tastes. The sausage grinder is brought out and fastened to the end of the kitchen table and a strong man begins the task of grinding the meat. After all the meat is ground it is mixed thoroughly with the hands and a patty or two is put in the skillet to fry for taste. If more seasoning is needed, it is added and more mixing done.

Then the sausage grinder is turned into a stuffer with an extension made of aluminum on which the hog intestine is placed and the long links of sausage begin to form on the table. Three or four of the lower large intestines are stuffed and they are called "Tom Thumbs." They will be eaten later on when they are thoroughly dried.

In the yard, the blocks of fat meat are now golden brown and the lard is ready to be dipped and put into stands that hold 25 or 50 pounds. The "cracklings" that have all risen to the top of the pot are removed first and they will be salted and eaten as they are with sweet potatoes, ground and used to make "crackling bread" or as seasoning for biscuits. "Cracklings" are considered a delicacy by many.

When the sausage is hung in the smokehouse it is the end of the day and bodies are bone-tired. Other chores lie ahead for souse has to be made, chitlins cooked, livers cooked and hash made, feet, ears and noses cleaned and cooked and made into souse meat, and some of the liver made into liver pudding, but those things can wait until another day.

Neighbors are given "freshes" for their labors — some of the livers, lean meat pulled from around the backbone (there were no pork chops or bacon in rural eastern N.C. a half-century ago), "cracklings," part of the sweetbreads and melts, links of sausage, and brains to go with their eggs for breakfast. This was standard at all hog-killings and each shared with the other and the giving was reversed when the neighbors killed hogs.

After some six or eight weeks when the meat has "taken" the salt, it will be washed off, borax and black pepper rubbed on it, and hung in the smokehouse with hay wire on nails driven into the rafters. That meat is a big source of the diet of farmers throughout the year.   □

Many Lived In Old Houses Like This

A Visit To Old Houses

I f I could glamorize those houses that we grew up in half-a-century ago, I would give them all the aesthetic beauty we are accustomed to today so that they would appeal to the present generation and give to the structures something of artistic value. I would paint them snow-white and have old brick walkways leading to every home, green lawns and a magnolia tree by every door, grounds sloping down to a pool surrounded by trees and shrubbery reflected in crystal-clear water.

I would place crisp, white curtains at every window, plush carpeting on every floor, antique furniture in the rooms and bowls of colorful flowers in appropriate places.

However, that isn't the way it was. If those houses were ceiled the occupants were lucky. If the walls were finished, either in wood, or in a few cases plaster, the occupants were extremely lucky. In many cases tenant houses were only weatherboarded and the rooms separated by a single wall. Where there were knotholes in the weatherboarding, on starlit nights in a darkened room, a star could be focused and boys and girls could fall asleep while star-gazing.

There were thick, goose-down feather beds in winter and they would be so cold when we jumped into bed the feather bed would encompass us and for a moment it felt like we were in an ice box. But almost immediately the body heat would warm the feathers and even on the coldest nights we were snug. It was a little different, however, if a child wet the bed. In that case, the wet child would move nearer to the other bed partner, for in sub-freezing temperatures, it was too cold for changing bedclothes.

Beds were of two styles generally. One style was the high, wooden headboard with fancy curlicues at the top. They were usually made of oak and painted so that the grain of the wood didn't show through. The other was a regular metal stead with vertical round spokes. Most of the metal steads had been painted many times but the paint was always popping off from the accumulation of coats so there would be a basic color but with a flecked appearance. No brass beds in my neighborhood.

The front bedroom where the "old folks" slept was almost always the family sitting room. That's where the fireplace was and where the fires were kept going in winter. That's where the old, ladder-back chairs — made of pine that had been shellacked in yellow when new — sat in a half-circle around the open fire. Ma's and Pa's old rockers usually sat on either side of the hearth. The straw bottoms of the chairs became ragged with time and the rough straw pricked the skin.

Most front rooms also held an old, shackly wardrobe that was much larger than is seen today. They were almost always a dark, mahogany color, but as in other cases, the grain of the wood was covered with paint rather than varnish. And there was always a bureau with a mirror but some of the backing on the mirror was gone and it didn't always give a full image.

The kerosene lamp sat on the bureau and if the chimney was kept clean it gave off enough light to see over the room. The secret to a clean shade was in keeping the wick trimmed perfectly straight so that one side wouldn't be a little high. When that was the case soot would gather on the chimney. Occasionally there would be a decorated chimney with very delicate white etching that appeared to be sheaves of wheat or some kind of grain.

There were not lamps for every room and most people came nearer having two than three. The lamp would be taken from the sitting room to the kitchen when supper was being prepared and darkness came early. From the kitchen it would be taken to the dining room, and back to the sitting room.

Reflecting across a span of more than 50 years, I can see someone carrying a kerosene lamp from one room to another when the wind was stirring and how they would cup a hand around the top of the lamp chimney in an attempt to keep the light from going out. I also remember the eerie shadows created by those old lamps as they flickered in the nights of long ago.

There was little or no closet space and clothes were usually hung on rows of nails and a corner of a room was sometimes curtained off for closet space.

There were no chintz curtains or Martha Washington bedspreads. There was almost always a counterpane in the front room. We called them "county pins." There were some sort of curtains at the windows and there might even be white tiebacks with ruffled edges made from homespun that bleached into pure white with the passing of time.

Patchwork quilts as colorful as dining room oil cloths adorned the other beds. Old washstands or bureaus were the other furnishings in the bedrooms.

The floors were bare unless there was an old rug in the parlor, and a linoleum cover in the kitchen. Those shellacked linoleum rugs would shine in the sunlight for a short spell, but with uneven floors and many feet scampering around, the new look soon faded and the slick surface wore away, exposing the black beneath.

On every piazza, as most of the old folks called the back porch, there was a board nailed at the side of the house and extending to a post that held up the roof, and that is where the water bucket sat with either a tin dipper or a gourd with which to dip the water. There was a wash basin that sat on the shelf and if there was "sweet" soap it was placed there with the lye soap for washing the hands and face. After the washing, the water was dashed into the yard and faces and hands were dried in towels made from salt sacks or flour sacks, hanging on a nail over which was placed a part of an old mirror.

There is no way to compare the dwellings of that era with those of today. They would now be called hovels and most would be condemned as unfit for human habitation. But don't shed your pity for us. They were a lot more than met the eye for present-day senior citizens who live in comfort. They were home and we didn't see their appearance nearly as much as we saw the love that was shared there. Home was our haven from the world, where families were much more closely knit than today and despite the gloom of the surroundings there seemed to be a halo over those old places for it was there that we dreamed the dreams of youth. ☐

Cane, Candy And Youth

S yrup that is made from cane grown in small patches on the farm is sweet to the taste with a flavor all its own and it added to the family food supply half a century ago, but take it from a cane "expert," it wasn't worth it.

Cane stalks are extremely heavy with their joints of sweet juice, and lifting the cane and getting it onto the wagon is a big chore. But that is the least unsatisfactory factor.

The cane is top-heavy with its abundant pods of seeds, and it is easy for it to blow over, and the September "gust" always came before the cane was harvested and the stalks were criss-crossed all over the patch and each stalk had to be separated, held up and stripped of its blades that looked like corn. It was an almost impossible task and if the patch had been large it would have been impossible. Fortunately, a small plot of land would yield enough syrup for a family during the winter months or until it sugared in the lard stands in which it was usually stored.

The stalks were stripped, the seeds cut off and each stalk cut with a grubbing hoe and placed in a pile to be loaded on the wagon later. Once this was completed the cane was loaded on the wagon and taken to the homemade cane mill in a clearing just beyond a patch of woods along the country road.

In that long trail of memory there is a scene that lives even today of an old "plug" of a mule walking round and round all day as she slowly ground the juice that flowed into the vats to be cooked into syrup. It was apparently the same mule every year, for she was a faded brown, with hip bones prominent and her coat in need of brushing, and rather small as far as mule size goes. Round and round and round she went as if walking in circles did nothing to her equilibrium. She may have fallen when unhitched to the cane crusher for all I know.

You don't describe the smell of cooking syrup, but it filled the air and had an aroma all its own as does chocolate cooking or any other delicious food. The attendant used wooden paddles to stir the syrup as it cooked, and yellow jackets swarmed around the cooking vats and pitched wherever the sweet juice was spilled.

The site of the cane mill never changed and piles of cane stalks from years before stood as evidence that the mill was permanently located on its spot.

There was a sandy field across the path from the cane mill and cotton was planted there every year and only the land must have been poorer than the old mule, for the stalks of cotton were no more than a foot tall and with barely a dozen bolls of white cotton on each stalk.

The old shack across the field where the cane mill owner lived bore more testimony to the fact that times were hard, for that old shanty looked like it would fall to the ground any day. It had the appearance of being older than Methuselah and the boards were as dull a gray as is possible with scrub pines in the background adding to the drabness of the scene. It was so lonely there and there was such a look of desolation about the setting it made you want to cry.

I don't know whether the owner of the mill received part of the syrup as pay or whether he was paid a certain amount for cooking the syrup. I just know it was a yearly ritual and the hot syrup was poured into the 25-pound lard stands and taken home and placed in the pantries and families "sopped" the newly-made syrup with buttermilk biscuits with hunks of home-churned butter, and it was a rarity at first but became old hat after a while and we wanted some store-bought syrup like Golden Crown, Turkey brand, or Karo.

I do remember that there was a large picture of a crown on Golden Crown brand, a large picture of a turkey gobbler with his feathers spread on Turkey brand, but I can't recall what was on the Karo cans. But poor folks 50 years ago did a lot of syrup "sopping." And when I say sopping, that is what we did. We'd break off a piece of biscuit, wind it around in the syrup until we had all we could get on the biscuit, hold our heads over our plates and take all that finger-licking sweetness into our mouths, followed by a bite of white side or fatback. Not bad! We fattened like hogs on such diets.

If today's diet-conscious generation thinks eating was one of the big pleasures in life half-a-century ago, they're right. To the slim-trim group, it is at the expense of good food, and with few other ingredients in life in that era, good eating was the essence of a good life. However, there is no way to compare the two groups, for if we ate huge amounts of food, we worked those calories off from meal to meal in doing manual labor on the farm. There is no way we could eat the amount of food we consumed in those days and survive today. A growing teen-ager then could eat from a dozen to 15 biscuits at one meal and go into the fields and work the calories off between dinner and supper. (We didn't have lunch then.)

Along about the time cane was harvested, it was time to get up the peanuts in the short rows at the side of a field. Some of the old folks called them "ground peas" then and we thought that was one of the worst sayings in the vocabulary of that time. If we could get a little lime to put down beside them and the weather was good, we could get enough peanuts to last us during the longer winter months.

After they were dried in tow sacks, panfuls would be put in the stoves to parch and we would feast on them at night and throw the hulls into the open fire and see the little spurt they created among the coals, lighting up the dim rooms for a moment. But sometimes we didn't have the lime and the weather would be dry and all we reaped were hulls.

And sometimes there were candy pullings and somewhere for the young folks to gather. The girls would cook sugar, water and vinegar into taffy until it would spin a thread and harden in water, and pour it onto greased plates or platters until it cooled just enough to be handled with the hands (and it was really hot at first). The boys and girls would grease their hands and pairs would take up the candy and begin pulling it and doubling it with each taking part in the ritual. This continued until the taffy turned white and was hard enough to be rounded and placed into plates and cut into lengths.

Then there would be the feast on the sweet-sour taste that lingers on even now in the memory. But it really wasn't the candy. It was the meeting of the sexes and the interchange of looks with the eyes saying much that could not be said in words. It was young love and innocence. ☐

Christmas Season's Here

W hat? No ornaments in the attic to put on the tree? No strings of lights to brighten the occasion? No lighted plastic Santa Clauses to glow in the rooms? No red candles and silver holders to make the occasion festive? No lights to place in windows? No reindeer scenes to place on roofs? No red stockings with embroidered names to hang at the mantel? How on earth can there be Christmas without any of these things?

There were none of those ornaments in rural eastern North Carolina 50 years ago. Most of those things are associated with electricity, and we didn't even have that, to say nothing of the things that we associate with Christmas today. No tinsel, no angel hair, no glittering icicles, no fancy-wrapped packages with ribbons and bows. So what could there possibly be to make something beautiful out of the greatest of all occasions? Let us see.

Rural neighborhoods, far removed from city sights and customs, speak nothing of Christmas or of the true meaning of the season. Winding dirt roads and dull gray houses and outbuildings with farming implements scattered around the barnyards would be picturesque scenes today, but they wouldn't impart a feeling of Christmas.

It isn't in the setting. Rather, it is in the spirit. It is enchantment. The mood of the people says it all. Everything is geared around Christmas and it is celebrated in rural eastern North Carolina more than any other season of the year. It is the season in which hardship or lack of money fails to dampen the spirits. The people prepare for Christmas. Somehow, some way, Christmas is always a festive occasion and young and old alike show a joviality not evidenced at any other time of the year.

If the farmer doesn't pay out, he still saves enough money to tide the family over through the holidays. There just has to be Christmas in every home. But planning for the big day begins weeks ahead.

Curtains are washed, starched, ironed and hung at windows that have been cleaned inside and outside until they sparkle. Never mind the broken panes where pasteboard replaces the glass. Bed quilts are hung on clotheslines to air, as are feather beds, pillows and bolsters. No need to scour the floors until a day or two before the holiday. They would only get dirty again and have to be scoured all over.

All the quilts and feather beds will be put to use during the holidays when the married children and their families come to spend two or three days. It isn't just a one-day celebration. It goes on and on. Feather beds will be pulled to the floor to serve as extra beds.

Extra corn is fed to the barbecue-sized pigs in order to fatten them a little more, for one will be dressed as part of the Christmas feast. Laying hens are given a lot of corn that is scattered all over the barnyard morning and night for it takes dozens of eggs, and several of the hens will also be sacrificed for the feast.

Plenty of hay is thrown into the cow stable if she is milking, for a lot of butter will be needed in all the things the women will cook as well as milk for custards and pies. And the turkey gobbler struts around with his feathers spread and gobbling as he gulps down the corn.

Kegs of scuppernong wine are in some smokehouses, kept under lock and key along with the meat and sausage, for there are imbibers in some families and the temptation to take a sip will be too great if doors are left unlocked. But there is 'simmon beer in a keg under the shelter for anybody wanting it. There will be many sips of wine taken during the holidays to add to the gaiety.

In retrospect, it seemed as peaceful during that period before Christmas as it must have seemed in Bethlehem on the night of Christ's birth. It had the feeling of a magical spell hovering over the earth with a special focus on our community.

The cold air and threatening skies brought visions of snow that never quite made it during the holiday season. There were a few times when a little snow was on the ground at Christmas, but for the most part, snow fell in January and February and once in a great while in March.

Far from the trend of today when Christmas buying is spread out over the entire year, it wasn't that way at all in the 1930s. Everybody went to town the last few days before Christmas. There was about a week's span when the streets were so filled with shoppers it was hard to walk, and the stores were literally crammed with people. That was all part of the spirit of Christmas.

Those few days were when the public did all its buying for the holidays. And it certainly wasn't all for presents. There wasn't money for gift-giving then as there is today, and gifts were very small and inexpensive.

There was no general giving among the families that I knew. The parents would get small gifts for some of the children and if others didn't have money for a gift nothing was thought of it. Maybe a dish or a fancy handkerchief for mothers and a shirt or handkerchief for the fathers. And I don't recall them being wrapped in holiday paper or tied with ribbon.

Sure, there were orders for Santa Claus, but they were insignificant compared to his visits today. Children today would scorn what children received in those days. And fruits and nuts were appreciated as much as the toys, for they were mostly Christmas-only luxuries. Compared to what children get from Santa today, it would be about a 50 to 1 ratio.

But the poor children of that era were far happier with their gifts and goodies than the little ones of today. Those gifts were genuinely appreciated and the only toys they got for a year, and if only today's generation could have seen the look on their faces and their exuberance at the joys of Christmas, they would know the true spirit of the season.

But many other things have to be done, for Christmas is still a week away. □

Cooking For Christmas

T he fireworks have arrived at the freight station and the boys have to find a way to get them home, even if the wagon has to be driven to town. Every year the neighborhood boys get together and order fireworks from far-away places. And the old neighborhood sparkles at night. Sky rockets, Roman candles, torpedoes, strings of tiny firecrackers, spit devils, sparklers, they are all included. Children get most of their Christmas spending money from scrap cotton that is sold at the gin.

But first things first.

Go to the woodpile, boys, with your hatchet and hammer. Get the sack of black walnuts out and turn a round piece of wood on end and crack the nuts on it. Turn them at an angle so there will be large pieces of meat instead of mush.

Pick out the pecans, girls, plenty of them. They'll be used in a lot of things, and don't try cracking them with a flat iron. It'll mash them to pieces. And don't try to crack the hard ones with your teeth.

Check on all the ingredients in the pantry to see if anything is missing. Yeah, vanilla flavoring is about out and some will have to be bought. Nutmeg is sufficient. Spice supply adequate. Ginger a plenty. Chocolate's a mite low. Add that to the list. Coconuts sound all right from shaking them.

Go out to the pasture and kill that pig, boys. Dress him out and get him ready for a good portion will be baked Christmas Eve. The oven will be reserved for that 35-pound turkey gobbler all night so he'll be tender enough to fall off the bone Christmas Day. Find paper sacks to place over him so he won't get too brown while cooking.

Grate that coconut, girls, and be careful with that grater. You could ruin a finger if you don't watch what you're doing and grate a hunk of flesh. Measure out a sifter full of flour for each bowl and don't bother about measuring out lard in a cup. Takes too long. Dip down in the lard stand and come up with a good-sized chunk and do the same for every cake. And remember that you want a cake to be good and short. Not enough butter for all the cakes. Cow's about to dry up.

But do measure out the sugar and break six eggs for each cake and beat all of it together until you can't beat no more. Dip a finger in the batter to see if it's sweetened to taste. Dash in a little vanilla if it's needed. Bake four layers for each cake and hurry, for other things have to be fixed. All the good smells make you hungry.

Boil the sweet taters, slip the skins off and mash them through the strainer to get out the strings. Grate some raw tater for there's tater pudding to be cooked. Could do without that but somebody would complain.

Make those pie crusts right now. Too little lard and they'll be tough. And don't put too much water in the dough. Just enough to roll them out and get them into the pie tins. As many pies as are being cooked it will take forever to get 'em all done, then no place to put them.

Take the chocolate box and start pouring, but don't overdo it. When you think it's dark enough, taste of it. Better to add a little than to put too much and have bitter pies. "Receipt's" in the head, not on paper. Same for cakes. A good cook's supposed to know how to fix things without forever running to a wrote-down "receipt."

Put the sugar and water on for the cake icings, and stir that stuff every second while it's boiling, and test it for that thread. As soon as you see the thread, put a drop in water and see if it's hard. If so, get that stuff off the stove. Are all the eggs beaten? Beat every bowl until the white is stiff, then add a little sugar and beat some more.

Take that coconut juice and pour it slowly over the cake layers and let it seep into the cakes to make them more moist. Pile the coconut high between the layers and be sure the coconut's sweet enough.

Drain the juice from the pineapple. Grate the lemon good and let a little juice seep in. Let the chocolate boil long enough to get some thickness to it, then pour it over the cake and it will go all the way through.

Don't cut the bananas too thick. They're going to turn brown anyway before all the cake's eaten. But somebody's just got to have banana cake.

Wash the sweet taters and fill the pan. Anybody washed the collards? Cook all the big pot will hold.

Go out boys and catch half-a-dozen fat hens — the ones with the reddest combs — and get them ready for scalding. And try not to wring their heads off, for it gets dirt around the neck and makes them harder to clean. No, don't bother to save heads at Christmas. Dress all of them whole, for some will be baked. The ones used for pastry can be cut up later.

Twist up a piece of newspaper and put it on top of the stove and set it afire. Take the hens by the feet and heads and singe the "hairs" off of them. Be sure to get out all the pinfeathers. May have to scrape them for that.

Now go kill the turkey gobbler and pluck out the feathers. Save the part of the wing that ain't good for eating. Makes good dusters for the house. That little bit of meat and gristle will dry out and they're good for dusting off the furniture. Reckon will there be enough to feed 'em all? It would be a shame not to have enough.

It's a hard job, getting ready for Christmas. No end to the work, but what would it be without all this? Been too busy to even know what the weather's like. Christmas is at hand and it's still cold. Has turned cloudy too. Looks snowy, but don't count on that, for snow just stays away at Christmas. Ice was two-inches thick on watering troughs this morning. Will be as cold tonight. All the folks will be coming in pretty soon. There'll sure be a crowd around. But it seems just like Christmas.   □

Christmas And Fireworks

I t's Christmas Eve and a lot to be done. A light frost but it might get colder. Wind's from the north and it goes right through the clothes and makes the teeth chatter. Seems good to be cold at Christmas though. A few years there have been hot Christmases with no fire and the doors open. Seems like that's a bad sign. Old saying goes: "Hot Christmas, fat graveyard." Seems like the graveyards grow whether hot or cold.

Go to the woods boys and find a little tree to go in the corner. A little one now. No room for a big one. Look at the shape and get one that's round — holly or cedar or pine.

Pop the popcorn girls and string it to go on the tree. String enough so it can dip down and won't have to be stretched to go around. Then get out the tub and scouring broom and scour every floor in the house. Scrub hard around the fireplace for kerosene and something else greasy have been spilled. Around the kitchen stove is greasy too. And move the slop bucket and scour there good. Now don't just scour around it.

Everybody get out there and sweep the yard. Then burn all the trash. The myrtle bush brooms will do better than the reed ones. Seems like the reed ones are about wore out.

There's mistletoe growing on some of the trees in the thicket. And holly's out there too. Find some holly with a lot of berries on it.

Got to wash the bedclothes too. Won't be no more sheets washed until after old Christmas. It's bad luck, they say.

That hind quarter of pig sure smells good cooking. Fix a cup of vinegar and hot pepper to dab over it and let the flavor seep in. And young'uns must keep wood in the stove and check on it every few minutes.

Go and find stockings for all the young'uns and wash them out. Darn the holes in the heels and put nails in the mantelpiece, enough for every stocking.

Stack the wood high on the porch and cut plenty of "lidard" to get the fires started. Shuck plenty of corn so it won't take a lot of time for feeding up.

Tree's right pretty. Cedar. Smells good. A clean smell. Do what you have to do to make it stand and then drape a sheet around it on the floor to make it look like snow. Start at the top with the popcorn string and go round and round and if there's not enough, pop some more corn and do some more stringing.

Now take the holly and make little nests at each end of the mantelpiece and put one on the bureau too. And the lamp chimneys have got to be washed and oil put in the lamps. And trim the wicks. But be sure to trim them straight across. And wipe off the looking glass to the bureau.

Got to get the ashes out of the fireplace too. They're sure packed in there.

Use the little shovel in the kitchen, and be careful when you take them out. There's live coals in them ashes.

And go pour that water out of the skillet and wring that rag out and then wash it or throw it away and tear off another one from the rag bag. Just throw the old one away.

What's happened to the day? It's already getting night and more to be done. It's not Saturday night but it seems like it. The little ones have to be bathed from head to toe. Hard to clean young'uns with chapped hands and elbows and heels. Them elbows feel like pure scales and dirt just seeps in, and around the wrist too. See if there's some Cloverine salve anywhere to put on them. Rubbing them clean makes 'em red and they burn. There's some Cloverine salve in the machine drawer at the top.

Christmas is on the dark of the moon this year and the Roman candles and sky rockets just light up the sky all over the neighborhood. The red and green and blue balls of fire look like they're going to fall on the houses.

And the firecrackers must be the biggest the boys ever bought. They sound like they're going to tear everything to pieces. Look at that one! All the colors and something like sparklers too. Listen to all the laughing and hollering. Every young'un in the neighborhood must be out there.

Uh oh! Something's smelling. A young'uns busted one of them stink bombs. Git in the yard with that mess and them spit devils too. Git on the doorstep or on a brick bat with them things.

Fire that stove for the turkey.

Bring in the fruit and stuff while all the young'uns are on the outside. Full bushel of oranges. Full bushel of red delicious apples. Three dozen tangerines. Five pounds of bananas. Five pounds of weighed-out raisins. Four pounds of English walnuts. Four pounds of "niggertoes." Ten pounds of weighed-out candy in all.

Enough for a feast and that's what it is, but it's just once a year. Whole lot of folks don't even have this though. 'Specially the poor folks in town. They're pulling weatherboarding off of them half-rotten houses and burning it. We're blessed.

Them firecrackers are sure going off everywhere. Hope no boy gets caught with one in his hand when it explodes. Lord! Them things are dangerous.

Stars a shining and it's cold. Young'uns feet will get cold out there. Listen. Somebody's singing. A whole gang of them. They're on the road. I hear "Silent Night." Sure seems like Christmas this year.

Put more wood in the stove to cook the turkey. That'll have to go on all night.

Now they're singing "Away In A Manger." Closer by too.

Time for little ones to go to bed now. All cleaned up and cheek's a shining but some of that's from being chapped. Bring the Cloverine salve and rub them in it. And get the "pneumonia cure" (Vick's Vaporub) and rub on their chests. They're rattling inside. Let them swallow a little dab too. It'll help to break up them colds. Fix the feather beds on the floor and let the children pile down. They're excited and may not sleep too good. Put plenty of cover over them.

It's getting late. Fire's burning down. Now hang up the stockings and get the room in order. Time for everybody to quieten down for Santa Claus is coming tonight. □

All The Joys Of Christmas

T emperature in the 20s. Skies dark except for morning stars low on the horizon. Wind calm. A mouse scampers across the floor, startled by the sound of muffled voices from a bedroom. Whispers almost, then becoming louder. Children are awake, tense.

A hand finds the matchbox on the mantel, rubs the match across the rough side of the box. Light flickers and a lamp shade is removed and the wick is ignited. A small amount of kerosene is poured over the wood in the fireplace and the fire flares up quickly, giving added heat to get the wood burning.

Stockings are hung close together on the mantel, for children and grandchildren are there. Stuffed full, they look grotesque.

Chairs are pushed back or removed from the room, to allow space for the children to play. Each child knows the order in which the stockings were hung and shoes are placed in that order around the fireplace.

There is a baby doll with painted-on hair and eyes and two teeth showing from a tiny, half-opened mouth, wrapped in a flannel blanket, lying in a pasteboard box. This one is brunette. Next is a duplicate, except this doll is blonde. They say "Mama" when turned on their faces.

A very small, shining red wagon for a toddler; a tiny dancing man that turns all the way around and shakes his legs and arms when the spring is wound; a tin tea set and a little stove with cooking utensils; a tricycle and a multi-colored horn lying on the seat;

A dump truck that runs with a lever to release the body, with a harp placed in the part that dumps; a horse with bridle and reins with wheels so that it can be rolled — gray with black mane; a top of many colors that spins for a full minute. For Ma a new potato grater and a little blue dish with a pin cushion inside. For Pa a pair of socks and a new pair of "galluces."

Boys of 10-11 don't expect visits from Santa but gifts are there with their names on them. Lying on the bureau in small boxes are pocketknives with real steel blades.

Children converge around the fireplace and their eyes and faces tell the whole story of Christmas. Stockings are taken down and part of the contents dumped on the floor, and all the fruit and nuts and toys are too much and they try to eat and play at the same time and oranges, apples and tangerines roll all over the floor and they try to gather them up and hold to their toys too and everything falls.

All the family gathers around the children, sitting on the floor and sharing the joys of the season. The boys with the knives say nothing, but smile when they remove them from their overalls' pockets, feel their weight in their hands, observe their shininess and count the number of blades. Just the thing for playing "stick frog" and for making sling shots.

The fire burns brightly. Warmth fills the room. Everybody's laughing. Everybody's happy. Children scream with pleasure.

Outside, the air is cold. The first signs of dawn are appearing in the east. In every house as far as the eye can see, light is showing from the windows.

Sunrise reveals a heavy coating of frost and a white world for a little while. Smoke rises from the chimneys straight up into the blue skies. Neighborhood children begin to run up and down the roads and visit all the houses to see what Santa has brought. Their breath appears as steam as it meets the cold air. Toboggans are pulled over the ears to keep out the cold.

All the family scatters over the neighborhood and children are bundled up so they can play. The "old man" and the "old lady" are left alone with their own thoughts for a little while. They say nothing, just stare into the fire and watch the spirals of smoke go up the chimney.

She looks at him and he takes her hand into his and gives it a pat.

The little nests of holly on the mantel and the bureau and the sprigs of mistletoe over the doors say the message of Christmas and the scent of cedar fills the room from the little tree over in the corner with its strings of popcorn as decorations.

Children return to their stockings to retrieve raisins, "niggertoes," English walnuts, coconut creams, peanut squares and chocolate drops. Oranges with a patch of peeling pulled off are lying around. Large delicious apples show one bite from a child's mouth. Raisins are mashed flat on the floor.

The skies become cloudy and some wind is stirring. It's beginning to look like snow. The road is filled with children and grown-ups running from house to house. Smoke from the chimneys now blows southward from the movement of the north wind.

Things are stirring in the kitchen. The table is overlaid with the white, starched linen cloth kept in the safe drawer for such special occasions.

Round up the nail kegs and the wooden boxes in the outbuildings. Fetch them in for every child will have a seat on Christmas Day. The food is steaming and the table is laden. Everyone gathers around the dining room table and the side table in the kitchen.

"Now heavenly Father, we thank You for the joys of Christmas and that You came to us as a little baby and changed the whole course of history. Let us remember the real meaning of Christmas and give You the honor You deserve. We thank You for all the blessings of life, for family and friends and the closeness of this occasion. Bless this food to the nourishment of our bodies for Christ's sake, amen."

The menu: Turkey with brown gravy and sage and onion dressing made from corn-bread and biscuit crumbs combined; baked pork with tender, crisp skin and natural brown gravy; rice with each grain standing apart; baked hen; chicken pastry; collards; home-canned corn and string beans; baked sweet potatoes; chow chow, pepper relish, beets, cucumbers, pickled peaches, watermelon rind pickles; buttermilk biscuits; baked corn bread;

Cakes: coconut, chocolate, black walnut, pineapple, lemon and fruitcake;

Pies: chocolate, lemon, coconut, dried apple, and sweet potato; sweet potato pudding; ambrosia; coffee.

The day wanes and soon night will appear. Children run around the yards with their toys and fruits. Somebody high on wine hollers "Yippee" somewhere up the road. Boys pull their new knives from their pockets and inspect them, then pull out a blade and cut a limb from a tree and begin whittling off small slices. It sure looks like snow.

A larger boy takes a child's harp far down the path toward the hog pen and the first six notes of "Jingle Bells," all with the same sound, are heard up at the house.

"Feeding up," is done, more wood is piled on the porch, the fire burns brightly in the fireplace. Night appears and across the way a girl in a clear voice sings "O Little Town of Bethlehem." The night is dark. The air is cold. It sure looks like snow but the "old man" says he doesn't feel it in his bones.

Christmas in the 1930s. ☐

New Year's Day In The '30s

N ew Year's Day was no big deal back when I was a boy. Fortunately, we usually observed the day because the weather wasn't favorable for outside work and it was a school holiday even back then. But there were no New Year's Eve parties out in the sticks or in town either that I knew of. And if people stayed up to see the new year in, I sure didn't.

We did one thing that is still traditional today. We always had hog jowls (we called them jaws) and black-eyed peas. That same old saying about a dollar for every pea eaten was around then and I guess it filtered down to us from earlier days just as it has done from my generation to the present. Now hog jaw was never my favorite food, no matter how it was fixed. And Ma would try to doctor up hog heads with the jaws on them by baking them and putting vinegar and hot pepper on them. But somehow there was too much fat there and even what lean there was didn't taste too good. The lean part seemed to be a little bit knotty or something, like the heads might have had kernels in them. But I'm sure that wasn't the case for they were always like that.

So we always knew what we were eating on New Year's Day.

There was something else of a superstitious nature that was a part of the new year. Everybody wanted a man to visit a house before a woman on that day. It was bad luck if a woman visitor came first. But I never found out what the bad luck would be, but they had all sorts of ideas, like if a rooster crowed in the doorway of a house there would be a death in the family and bells ringing in the ears meant a person would die in the direction of the ear that was ringing. No axes or saws or pitchforks or hoes or things like that could be brought in the house. Bad luck. The same about breaking mirrors or walking under a ladder. To tell the truth, I didn't believe in all that mess even then, but it was the grown-ups that were all fired up about such things.

The worst thing about New Year's was that school started the next day, and after all the loafing during Christmas that was the one place we didn't want to return to.

It was a letdown — post-Christmas blues if you please — that sort of gave us the blahs. And most of us were stuffed full of cold after traipsing around so much during Christmas. We'd cough our heads off and hawk and spit and the more we did that the more phlegm seemed to accumulate. And sometimes people got flu and were laid up. It just wasn't the best time of the year and everybody was as ill as a hornet and snapping at each other and we young'uns would fight and the "old man" would threaten to kill us.

All the calendars were turned to January and if Pa had been lucky there were one or two calendars for every room. They served an artistic purpose for us with their colorful pictures and we needed those without pictures to mark dates throughout the year. Ma would mark the dates that hens were set and when they were due to hatch in the kitchen calendar. Pa would mark the dates sows and cows were bred and when their young were due.

And the moon changes were very important for all manner of farming activities — cutting wood, making soap, planting underground crops and other crops as well.

And the almanacs that Pa bought every year were read religiously, even to the jokes. The signs of the Zodiac were important too. For instance, they didn't want to have teeth pulled when the sign was in the head. We read those long-range weather forecasts and really relied on them to an extent, although we seldom referred back to them for accuracy.

Along about the first of the year the seed catalogs had arrived and they also held our interest, for they were colorful. There is a much wider variety offered in seed catalogs today, but in general the practice of sending out catalogs has continued for as long as I can remember.

And we knew that sometime before Good Friday, when just about everybody planted their gardens, several neighborhood children would come around with their packets of garden seeds and flowers, and that practically every home would buy several varieties of seeds.

It was also the neighborhood children who brought around the Cloverine salve and the Rosebud salve every year. The salve would be in round cardboard containers, one box stacked on top of the other, and there were also color pictures that were given away with a box of salve. Somehow I remember they'd take the pictures out of the same box with the salve, unroll them and show kittens at play or maybe collie dogs, or Jesus. This is a little fuzzy but I know that pictures were associated with the salve.

And we used that salve too. There wasn't any chapstick as such then and that old Cloverine salve was mighty soothing to lips that were raw from the wind and cold. We also used the salves on cuts and things like that. Smelled good too. Especially the Rosebud salve.

We also made New Year's resolutions just as people do today, and just as now, we never kept them. Ma was going to raise more biddies so there'd be more chicken for the family, but she failed to take into account the number that might be eaten by a pack of hungry hogs, or how many the hawks might scoop up and carry to the woods, despite the "Nox Varmit" she mixed in their food to kill the birds, or the scarecrow in the area where the chicken coops stood. Now I can't find the words "Nox Varmit" in the dictionary, but I swear that's what it was called. It was a powder that was supposed to be poisonous to hawks but not domestic fowl. When I looked for "Nox Varmica" the words were in the dictionary.

But whatever Pa may have resolved to do, he didn't tell any of us anything about it. He no doubt resolved to find more work for we boys to do to keep us out of a little less mischief, knowing Pa like I did. He knew he had a problem with five growing boys, and his best recourse was to keep them busy. I'm sure that was Pa's biggest New Year's resolution.   □

A Winter Night Long Ago

B itter cold would sweep down on the area sometimes without any warning signals. With no weather forecasts except those outdated in the newspaper that arrived a day after it was printed, cold snaps were to be expected after a warm spell in which the once-frozen soil would become mushy and people would go without coats for a little while and worry about their fresh meat in the smokehouse.

At such times it was so cold the stars appeared frozen in the vastness of space and the howling winter winds only added to the hardships. The open fields allowed ample space for the north winds to sweep full-force around the buildings and roar and whistle as they spent their fury on their way to oblivion.

Frozen limbs on trees appeared arthritic as they creaked and broke against the force of the winds and tin tubs and buckets were blown from benches and piazzas to roll erratically across yards and cause ghostly sounds as they slammed against clothesline posts or fence posts or the wood blocks that served as the underpinning of most of the shackly houses.

Inside, the fireplace was piled high with oak wood that generated good heat in the one warm room in the house. It was even cheerful and bright after the wood burned down to red embers, especially with the light from the lamp on the bureau. After supper the entire family would gather in the room, for families were especially close in those winters of necessity. Keeping warm was the prime concern when the weather was severe.

The water bucket would freeze over, even if it were set in the hall, and the dipper would have to be freed from the ice before children could quench their thirst.

Each child and the parents had their places around the half-circle, with Ma and Pa situated on either side of the fireplace in their old rockers, and the children in the straight-backed chairs with their ragged straw bottoms. Although frigid on the outside, it was cozy around the fire and the girls' legs would burn from the heat and they would have to turn sideways to be comfortable. Heat from the fireplace turned their shins red-spotted. But the heat didn't penetrate to the back so well, so part of the body would be overheated while the other was a little chilly.

School-age children would take their books from homemade booksacks fashioned from bed ticking and do their studying for the night. They would trim their pencils with a knife, leaving a blunt end to the lead, and put the pencils in their mouths to make the writing darker as they worked on their rough paper tablets.

The wind would rattle the windowpanes and ruffle the curtains. With no underpinning, the wind came up through the cracks in the floor and Pa would take the firestick and punch the half-burned oak or pine saplings and hundreds of sparks would fly up the chimney, but sometimes a drift of wind would sweep down the chimney and ashes would be blown on the hearth and they would be swept back with the broom that sat in the corner near the hearth.

A pre-teener would be sent to fetch more wood from the piazza, and an instant fear would well up in his chest, for he had to penetrate the darkness of the hall and actually go outside to gather the wood. Two graveyards were visible from the back porch and he dared not look toward them for fear of seeing a "haint." It was never ghosts in those days, or haunted houses. It was always "haints" or "hainted houses." And there were tall tales about "haints" that roamed the countryside.

The feet were a little too fast for the body and they felt as light as a feather and something seemed to be just behind them, and the trip from the piazza to the front room was only a matter of seconds. Doors could not be left open for that would allow heat to escape. And a boy dared not ask a brother to go with him for the wood for that would have been a sissy thing to do.

Among the family group, if there were grown girls they would do tatting or look at the farm journals that came once a month, Ma would knit socks from left-over tobacco twine, and Pa would nod if the noise wasn't too great. If it was, he would take one look at the noise-makers, and things would quieten down. Older boys who would become bored with it all would go to their ice-cold beds and turn in for the night.

The water in the black wrought-iron skillet that was placed in the coals earlier is hot, actually too hot without adding cold water that is brought in from the water bucket. Ashes that have blown into the water are ignored as the children begin their nightly ritual of washing their ears, necks, faces, and hands in preparation for school the next day. A piece of cloth torn from a ragged sheet or some article of clothing serves as a washcloth, and each child uses the same water and the same cloth. If there is "sweet" soap it is on the hearth and if there isn't, lye soap suffices and no comment is made regardless of which kind it is.

Each child removes his shoes and long black socks and places them on the hearth so that they can be put on before the fire in the morning rather than in the cold bedrooms.

The fire has now become only dying embers and the flickering light from the lamp casts shadows over the room. The wind continues to blow and the windowpanes rattle on.

The old clock on the mantel chimes nine times and the cold begins to penetrate the room. The children finish their semi-baths and Ma checks the ears and sometimes runs a finger deep enough to get a yell from a youngster who has failed to remove all the grime and dirt that accumulated during the day. If wrists still show signs of dirt, they have to be scrubbed again, even if it means twisting the flesh to remove the dirt. Children begin to yawn and stretch and after the covers are turned back on the beds, they dive under the covers and feel for a moment as if they are in an ice box until the feather bed warms around them from the heat of their bodies, and their day is ended.

Soon all becomes quiet except for the whistling of the wind around the corners of the house and under their heavy load of quilts, a family sleeps snugly during a winter night of long ago.   □

Quiltings Held Yearly

From the time the deep freezes were upon the land to early spring when the wild violets appeared along ditch banks and robins began to pitch in the yards, women of the 1930s became involved in making quilt tops.

When they were through with dinner they got out their scrap bags and began cutting pieces from patterns made of newspaper that would be shaped to make the squares. Sometimes they would take several scraps and pin them to the pattern to speed up the cutting process.

Now I know that all scraps from clothing made at home were saved, but I have a feeling that such material was also available at the stores in town, for I don't recall ever seeing all the bright colors in quilts being a part of wearing apparel.

And there were numerous quilt designs — diamonds, squares, stars, oblongs, etc.

Quilting in those days was a necessity rather than an art form. It took a lot of cover to keep large families warm in winter, and quilts did wear out with the passing of time, and after several washings the cotton underneath would begin to show where stitches came loose in the quilt top.

Also, when children married and set up housekeeping, mothers on both sides usually gave the bride and groom a couple of quilts for starts. They would also give them two or three hens and a rooster. These were the major contributions of parents in helping their children set up housekeeping.

But just because quilts were a necessity to families of the 1930s it didn't mean the women were not artistic in their craft. They were accomplished seamstresses and were proud of their fine stitching. They would sew the scraps together, then admire their handiwork as they held it up for inspection.

Fine quilts hang in headquarters of giant corporations and in art galleries today as examples of fine art, and some bring astronomical prices — in the hundreds of thousands of dollars. And some of those quilts of the 1930s era could have competed with the best of them, but they served their purpose well.

But there is no doubt that if those women could have known the value that would be placed on them in the latter part of the century, they would have put a few aside to cushion their Social Security payments in the 1980s.

During the course of the winter and spring several quilt tops might be pieced together in preparation for a "quilting" after the weather warmed up. And by whatever names they are called today — "quilting bees" or "quilting parties — " there was no sophistication attached to the affair in those days. They were "quiltings" period.

But other work had to be done before a "quilting" could be held, a lot of it. The solid back of the quilt, made from homespun, flour sacks or muslin, had to be dyed, and several colors were chosen for the backs.

One very important part of the quilting process was carding the bats that gave the warmth to the finished quilt. These were made from cotton and homemakers would have a tow sack or two filled and saved from scrap cotton pickings to make the bats.

A simple pair of cards with hundreds of stiff steel prongs on each card were used in making the bats.

A thin coating of cotton was put on one of the cards and the process began by taking one card in each hand and working the lint into the steel prongs that removed any knots or other impurities. When this was accomplished one of the cards was used to loosen the cotton from the other, and the result was about a 3x6-inch bat as light as a feather.

The bats were placed into a straight pile and when the quilt backs were attached to the quilting frames, the cotton bats were placed in rows over the quilt back and the top placed over the cotton to be quilted.

The quilting frames must have been professionally made, for there were literally hundreds of holes bored in them of fairly small dimensions to accommodate the pegs used as the quilt was rolled after a course was quilted.

The back of the quilt was attached to the frame with tobacco twine that was run through the holes in the frame and into the quilt back.

Hooks were screwed into the ceilings in most cases and heavy cord extended from the hooks and held up the frames, although sometimes the frames were held up with chairs placed at each corner.

So when the big day came, the neighborhood women gathered for the "quilting" in clean frocks and starched aprons with freshly combed hair twisted into large balls and held up with horn hairpins and combs that made their faces appear almost drawn.

Tucked into their apron pockets were their thimbles and snuff boxes and handkerchiefs to wipe the corners of their mouths when they "dipped." And in reporting on how we really were, I must say that a majority of rural housekeepers in those days partook of snuff, but none that I knew smoked. They would either fill a jaw with the powder or use a toothbrush to fill their mouths with the powdered tobacco.

And this caused problems for they had to have something to use as spittoons and in many cases they were tin cans, and it was dangerous to place them on the floors for the young children were there too, playing underneath the quilts while the mothers worked. Sometimes a "spit cup" would get overturned and a "mess" was the result.

Deftly they made their fine stitches, following the design marked off with chalk, transforming the layers of cloth and cotton into works of beauty. As the courses were quilted the quilt was rolled and the quilters drew closer and closer together. One hand was under the quilt and the other stitching the material in a manner similar to an accordion player that uses one hand at the back of the instrument to bring out the desired sound.

Quilts were taking form in several rooms and the usual small talk was carried on among the quilters with an occasional outburst of laughter.

There was the usual feast at dinner time as was the case whenever a group gathered for the day on special occasions. "Quiltings" were the only times when it was an all-woman gathering but I can't recall what became of the menfolks on those occasions. Maybe it was the one time of the year when the women had an opportunity to "run" the men out of their domain.

After the "quilting" the quilts were removed from the frame and the larger extension of the back folded over the top and stitched down, making the finished product. And it was a yearly ritual after the weather warmed up and the birds were singing and crops were beginning to grow.   □

Silent Snows Of Winter

T he snows sneaked in like thieves in those winters of long ago. With no up-to-the-minute weather reports telling about low-pressure systems moving up the coast from the Gulf of Mexico and a cold front moving in, there was no way of knowing what the weather would be from day to day. We did have the Turner's and Farmers' almanacs with their projections for an entire year, and that was about as reliable as Pa's "feeling" about snow.

We'd go to bed at night with the stars shining to be awakened before day with something cold and powdery falling on our faces and we knew that the snow had come and it was finding its way into the house through the cracks under the eaves.

That made it seem colder than it was, for snow didn't usually fall when the weather was too cold. Just a little below the freezing point was ideal for snow. The coldest weather usually came after the snowfall.

If the snow came in daylight, the first etching of white showed on cotton, corn and tobacco stalks in the fields, and on the grass around the garden fences. It was a contrast in black and white at first, with the dirt appearing even blacker than normal, but as the snow piled up, everything was covered except for the mule lots. They were so wet even a four- or five-inch snowfall would leave dark places in the lots where water remained in the accumulation of mush.

But there was no school and we were as happy as a jaybird sitting in a pine when it snowed. We'd go outside and look up into the sky, open our mouths and let the snowflakes fall in. As soon as there was enough accumulation, we started throwing snowballs, and the harder it snowed the happier we were. Of course we had to get out to the woodpile and stack every bit of wood we could get on the porch. It took a lot of wood to halfway heat the front room and it kept us constantly in the woods cutting, sawing and hauling.

Where there was a clean place, we'd scrape up a ball of snow and take it inside and hold it over the fire and let the smoke taste seep in. Then we'd eat our fills.

And Ma would fuss and quarrel and threaten to kill us if we didn't clean off our shoes when we came in from the outside. She had placed a guano sack on the porch steps for us to use to clean our feet on. But we'd forget and come inside with snow on our brogans and the snow would melt, leaving little puddles of water everywhere. Ma hated for it to snow.

Sometimes the white stuff would pile up all day and it was the prettiest sight in the world to look as far as the eye could see with nothing but white. It was the only time when our house was prettier than the "boss man's" down the road. His house had been painted at some time and it still had a grayish look about it where it had once been white before time and the elements faded the white to gray. His was better built too. But our house and the other tenant houses in the neighborhood stood out like little white castles. A little bit of the dark gray weatherboarding showed, but for the most part, everything was painted white by the snow fairy.

And snow just brought out the beauty of things we didn't pay any attention to most of the time. The hay rake was in the barnyard all year and was hardly noticed, but when it snowed every rake was ridged with snow an inch or more deep. Same with the disk harrow and the mowing maching. And insignificant wire fences, hardly observed at any other time, became squares of white where the snow settled on them. It was a world of fantasy for a little while.

Sometimes it would get colder while precipitation was still falling, and snow would turn to sleet, and then rain that froze over and gave us a world of ice. Long icicles would form on the eaves of the porch and around the top of the house and when there was a little melting we'd break off long pieces of ice and eat them as if it were the heat of summer. If the ax had been left on the ground, it would be frozen over and boys would have to go out and break the crust to find it, for more wood would have to be cut.

Ma would put on a pot of peas and let them simmer slowly, or a ham bone and put rice in it after it had boiled until it was tender. We boys would get sweet potatoes and put them in the coals and let them get about half done and have a tater feast.

Then we'd have a fit for snow cream. We liked canned milk for snow cream since it was thicker than regular milk, so somebody would have to trek to the store for the milk and vanilla if there wasn't any around after Christmas. That is if there was any money around. If not, there might be enough eggs to sell to get the items. But cold weather cut down on egg production, so eggs could be scarce, too.

But Pa was so curious he wouldn't eat anything with milk in it, not if there was any milk taste there. He'd take snow and add sugar and lemon flavoring and a little water. I don't know what he called it, but it sure wasn't snow cream.

To kill the boredom of being inside, we would get pieces of stove wood, take butcher knives and the hammer, and split the wood into small pieces and build bird traps. We'd build them in the same fashion they made pens to hold the hens and biddies in spring from tobacco sticks. With the bird traps, we would fasten the pieces together with tobacco twine. Then we would take a long string of twine and attach it to the trap and put biscuit crumbs inside, wait from the barn door until the birds went in to get the crumbs, and pull the string.

All the neighborhood boys would get together and we'd run and slide on the snow and ice and wallow each other in the frozen mess and throw snowballs at each other and we were apparently immune to the cold until the games ended and we suddenly realized that our feet were numb with cold.

We'd go home, pull off our brogans, hold our feet before the fire and put our wet socks on the hearth to dry and the steam would rise from the wet socks and that smell of dirty socks would fill the room and everybody would look disgusted, 'specially Pa. I reckon he just figured there was no real way to handle a pack of boys except to let them grow up and get out of the way. And Ma continued to get on us about traipsing in and out, in and out, toting in snow and dirt and messing up the whole house. Winter in the 1930s.   □

Tobacco: A 12-Month Job

With tobacco a 12-month operation, the process begins in January. Tobacco beds have to be prepared and cloths made to cover them with after the seeds have been sown, so both men and women are involved.

As for the site of the beds, there are two choices. One is to clear up a new ground that is not saturated with all manner of weed and grass seeds, and the other is to plant the bed in a rich place and let it be taken over by grass and weeds. So there are no easy choices.

Clearing a new ground for tobacco beds requires an awful lot of digging and cutting and carrying out roots and cutting around stumps to loosen them up so the mules can be hitched to trace chains and the chains placed around the stump to get it out of the way. Before a new ground is finally cleared you always wonder whether it is worth it to be less plagued with growth that you don't want among the tobacco seedlings. That is until the beds are planted and the tiny plants can't be seen for grass and weeds, and every inch of ground must be picked, over and over.

In case anybody is wondering, there were no fumigants to put on beds 50 years ago, no weed killers, no plastic even. Man, we did everything the hard way.

But it was a joint effort in getting the tobacco beds sown. First, the "old man" had made a trip to town on the wagon to purchase the covering for the beds from the farm supply places. And there were two or three qualities of tobacco cloth. The best quality was closer woven than the other grades (and cost more) so the tenant farmer always chose the second quality for he had to buy the cloth out of the money he got from the landlord to run himself on for the year.

I think the cloth came in two-foot widths and the widths had to be sewn together either by hand or on the sewing machine and Ma chose the sewing maching for it was faster, so she always cautioned Pa to go to a department store and buy some coarse white Clark's sewing thread and it took several large spools to sew the cloth together. And he may have had to tie a string around his finger to remember for all I know, but he'd better not forget that thread.

And we fudged on tobacco cloth sometimes anyway. We'd save a cloth and use it for two years, but in all truthfulness, it didn't give the proper protection to the young tobacco plants, for a few holes always came in the cloth and we'd have been better off if Pa had sacrificed the money and bought new cloth every year. But those few dollars were too precious and were needed too badly not to cut every corner possible.

After the cloth was removed from the beds when the weather warmed up, we would roll up the cloth and fashion it into a slip knot to reduce the bulk and also to make it easier to handle, and hang it on pegs under the shelter. But still, part of the beds had to have new cloth every year.

And to be truthful, we didn't do a lot of grubbing tobacco beds. We did do it a time or two, but most of the time we prepared the beds on open land, then cut pine saplings and placed around them and drove nails all around the logs to attach the cloth to. Each bed would be about 20 feet wide by 50 feet long.

So we boys prepared the beds and raked them clean and the little bitty seeds that could hardly be seen were mixed in a little fertilizer and broadcast over the bed and the guano showed where the seeds had been sown. Then we used a light-weight homemade roller to settle the seeds in the ground.

In the meantime, Ma had filled the bobbin to the old Singer and stitched up all those lengths of cloth and after we cut switches and stuck them in the ground in straight rows, each end inserted into the soil to make a half-circle to hold up the tobacco cloth, the cloths were placed over the beds and attached to the nails all around the beds. Then some switches would come loose at one end and poke up and make small holes in the cloth.

We waited for several weeks before even peeping through the cloth to see whether the infinitesimal plants had come up, for the germinating process is slow for tobacco seeds, especially when the ground is cold.

And tobacco plants have always been compared with coins in determining their size . . . as big as a dime, a penny, a nickel, a quarter, a half-dollar, until they turn up and the real growth process begins.

But this was only the beginning, for by the time tobacco plants were seen, the grass had already made its appearance, and under the protective covering, it was growing up a storm. By the time the weather warmed up enough, everybody available was put to picking plant beds. We made scaffolds to go across the entire width of the bed for the pickers to sit on, and low stools were utilized and pickers had buckets and cans to put the grass and weeds in. And we were cautioned, under the threat of death, not to dig our feet into the beds and tear up the ground. But no matter what was said, when I was on a plant bed, it looked as if a mule had been in there with its hooves. They made me pull off my shoes, but I still managed to tear up the soil, and I even tried lying on a scaffold and not even putting my feet on the ground. But that didn't last long.

And we used every "little" spoon Ma had and were again threatened with death if we didn't bring them home when we left the plant bed. "Little" spoons made it much easier to pluck the grass and weeds from between the plants than trying to pull it up with just the fingers. Everybody that had a pocketknife used it also.

It would take days sometimes to pick the beds, and it wasn't long until they had to be gone over again. But once the plants turned up and the nights grew warmer, they overtook the grass and it was no longer a problem. So January got the tobacco process off to its start, and it was at least Thanksgiving before it all ended for the year.   □

Coping With Itch And Lice

O ur mothers of yesteryear were a generally dedicated, home-loving, compassionate group who showed a great love for families, neighbors and friends. Proper in deportment, they soothed the hurt child, comforted it at their bosoms and blew on the wound to lessen the pain. They usually kept peace in the family. It was unusual for them to get fired up over anything, but there were two things that would get them out of kilter in one second. One was when a young'un would come home from school with head lice and the other was when he brought in the itch.

Whoopee! You never heard such ranting and raving with throwing dish rags or baby diapers around. They were infuriated. Both head lice and scabies were associated with filth to them, and they felt that it was a reflection on them as parents. They would automatically begin to scratch their heads and under their shoulder blades as they took the child down for a head inspection or have it spread the fingers to see if there was roughness with reddened skin.

Luckily, in most cases there were not head lice and itch at the same time for that would have been a little too much to take. If they were searching for lice and they saw the first infinitesimal white nit on a strand of hair, they absolutely went crazy, realizing that every person in the family would have to be checked and "deloused." The very idea of the "old man" getting them caused a chill to go up and down their spines. If women were intolerant of such things, they were mild compared to a man with head lice or itch.

Every child's head was gone over with a fine-toothed comb and the newspaper over which the head bent was observed for those pale, sickly-looking tiny insects that were causing all the trouble. If they were heavily infested there would be several lice observed among the dandruff and nits that came off with the scraping, for those combs raked the pure scalp and sometimes left sore places due to the thoroughness of the mothers' combings.

The more this went on the more everyone in the family scratched their heads and the grown-up children were so disgusted some would immediately saturate their hair in kerosene and leave it on the scalp for a while. The mothers would question the children as to whom they had played with or sat near in school in an effort to determine the source of the lice. But just as is the case today, there was no pinpointing the source.

Mothers would feel that they had been negligent and had not been clean enough in their housekeeping. They wanted to gather up every piece of bed clothing and all wearing apparel and boil everything to get out the taint. But they learned that when lice and itch made the rounds at school, they usually affected most of the students and this helped to ease their conscience to a degree.

Within a short time the lice would be killed and a normal pattern of life would return.

When the itch struck, it was something else. Sterner measures had to be resorted to then. Mites were under the skin and they had to be killed before the lesions could be cured. Somebody had to go to town then to get some 30 Minute Itch Cure. That stuff wasn't kept in family medicine cabinets (a shelf in the pantry where the usual drugs used by families were stored).

At some time during their school years, most children became victims of lice and scabies, and one round with 30 Minute Itch Cure gave them all they ever wanted in treatment for the itch. In the first place, the medication smelled like rotten eggs and in the second place, it was pretty strong stuff. It had to be if it was to kill mites that had worked their way under the skin.

So every child that showed any signs of itch was medicated — from head to toe. Water was heated and poured into a wash tub and cooled down to a reasonable level. The child was stripped and placed in the tub and a thorough wash job done by the mother instead of the child. The child was dried off and placed on the floor and then the dirty work began. Medication was rubbed on every inch of the body, from the scalp to the toes. Even the stink became secondary to the burning caused by the medicine. It literally burned the child up. After a thorough saturation the child would sometimes run naked around the house in an effort to cool the burning. And the smell was awful and there surely must have been at least one rotten egg in every bottle. But if that 30 Minute Itch Cure was applied in the right way, it cured the itch in a little while and the pattern of life again became normal.

Every piece of the child's clothing was gathered up with thumb and forefinger and taken to a tub on the outside and put in soak, along with the bed clothing. Potash (box lye) was added to the water as a killing agent and almost everything in the house was boiled.

Come to think of it, it is a thousand wonders that many, many children of a long time ago didn't die from box lye, considering the amount of it that was used by families. It was a must in laundering clothes for there were no regular cleaning agents as we have today and it was generously used in washpots and it would cut grease and whiten dingy clothes. We saw plenty of those red devils with their pitchforks on the can labels in those days. And once in a great while there would be a report of a child getting into the lye box, but that was very rare.

Also, with kerosene sitting on the premises all the time to replenish the oil supply in the lamps and to get fires started when fat lightwood was scarce, once in a while a toddler would drink kerosene and had to be taken to town to have the stomach pumped out, but that was also a very seldom occurrence. □

Wood-Cutting: Yearly Ritual

With Christmas past, the new year well begun and a break in the winter weather, it's time to get the saws and axes ready for cutting stove wood and tobacco wood for the year. With their outing-lined denim jackets to keep them warm, the men congregate under the shelters and begin preparing the tools for the task at hand. When the season and the moon are right, they will take to the woods for the annual ritual and the tools of the trade must be ready and waiting.

The cross-cut saw is taken down from nails that held it to the side of the shelter and one end placed in the vise in order to sharpen the teeth for smooth cutting when the trees are felled and sawed up into the desired lengths. A special file is used to sharpen the teeth and one person holds the part of the saw not held by the vise. It takes an experienced hand to sharpen saw teeth.

The heavy wooden mallet is pulled fom the eaves of the shelter and checked out. Mallets are homemade from hard wood and are in one piece with the hand-hewn handle and the mallet itself round and sturdy to get the wedge into a piece of wood so it can be split.

The wedge isn't in its place on the plate of the shelter and a search has to be made, for the steel tool is a requirement in splitting wood. Some young'un has misplaced it, and the most likely place to find it is on the woodpile among the chips and other debris. So rakes and pitchforks are taken to the woodpile and chips raked gently in an effort to uncover the wedge. An extensive search is made around the saw horse but nothing is found there.

By this time a father is becoming angry with a pack of boys and starts kicking at stray pieces of wood lying around, and there is the wedge half immersed in the center of a tough piece of gum wood rather than on the edge where it could have been split.

The axes are taken to the whet rock with its handle that turns and one person maneuvers the grinding stone while another holds the ax to the stone to whet it to razor sharpness. Axes and hatchets are sharpened thoroughly for the woodcutting ahead.

It's also a good time to grease wagon wheels for there's a lot of hauling to be done and it will make the job easier if the axles are well-greased. So a hub is loosened and a piece of wood of the proper length found to hold up the wagon while the wheel is removed. The wood is inserted under the wagon, the wheel taken off and the axle greased thoroughly with heavy, black grease rubbed around the axle with a flat stick. This continues until all the wheels are greased.

So everything is placed in readiness and when the time is right, all the available men and boys climb into the wagon for a trip far up into the woods. They have a pop bottle filled with kerosene and a cut-off pine bough for a stopper stuck in the hind pocket of their overalls to pour on the saw to make sawing easier. A seasoned woodsman, weighing at least 200 pounds, is hired to help in the sawing process. The area where the trees are to be felled is cleared of high underbrush before the sawing begins. There has to be some planning in cutting the trees down so they will fall across each other to allow for sawing without the wood binding the saw.

A chip is cut from the pine that is to be felled so that it will fall in the desired direction, and then the actual sawing begins. The bottoms of those trees look gigantic as the saw, placed at a side angle, begins to cut into them.

And buddy, this separates the boys from the men, or to say it more correctly, it makes men out of the boys. Take a 16-, 17-, 18-year-old boy with some belly flabbiness from overeating and with less exercise during the winter months and put him at one end of a cross-cut saw and a real man at the other end that exerts some pressure on that saw, and pulling it through that wood for a full day half-kills them. It gets all the breath and cutting all the way through those trees seems interminable.

All the trees are cut down and the limbs containing the pine boughs trimmed off and taken out of the way, and then the sawing begins in earnest. The smoothest, best-looking trees are sawed up into stove wood and those twisted or with a lot of knots are used for tobacco wood.

It is impossible to determine the amount of wood that will be needed to fire the kitchen stove, but one good way is to decide on the number of trees that might supply enough wood for the year, then add at least three more, and then usually wind up around Thanksgiving with nothing left but four-foot lengths still lying in a pile at the tobacco barn. This is hauled up to the woodpile on the tobacco truck and sawed in lengths for the stove by boys after they get home from school. And seasoned pine and a shackly saw horse with a dull saw can result in a demeaning chore and a boy might get torn down by an irate mother with supper to cook and no wood to cook with.

After the stove wood is sawed into the desired lengths it is slabbed up in the woods and then thrown into the wagon and will be split into burning-size pieces on the woodpile. Slabbing up stove wood and splitting it is the easiest part of the wood-cutting process.

The four-foot lengths of tobacco wood are split in the woods and hauled out ready for the curing season. There are also a lot of saplings or other species besides pine cut up for tobacco wood. A lot of gums are cut from the low places, and these can be a mess to split.

The really sad part of it all is that most of the women folks, who do all of the wood burning for the stove, never know the real work involved in getting that wood out of the woods and on the woodpile for easy access. Then they complain if the wood isn't immediately split and penned up so the air can get to it and dry it out quickly so it will produce plenty of heat to cook three square meals a day. And young'uns complain if the meal isn't on the table on time.

After working in the woods all day, we come home at night and eat everything on the table and resort to raw sweet potatoes to fill us up. By now, only a few small ones with rotten spots in them, are left in the hills, but we scratch around until we find some that are still edible.

Once the sawing is completed, on fair days the wagon makes several trips into the woods daily to haul out the wood, and when there is nothing else pressing to do, the "old man" can always send the boys out to the woodpile rather than allowing any loafing.   □

Time For A Little Thinking

After the new year begins and during warm spells, farm life starts up all over. With so many things to be done, farmers pick their times to do outside work. Ditchbanks have to be he shrubbed, stalks cut, land disked, broken up and planted in due time. Unless farming operations are pushed, they can pile up on you and it's hard catching up.

The "old man" can send the grownup boys out with their shrubbing blades and pitchforks to the ditchbanks to cut down the healthy growth of brush that has accumulated over the past year. The soil on the ditchbanks must be the best, for the bushes are always rank and thick there, and if a farmer were to leave the growth unchecked it would spread and begin taking up valuable farmland. But it would also be a disgrace. Farmers must keep those ditchbanks relatively free of that heavy growth.

Shrubbing requires muscle and strength, and young men have all the necessary equipment to carry out the process. But the "old man" can utilize his services by hitchig the mules to the riding stalk-cutter without manual labor. And all the stalks have to be cut before the land is disked. The legs have become permanently tired from endless walking in plowing the fields over the years, millions of steps that eventually take their toll.

So he takes the stalk-cutter to the fields and begins cutting the stalks into small pieces that will go back into the soil and rot to benefit the topsoil. It seems good to be outside after being cooped up in the house for so long with all the family members in a little too close proximity to each other during the cold months.

With a warm sun shining down and the heavy jacket almost unncessary, it is pleasant out in the fields and allows for a little thinking.

First and foremost, there is the hope for a good crop year. Without a good crop, there is no other hope for the farmer. Hope is all he has to go on, for the seasons determine what kind of harvests there will be, and no matter how hard he tries, if the weather is uncooperative, yields will be small.

He would like to expand his thoughts beyond the menial tasks of farming, to know the real story beyond the confines of his small world. And he does know some of that world from newspaper accounts. There is always war some place and Ethiopia and Haile Selassie dominate the war headlines in that remote country that he cannot associate with himself or his world.

There are also stories about Mahatma Gandhi and his hunger strikes in

India, and pictures of a little man in white sackcloth and a turban that looks so emaciated he appears at the point of death. And always there are stories about Herbert Hoover and the Great Depression that has strangled the nation. But it's hard to understand a lot of things in the newspaper and with a fourth-grade education, getting the real meaning of it all is impossible.

What does it all mean? Where is the hope? Times were better for the farmer during World War I and a little while after, but all that faded and everything started downhill again.

The farmer is really a victim. He has no choice. He has followed in the footsteps of his ancestors and tilled the land. He is uneducated. How could he have been educated if that had been his desire? He is doomed to the land, but he consoles himself that there's no other place on earth he'd want to be. But he would like to reap a few more rewards for his efforts. Always owing the landlord after settling up in the fall. Always starting another year with a debt on his back.

There are dreams of another way of life, but they fade and die in the face of reality. If a farmer were to go into other work it would still be the manual labor jobs. Without education and training, he would be no better off as far as physical labor is concerned. He'd have to settle for the menial jobs, even if there were jobs. And if he lived in town with no means of growing food for a family and having to buy wood or coal, he'd be even worse off.

It just seems that everything is at a standstill. Nothing seems to be moving forward and there doesn't seem to be any leadership. If a whole nation has no faith in its president, what can you expect of all the poor folks that look to him as a sort of savior? The poor are always with you, but if people that had been considered on a higher level than poverty are brought down to the level of the dirt farmer, what hope is there?

If it is brought down to the neighborhood level, there is no leader among the people. Oh, they're good folks and willing to help a neighbor, but there appears to be no real cause to plead for and if there were, everybody's just about in the same boat as far as leadership qualities go.

There are no neighborhood meetings, no drives to help specific causes. Everybody is just bogged down in trying to survive. If somebody gets sick, they pitch in and plant or plow his crops and do whatever they can to help out. But that's saying a lot for poor people.

Whatever the future may hold, the "old man" knows that it is all cut out for him for it's too late for any changes in his lifetime. And it does no good to try to think into the future, for nobody knows what that will be. It's all sort of hopeless and too much thinking gets the mind upset.

The farmer's just got to keep on doing what he knows how to do — shrubbing the ditchbanks, plowing the land, planting crops and trying to stay alive. It's more than a 12-month job, for there's that "13th" month in summer when he's up at night as well as during the day when tobacco has to be cured. It never ends and no matter how boresome it may be, it's the only life he knows, so he just works on and reads the newspapers and looks at the pictures of all the people in the streets in the big towns and those periodic pictures of old Gandhi and Selassie as if they mean something to him. But they've got to fill up the papers with something. ☐

Stables Cleaned Out Yearly

T he "old man" saves a good one to spring on the boys in the early part of the year. And there is no forewarning about this task. It isn't that the boys aren't aware it's coming, but just when is the unknown. And the "old man" doesn't want to hear the belly-aching and griping. It has to be done, and so at some unsuspecting time, he just comes out with it at the breakfast table. It's time to clean out the stables and haul the manure to the fields and spread it in places where the soil is poor.

It's a once-a-year job, and the best that can be said for it is that it stinks. And it's no easy job to loosen up the accumulation of manure and other debris over a year's period, not when the mules and cows are in those stables every day and mashing it all down with their heavy weights.

Getting the pitchforks to sink down into all the mess is a problem, and as the digging process begins, the manure comes up in layers and the large pieces have to be broken up so they can be spread more evenly in the fields.

And hauling stable manure is as much a part of rural life as chopping cotton or putting in tobacco, and I'm telling about us as we really were.

The very worst part of digging up stable manure is the almost-overwhelming smell of ammonia from the urine deposits. Sometimes the smell almost knocks you out. But that is no excuse not to clean out those stables. And they really do need that annual cleaning, for animal waste might be at least two feet deep in one area of the stable, apparently their favorite place for disposing of their wastes. It is always in a back corner.

The front of the stables where the mules enter and leave their quarters is a good deal lower than the back of their domain.

So we boys dig in and get the odors flying everywhere and the wagon is backed up to the door so we can throw the debris out of the stables as it is loosened up. We cuss and fuss and swear revenge on the whole human race for having to do such things, but the "old man" never hears a crying word of it. If he had, it wouldn't have made any difference anyway. It hurts our pride and offends our nostrils more than anything else.

The odor isn't all that unbearable until we dig down to where moisture has kept the dung wet all year, and it is then that we get the worst odor of ammonia as well as soft refuse.

Anyhow, we load the wagon down, crawl on top of the mess and make our way into the designated areas of the fields and start our broadcasting process. We sling that manure with a vengeance and the little dark particles lay as innocently in the fields as if they are of the purest components. But it serves its purpose for it is good fertilizer and sometimes the areas where the manure is distributed are greener than the others.

Cleaning out the stables is a job that takes several days, and once we are into it, we don't want to stop until it is finished. So we take off our smelly clothes at the end of the day and put on our Sunday shoes so the soiled brogans stay outside. We hang the clothes outside to keep from smelling up the house and go back to them and the brogans in the morning.

So we dig and dig and dig and sling manure for days, never accepting it as a routine job, but rather something that we have to tolerate. At this time in life our thoughts are their farthest from horse droppings. We have our minds on girls and the sweet smell of face powder and the dime-store perfume they splash on themselves. We wouldn't have them come up on us when we are cleaning out stables for anything in the world.

So we finally get all the stables cleaned out and the animals have clean quarters again, and the "old man" can't throw that one at us for another year. But the chicken house droppings still have to be moved, so after the garden plot is burned off, we clean out the henhouse and broadcast the droppings.

And we wash all over every night when we are hauling manure. Somebody has to make sure the reservoir is full of warm water and everybody has to get out of the kitchen after supper so we can strip off and get in the tin tub and try to wash off that smell. Then we don't feel clean until every stable and the henhouse are spick and span and we don't have to return to those smelly clothes again. But cleaning our brogans is the worst job of all. We actually have to take a rag to them sometimes and there is also a lot of scraping going on.

Our clothes are put in soak for a day or so with a lot of potash and soap cut up in the water. Then they are put in the pot and boiled and after a thorough washing those shirts and overalls come out smelling like a rose!

There were many things we disliked about farming during our teen years. Pulling fodder was a bad one. Flat-weeding sweet potatoes and making a ridge on top and turning the vines so they could be plowed and then crisscrossing them across the row again was another. Suckering tobacco was no easy task. But none of those jobs compared with hauling stable manure as far as we boys were concerned. That just went a little too far for human dignity. But then when we remembered that the women rid all of those hog chitlins, it made it all seem a little less defiling. Just another farm chore a half-century ago. □

Doctoring Babies In The '30s

O ur cultural and social values have changed so much over the years, many of the things about which I write don't seem to be a part of the 20th Century. Rather, they give an impression of being from a heathen land in which there was no sense of values. But when we think of all the world changes during the lifetimes of the over-50 age group, we realize that change has occurred at such a rapid pace it is almost incomprehensible.

Many people who are a generation younger than those born in the 1920s might be surprised to know that their first solid foods were chewed in their mothers' mouths and transferred to the babies' mouths. That was almost a trend in the late '20s and early '30s.

In those days pregnant women shied away from public view. It was customary for a woman in the "family way" to stay at home and be seen as little as possible.

But women magnified their pregnancies in those days. They didn't have maternity wardrobes and as a matter of fact, wore the same clothes during pregnancy that they wore before. As the pregnancy progressed, the front of the dress rose and the mid-section was so tight it appeared uncomfortable for the mother-to-be. And on top of that they all wore aprons tied at the waist, accentuating their swollen state.

Just about every mother nursed her newborn baby, and they openly bared their breasts for their babies, whether at home or elsewhere. There was no shame associated with feeding the babies, and neither did any of the population consider this distasteful.

Mamas with little ones were busy with the many chores associated with raising a family, and they had little time to soothe and play with their babies. If the infant cried, a "sugar tit" was one solution to the problem. The mother would take about a three-inch square of white rag, place a teaspoonful or so of sugar on it, twist it into a small ball and tie a string around it. They would place the "sugar tit" in the baby's mouth and once it got the sweet taste, it often went to sleep with the sweetener in its mouth.

Mothers not only nursed their babies when they were little, but the nursing period was extended far beyond the short period of today. And the older those babies became, the more adamant they were about nursing. Long after they could walk and talk, they would hang at their mothers' sides, pull at their clothing, stomp on the floor and cry for their "ninny." Little boys were worse about this than were little girls.

Babies were generally healthy in those days and they were robust and fat with rosy cheeks and dimples and little fat under-chins and if a baby didn't fit that category, they were considered "puny." There was one ailment, however, that people feared among their babies, and that was colitis. When a baby became ill and it was diagnosed colitis, in a great many cases it meant a dead baby. This disease of the large intestine has apparently been controlled with modern medicine, for we don't hear of it as the child-killer it was 50 years ago.

Whooping cough was another disease that was widespread during that era. Babies, as well as children well up in years, would contract the disease and almost whoop themselves to death. They would cough until they lost their breath sometimes and someone would beat them in the back until they could breathe again. This was a real problem among the population and children would whoop for several weeks.

The average medicine chest contained castoria, Black Draught, castor oil, camphorated oil, spirits of camphor and whisky, spirts of turpentine, calomel, laudanum and paregoric. And mothers of that time believed in doctoring their children.

Do you know how they would do us about taking medicine? All that a child had to do was to act a little puny and look a little peaked-faced, and they would take us by the chin and tell us to open up. They'd take one look and say, "uh, huh, that tongue's coated. You've got to have a purgative."

They'd fix that stuff and if a young'un rebelled, somebody would take the head and hold it back and place two fingers over the nose so we'd have to breathe out of our mouths, and when the mouth was opened, they'd poke the spoon in and if we gurgled and tried to keep from swallowing it, they'd run the spoon down to the "goozle" and we'd gag, and the liquid went down.

And they kept that spoon right there at the lips so that if the medicine started coming back they'd start raking it right back into the mouth. There was no way of getting around swallowing what they wanted us to take.

We got that Black Draught ever so often, whether we needed it or not. They would measure out a teaspoonful of the sage-colored powder and place it in a teacup. They would add boiling water almost to the brim, put a spoonful of sugar in it, set a saucer over the top to let it "steep" a while and cool off. When it was lukewarm, they stirred the ingredients and the child had to drink every drop, dregs and all. It was horrible. But they didn't have to go to school that day at least (if it was during the school season). If the child lost it, another cup was brewed.

Calomel was another no-no for the children, but they had to take it also. And it was a spaced-out process. Several of those pink tablets had to be taken at intervals of 10 or 15 minutes. I don't know why that was, but they said if calomel were not taken carefully it would salivate you. I presume they meant you would "slobber" yourself to death if that happened. So they would take those sickly, pink tablets and mash them up and put them in a teaspoon and fill it with water and "force" it down our throats. As I recall, calomel was just another of the laxatives used prolifically in those days. They believed in keeping you "cleaned out" and that's when castor oil came in if a deep cold developed. Half a bottle, no less, (and no orange juice in those days to follow the greasy stuff).

Turpentine was used on cuts to take out the soreness, and was also given internally for the same purpose. A teaspoon of sugar and 10 or 12 drops of turpentine were given if strenuous work of an unusual nature caused body soreness, like sawing wood or getting up corn. Paregoric was given to soothe babies when they had colic and as I remember, laudanum was given for this purpose also. Castoria was also usually given to babies and younger children who were unable to take Black Draught with its "griping" effect.

Yes, we were doctored in those days, if it was 99 percent home remedies. □

Country Store Was Important

C obwebs have accumulated at the top edges of the barred windows that on first appearance give the impression of being a jail. Fly specks dot the dust-covered glass panels. Dead flies lie on the windowsill and several signs — Coca-Cola, Fletcher's Castoria, and a man puffing on a Chesterfield, sit at unimposing angles. It is a country store-filling station combination.

On the outside, centered between the two columns that hold up the extension of the store to form the shelter area, is the gasoline tank. At the back of the shelter is the oil drum with grease prominent at the top of the container, the kerosene drum and several quart jars used in putting cylinder oil in automobiles.

A Rayo lantern hangs on each side of the shelter to provide light at night.

An entire exterior wall that shows prominently when travelers pass by is taken up with a faded painting of a camel and underneath in barely-intelligible writing the famous slogan, "I'd Walk A Mile for A Camel."

There aren't many touring cars in the area, but with more and more automobiles coming on the scene, store owners feel obligated to keep up with progress and also see a possible profit in the sale of gasoline and oil.

The glass bowl holds 10 gallons of gasoline with the measure beginning at the bottom of the bowl. When the number of gallons of the purchase is known, the attendant manipulates the hand pump and draws up the amount of gasoline wanted.

Inside, there is the pot-bellied stove sitting some five feet from a corner of the room with a wood frame about three feet square built around the stove. Dirt or sand may have been put inside the frame at some time to protect the floor from the hot stove. But if so, other items have long-since replaced dirt within the square. Ashes and small pieces of burnt coal lie around the heater with orange peels, apple skins, banana peels, all dotted with chewing tobacco juice.

Pop bottle cases turned on edge, along with nail kegs and one or two old ladder-back chairs are placed around the heater. These are sitting places for farmers that gather at the store regularly when working hours are over, or on rainy days.

A counter runs about three-fourths of the way across the width of the store, with shelves built behind the counter to display canned goods and other merchandise.

At one end of the counter is the glass candy case that contains all manner of sweets — all-day suckers of chocolate, lemon, strawberry and lime; flat sugar-coated coconut candy that looks like a flag; Baby Ruths, Mary Janes, Tootsie Rolls, peppermint gum in sticks (I think it was named Oh Boy or Big Boy, pink in color and as tough as whitleather.)

On the open counter is the hoop of cheese. A jar of pig feet sits there, as does a jar of Johnny cakes. A place is provided for men to eat sardines, Vienna sausages, and pork and beans while sitting on a nail keg. It seems that men getting off drunks especially crave sardines and pork and beans and they use plenty of salt, pepper and vinegar and complete the meal with a box of soda crackers. But there are other partakers also. In the absence of a spoon, sometimes a piece of the cracker box serves as a spoon. But the smells are delectable to boys without a dime in their pockets.

On the shelves are the general run of canned goods — salmon, pork brains, canned milk, and various vegetables. There are also flavorings, patent medicines such as castor oil, Black Draught, castoria and spirits of turpentine. There is an ample supply of chewing tobacco — Brown Mule, Black Mariah, Apple and other brands. Several brands of snuff are stocked and there is a sizable display of smoking tobacco. Cigarettes are plentiful also with Avalons and Wings big sellers because of their cheaper prices.

Once in a while a bunch of bananas hangs from the ceiling and in the fall and a while after Christmas there are boxes of apples and oranges around.

From the counter to the back of the store, general merchandise is stored. The vinegar barrel with its wooden faucet is up near the front as is the sugar in five-pound bags. A wooden stand holds white side and fat back meat. Ropes are hung on the walls as well as trace chains, singletrees, hames, mule collars, etc. Nails, various sizes of plow points and clothespins are in bins.

Buckets of various kinds are stacked together. There are well buckets and several sizes of galvanized pails. Tin tubs, wooden tubs, washboards, slop jars and various other household items are in stacks on the floor.

An old table and several chairs are also in the back and there is a kerosene lamp on the table with spit cups pushed under the table. Men gather here to play cards.

It's always lively at night when men gather around the stove and tell lies and burst out in laughter and scratch themselves. There's a lot of cussing going on too. And the dirty jokes they tell would make a sailor blush.

It has the distinct odor of a country store — sweet and sour, leather and kerosene, fruits and tobacco juice, cigarettes and sardines, molasses and spittoons — all combining to give a country store its unique odor.

Women don't usually come into the store if they have to have a box of snuff or a spool of thread — things they can't do without. They just knock on the door and when the storekeeper opens the door they tell him what they want. And whatever the men are talking about, they get as quiet as a mouse until the lady leaves.

Because of the carryings-on at the store, it's considered a place of sin, and some women have fits about their men hanging out there. But others become resigned to it, knowing that whatever they say will do no good and that they could be in worse places.

And as soon as a young'un gets a gawky voice and starts sprouting a beard, he's right down there at that store. It draws 'em like Rayo lanterns draw bugs in summer. When men try to sit under the store front they're constantly picking bugs from their hair and shirts.

A Model T pulls up for a gallon of gas. A boy with a five-gallon can buys a gallon of kerosene. A girl with a gallon jug wants molasses. She has a sack full of eggs. A boy buys a Johnny cake and another wants a box of Cracker Jacks.

Somebody has broken a plow point and needs a replacement. One sack of Golden Grain, please.

Pa needs a plow line but "hain't" got no money now. Can he git it now and pay for it the first of the month?

The country store. It's as much a part of the community as the church house, and a whole lot of people "druther" be there too. Both are essential in serving the needs of the people.   □

Hauling Guano In Spring

A postcard has been received saying that the year's supply of fertilizer has arrived at the siding, listing the number of days allowed to get the cars unloaded. All the area farmers get cards about the same time, for the fertilizer is picked up at the rural siding each year.

So those young upstarts who are always showing off their strength at the store will be called upon to use that muscle in loading, hauling and unloading that guano under the shelter. They show their might down at the store by picking up straight-backed chairs by the front bottom rounds and holding them straight out for a full minute, picking up 50-pound nail kegs at the top of the keg with a thumb and forefinger and placing them on the counter, or taking five-pound bags of sugar on an ax handle and picking them up off the counter and holding them straight out.

At that age — 16 to 20 — they are as strong as a bull and raring to go, and they can handle those 200-pound bags of guano with relative ease. But getting the fertilizer from the siding and placing it under the shelter is only the beginning of handling the heavy load.

So, on a clear day when the weather is warm enough, the mules are hitched to the wagon and two youths head off down the road toward the railroad crossing, where they have to turn off on a side road beside the cars that are holding the fertilizer. Several farmers' fertilizer is in one car, so there might be a waiting period while the wagons are being loaded.

The roads haven't been scraped recently and ruts are deep in places while in others sand is thick and along the pocosin that stretches for several miles along each side of the road trees and undergrowth extend out into the road. But there is a chain gang working up ahead, cutting back the growth and piling it at the edge of the woods before the road scraper comes by.

A sizable number of convicts is working along the road, some with chains dangling between their legs, while others go about their tasks untethered. A trusty is bringing water from a nearby well to quench the thirst of the laborers. A guard stands nearby with a shotgun in hand if there is any attempt to escape.

Both black and white, the convicts are chanting phrases of blues songs or spirituals that become a cacophony without meaning. They sing and the chains jingle while axes, shrubbing blades and pitchforks clear away the growth. With danger involved in the use of such tools, the guard is constantly on the alert and a falling limb catches his immediate attention.

It is a lonely ride through the pocosin, with its scrub pines, gums and reed beds that look forlorn and underdeveloped for a wooded area. Along the road there are a few three-room houses with overhanging front porches. Roofs show the ravages of time. Shingles are missing on some while rusted tin roofs show holes and it is a barren landscape with sand-covered yards and a washpot sitting forlornly on a bare woodpile, a few chickens with pale combs and dogs showing malnutrition with their ribs and hip bones prominent under dull coats.

But beyond the pocosin there is community life and a thickly-settled area near the railroad tracks.

The boys are able to get to the car and once they find where their fertilizer is located, they begin loading the sacks on the wagon with the help of a cart with wheels, so getting the fertilizer on the wagon isn't a big problem.

When they arrive back home they go to the tobacco barn where there is left-over wood for curing and bring enough to make an underpinning for the fertilizer to keep it off the ground. The wood is placed in two rows, lengthwise, and the fertilizer placed across the wood. It is important that the fertilizer be placed so it will not get wet from rain, for lumpy guano doesn't work well in a guano distributor, and it will be a few weeks before planting time.

All the land must be disked after the stalks are cut, then broken up and rows run, fertilizer sown, the rows ridged up before the crops are planted. It is a never-ending chore and preparing a farm for planting is a big job in itself, and that is just the beginning. Millions of steps are taken in the run of a year by all the people working the fields.

In retrospect, it is a wonder that all the processes involved in farming were carried out in those days. In a world without convenience, it is impossible for the younger generation to realize the hardships encountered in farming 50 years ago. The greatest convenience in those days was a riding cultivator that allowed the person plowing crops to ride as the plowing was done.

All the various process can be carried out by one person on a modern tractor today and chores that were backbreaking are made easy with modern equipment and know-how.

It may be that some readers even become tired in hearing about all the manual labor involved in farming in that distant past, but I am only telling about rural eastern North Carolina as we actually were, and not as we would liked to have been. But in remembering that past in the days when we were filled with the vigor of youth, the recuperation period was very short, and we seldom turned down a chance to have a good time, no matter how hard we worked during the day.

We were used to hard work. We were conditioned by our lifestyles and there was a "toughness" about us because of that conditioning that is missing in today's society.   □

Planting 'Ish Taters'

T here comes a time in early spring before the gardens produce fresh vegetables and after a long winter of eating out of the pantry, that the cupboards become sort of bare and there's some scampering around to put three square meals on the table every day.

Everybody's tired of sopping syrup and molasses and eating fresh side meat that still has a sort of green taste to it and rice and ham bone and black-eyed peas. All the sweet taters are gone except the ones with rotten ends and rotten specks on them, and a half-rotten tater don't taste so good.

All the big sausage is gone and most of the Tom Thumbs. Maybe one or two left but after they hang up so long they get kind of rank and they're cooked on top of the pot sometimes to season greens (if there are any greens).

The collards have been picked over so much there's little left of them and despite being turned down, the cold has hurt them to some extent. Something different would just taste good, like potato salad or turnip salad or mustard and kale, and it will be several weeks before that will be ready. The crowd could eat a peck of mustard and kale and drink every drop of the pot liquor, too. A cup of pot liquor with corn bread broken up in it is as delicious as the greens (almost).

But the collards have sprouts on them and their yellow flowers shine in the gardens, as do the turnips that have run up, and they are picked as clean as a bird picking cherries and every tiny leaf saved and washed and boiled in the pot. It's just a yearning for greens. Oh, if there were only some "ish-taters" to go with them.

Nothing on earth is better with greens than Irish potatoes and baked corn bread and that boiled meat that's used to season the greens. But there ain't no "ish-taters" around yet, and won't be until seed taters are bought and cut for planting. Then the "old man" thinks every bit of the heart ought to be cut with the eyes to give the taters a better start. But no young'un that I ever knew cut all the tater up. There was a heart left from every one, and that's what was out of this world after no taters through the winter.

(There was no way to keep white potatoes during the winter months in those days and when cold weather came it ended potato eating until the next spring.)

From the back porch, we saw the cabbage were green and spreading out and we'd go out to see if they were beginning to twist to form the heads. And we didn't wait until those heads were hard either. Man, we wanted those cabbage and pot liquor.

But a farmer just couldn't help but put a little bit of soda to cabbage and corn and things like that, and sometimes those early greens would tear our stomachs all to pieces and we would have the "trots."

And it wasn't long until the "old man" hitched up the mules to the wagon and went to town for the seed potatoes. They were the best-looking tow sacks we ever saw. We couldn't wait to get out the pans and knives and start cutting those potato eyes. The larger we could get those hearts the better we liked it, and after the eyes were cut they were put back in that tow bag in a hurry for we didn't want close scrutiny from the "old man."

So we stuffed our guts on those tater hearts and there were enough for several meals and we sopped every drop of that gravy too. And then it was time to plant the tater eyes and we were cautioned to drop them with the eye up. I reckon Pa thought they'd never sprout if they had to take root from the under side. But I have news for Pa in case he's listening. We dropped as many tater eyes with the potato showing on top as we did those with the eye showing, and we always got a good stand as I recall.

It took a couple of weeks at least for the vines to begin appearing on the rows and when it got really warm they began to take off and soon there were large vines and of course the terrapin bugs appeared every spring and there was the Paris green solution to be put on them. We didn't have any kind of sprayer or anything like that so we made our applicator from rags tied to the end of a tobacco stick broken half in two and poured the Paris green mixture into a bucket and saturated the tater vines with our homemade contraption.

And sometimes by mid-May we'd go out on the hunt for new potatoes. We were told to get anything as large as a guinea egg and not to bother those of marble size. So we'd scratch around the vines and finally get enough for a mess and the womenfolks would take paring knives and scrape those babies and there would be little specks in some of the eyes that remained a little red after the scraping but they'd put those buggers in a peck-size pot, for that's how many it took to fill everybody, and when they simmered down to a slow gravy there was all the tater taste in the world in those spuds and being fresh from the field, they were even better than the tater hearts.

They even made a little pastry and put in new potatoes sometimes and that was something good too. They did the same with garden peas. And we loved potato cakes for breakfast but there was seldom enough left over from supper for that. They'd mash the potatoes up and add enough flour to hold them together and fry them to a golden brown and there's no telling how many we could have eaten. Put plenty of black pepper over them and settle down to eat with scrambled eggs and slices of side meat and those tater cakes, and it was a meal fit for a king.

And that was just one of a hundred good things to eat back in the days when diet was no problem and excess calories didn't lie around to accumulate more fat. But there were plenty of people who worked every day but stayed plump and some downright fat. I wonder what they would have been like if they hadn't worked their butts off? □

Sowing Guano In The Wind

T he winds seemed to blow more and harder in the 1930s than today. Maybe they didn't, but it sure seemed that way. "Windy March" it has always been called, but the winds often extended into April also.

Sometimes there would actually be dust storms when the air was filled with particles of dirt and visibility was almost zero. The sky would become overcast and the sun subdued. It could barely be seen in the heavens and appeared as a dull red ball in the sky. It was an eerie sight.

Where the fields had been broken up, the strong winds stirred up the topsoil and whirlwinds played over the land.

When the dust storms came, no work could be done on the farm, for dirt filled the eyes when people exposed themselves to the dust. People just stayed inside and dragged chairs up to the windows and watched as Mother Nature played one of her tricks over the landscape.

If there were biddies in the yard, they looked half-dead and their eyes were almost closed. They were droopy and their wings hung from their sides.

Even the dogs would leave their tow-sack beds on the doorsteps and seek haven in an outbuilding or under the house.

Dust seeped into those open tenant houses from cracks in doors and windows as well as the eaves of the house. Furniture was coated over and children wrote their names on bureaus and tables and looking glasses. Dust penetrated into safes and caused the food to be gritty. It even felt gritty between the sheets on the beds. All the "something to eat" in the safes had to be dumped into the slop bucket.

But life had to go on, and farming too. Crops had to be planted and fertilizer put out so the rows could be ridged up. It was cotton-planting time and backer plants were growing by leaps and bounds in the beds. So when the storm subsides, it's back to work and all the guano under the shelter has to be hauled to the fields and distributed. Time for those strapping boys to show their young manhood.

The wagon is loaded down with sacks of guano and taken to the fields. The sacks have to be unloaded. The distance between the rows of fertilizer across the fields is determined by the amount of guano needed to go from one sack to the next. The best way to determine the distance is to fill up the distributor, set the lever on the sower for the number of pounds wanted per acre, sow the fertilizer until it gives out, and place a row of fertilizer across the fields.

Get the guano to the back of the wagon, then back up to a sack and pull it onto the back, holding it by the "ears" formed when the sack is sewn up. Get your balance and start across those rows with that 200 pounds on your back. Be careful, and when you get going, keep going or you'll lose your momentum and have to let the sack go before you want to. Can't afford to sprain the back and land up hurting.

Haul all the guano to the field and position it at the proper places, place a bucket where each row of fertilizer in standing, fill up the guano distributor and start sowing that guano, and then is when the wind rises.

It might be perfectly calm, and if a reed bed is burning, the smoke might rise straight into the skies, but when the guano distributor goes to work the wind starts blowing. And before the day is over the person sowing fertilizer looks exactly like a clown.

The guano settles on the face and makes it look an ashen-white. It covers the ears and whitens the eyebrows. The nose is covered and only the nostrils are free of the fertilizer, but sometimes a whiff gets up the nose, and that burns. But it accumulates around the openings of the nose and the lips are covered. If the mouth is opened there is the taste of guano and wiping it away does no good, for it gets right back on the lips.

The clothing becomes saturated with the stuff also and when the distributor is refilled, dipping the hands into the fertilizer causes it to get under the fingernails.

Another man with a plow is going behind the guano distributor and ridging up the rows so that cotton can be planted. The cotton sower is retrieved from the back of the shelter, since it is only used once a year, but it is important in getting the cottonseeds into the soil.

The planter will be filled with seeds and run on top of the ridge and the roller will push the seeds into the ground. But cottonseeds are planted at the top of the soil and many can be seen after the roller goes over them.

Cottonseeds are planted in a continuous stream and when they come up they are ugly, long-legged plants inclined to lean over rather than stand erect. And by the time the plants are ready to be thinned out, there is a growth of grass among them that results in "flat-weeding" the entire row.

The plants are thinned to the width of a hoe with two or three plants left at each hill. When the excess plants are cut down, those left want to fall over and they have to be propped up with dirt so they will stand. And those who are doing the chopping better be sure those plants are standing, too.

Sometimes small hills of grass have to be pulled from around the plants for grass grows everywhere in fields and when they are plowed the dirt doesn't overlap and cover over the small grass.

Good thing they had plenty of "hoers" around in those days, for chopping was a necessity to keep grass from eating up the crops. Young'uns from 10 years old up had to chop in the fields and the womenfolks got into the act too.

Women in those days wanted their skin to be white, and they would fashion long gloves from old stockings and pull them up their sleeves above the elbows. They would cut holes in the foot part to allow for a thumb to go through and a slit so the rest of the fingers would be free. They also wore large, slatted bonnets that had aprons dropping around their necks and they pinned up the fronts to keep the sun out (and almost smothered as well).

Once in a while a woman would have to go to the fields and plow, especially if there was a pack of girls and no boys in the family. But even in those days, plowing was considered a man's job, and the woman who had to be a "plowgirl" felt a certain shame in the area in which I lived.

It was a sight to behold all the people working in fields in those days.   □

The Beauty Of Springtime

When the fresh-plowed fields are flanked by flowering fruit trees — peach, pear, apple, plum, cherry — with pink and white splotches of color dominating the scene and every twig, bush and tree is green with new foliage, it is springtime in Carolina.

When dawn gives way to morning and birds are busy carrying straw, twigs and strings to their nesting places in the nearby trees, it is spring in Carolina.

When the purple martins return to their nests of gourds high on a pole in the edge of the yards and bluebirds, robins and redbirds, along with the sparrows and other somber-colored species pitch and sip water from mudholes in the yard, it is springtime in Carolina.

In spring, water runs faster in the ditches as excess moisture from winter finds its way to the tributaries that will take it to the sea. Sandy bottoms of the ditches are clear, the banks covered in wild violets, and the water spills over sticks caught in the stream, creating little ripples of white foam.

Daffodils, with their yellow and white flowers, come into full bloom in spring in their beds at the edges of the yards. Wisteria vines that have climbed into nearby trees are filled with their lavender blossoms that hang in clusters like grapes on the vine. And the most humble structures are decorated with climbing rose bushes that burst into colors of red, pink, white and yellow and shed their fragrance over the premises and add a certain dignity to the setting. And the lowly chinaberry trees are filled with their small, purple flowers.

In spring petunias bloom with their white, pink and purple flowers and their beds are marked off by tobacco twine attached to sticks driven into the ground to keep the children out. And in beds bordered either by zig-zag brick or old automobile tires, verbena grows as does moss (the kind that blooms). And the sweet Betsys smell to high heaven.

There are no spirals of smoke rising above the neighborhood from the tall chimneys in springtime and doors and windows are opened to allow fresh air and sunshine to come in. Instead, people take their chairs to the front porches for sunbaths after the winter hiatus, and children swing again under the tall trees.

The greening of spring, of rebirth, is a beautiful time in rural Carolina. It is then that the land comes alive and everything shows signs of life. Trees and bushes that have stood naked and forlorn during the fury of winter, are again green and stand proudly as part of the landscape. Seeds scattered by the cold winds that have lain dormant sprout and come from the earth and in the meadows and pastures, livestock savors the sweetness of tender grass after a dry diet during the winter months.

When the leaves have fully matured and it's a little too cool to sit in the shade and a little too warm in the sun, it is spring in Carolina. It is also then that men shed their heavy "union suits" and women their winter petticoats and take on more comfortable attire. The children take off their shoes and feel the cool earth on their feet, giving them a sense of freedom that only a child can appreciate. They find their small wheels and drive nails into the ends of sticks and start their annual pastime.

And in spring the cabbages in the garden rows start to twist and the scallions grow tall. Garden peas show their first blooms and corn, butterbeans, squash and cucumbers are green and growing. The sage bush at the end of the garden puts on new growth as does the parsley bed. And the first butterflies appear.

On clear nights people sit on their porches and watch the day end and darkness appear, with a buttermilk sky and a million stars in the firmament. And the first fireflies begin to appear as a prelude to summer when they light up the area yards.

In the barnyards, hens are cackling and roosters crowing and the egg basket overflows and sitting hens leave their nests and ruffle their feathers and cluck as they search for food to tide them over during the brooding period. And the geese leave the barnyard for solitude in the reed beds to build their large nests and prepare for raising a family.

The guineas also meander further in the back fields and habitate the places where the foliage is thick. They lay their eggs and sing their guinea songs and return to their roosting places in the trees at the edge of the yard at day's end until they take to the nests to raise their families. Children find their nests and remove some of the eggs with tablespoons so the human scent won't cause them to change nests.

When the setting sun sheds its last rays on the land and farmers come over the ridge with their mules following them for their well-earned rest, with a background of plowed fields looking barren and swept clean by time, they appear as nomads crossing a lonely desert. But that picture speaks the message of spring. It was as beautiful 50 years ago as today.

It is eastern North Carolina, where the beauty of spring greets you at eye level. Its beauty is before you, beside you, real and touchable. We can't boast the majesty of the mountains where the peaks and the sky seem to meet and where rhododendron and mountain laurel and many other wild flowers grow in spring. We lack the solitude of the sea where the sky and the big waters seem to merge and where the seaweed stands lonely among the sand washed ashore by tide and time.

But we are endowed with fertile soil, rich farmlands, tall pines, flowering honeysuckle, beautiful dogwoods and other flowering plants. This is our homeland and the only place on earth we who are natives of the area wish to be. Spring in eastern North Carolina! □

66

(N.C. Dept. Archives and History)

Look At The Dominecker Chickens

Biddy, Biddy, Biddy

With all those hens and biddies coming off, if anybody didn't know it was spring that in itself would let them know about a change in seasons. The hens have laid and laid and laid, but since they haven't been bred strictly for egg production, they lay out their so-called "latters" and get the instinct to sit on eggs and raise a family.

Tobacco-stick pens are made almost daily to make a place for each mother and her brood. Then problems arise when biddies from one mother enter the pens of another. Many hens won't tolerate biddies from other pens in with their brood. Some hens even pick on one of their own brood that might be a different color from all the others.

But there are still many sitting hens around and more pens will have to be built. It will almost look like a "biddy city" in the little bit of land where the apple and peach trees are planted between the barn and the tobacco barns. And a lot of corn will have to be cracked to feed all the biddies. They are too little to "gom" down whole kernels of corn and the grain has to be taken to the mill or beaten by hand to be cracked so the baby chicks can fill up those crops and feather out as fast as possible.

That old dominecker hen sitting in the barrel on top of the backer sticks under the shelter is as gentle and easy as she can be, and all her 15 eggs are under her and about ready to start pipping. Every egg is marked good with a pencil so if other hens crawl in and lay with her the eggs can be removed.

But that old hussy in an apple box nailed to the side of the shelter is as flighty as she can be. She's black with gold feathers on her neck and there's some game there. When you go to look under her she will either fly off the nest or give your hand a peck hard enough to make you pull it away from her right quick. Some of her eggs have been broken too, for there are yellow smudges of yolk on the other eggs. Must be 11 or 12 under her now. Fifteen eggs is the usual setting.

Stinks in the nest too, and a pan of warm water has to be brought out to wash off the eggs and she probably won't come off with many biddies. Seems like when the eggs get gommed up they just don't hatch as good. She'll be a good one to put in the pot for boiling one of these days.

Here's one with eggs pipped and one half-dry biddy already in the nest. She's hatching a day or so early. But she's a Rhode Island Red and they are usually docile and easy to manage. But that biddy's going to be a dominecker, for it has that light spot on its head with the black body.

Here comes a hen across the road with a passel of biddies, and nobody even knew she was sitting. She went over there among the briers and stole her nest and she's a light-speckled hen and them biddies are all colors. She'll have to be caught and put in a pen or something'll be eating them biddies in that brier patch.

The young'uns have a few bantams around and that little cocky red rooster with black wings and that purplish long tail is running every hen in the yard and there will be some half-bantams when these biddies grow up. That's a pure waste for a bantam ain't good for nothing except to crow and run around and look pretty. What this crowd needs is a chicken with some meat on it to put into the gut. Can't even sell the little white eggs. They're too little to make two mouthfuls of scrambled eggs.

There's 13 biddies with the hen in the tater hill that set early. They're already feathered out and the roosters' combs are starting to grow. There's 10 with another hen, 12 with another, eight in the next pen, only nine in the next but there were 12 to start with. So far there are 39 biddies, plus the 12 with the hen that stole her nest, making a total of 51 biddies.

But you can't count on them just because they're hatched. Cats or dogs or hawks are going to get a certain number, and if they start roaming around the hog pen some will be gobbled down by them hungry hogs. And rats are going to get a few too. Wherever there are biddies and cracked corn, rats are going to be around too.

Then there are the suck-egg dogs that are always roaming around hunting for a hen nest to rob. Nothing's hatefuller than a suck-egg dog.

A new scarecrow has to be fixed and put in the middle of the biddy pens. Hawks are bold enough at best, but a decent scarecrow might scare a few away. That ain't saying much for the scarecrows that are put in the corn fields, though. Crows sure don't pay them much mind. It's nothing to see a whole drove of crows in a corn field and sometimes one will pure pitch on a scarecrow.

Got to get a new supply of nox varmit (nux varmica) from the drug store too. It may not kill the first hawk, but if it kills just one it will be worth it. It's pure pitiful to see them rascals swoop down on a bunch of biddies and grab one in their claws and fly away towards the woods with that biddy just a crying.

There's a hen going into the backer barn. She's probably stole her nest too.

Yep, there's a nest in one corner where some backer trash was left and she has several eggs in the nest already. That ought to be a good place for a hen to sit so the eggs will just be left there and she'll take to the nest after a while.

Some boards will have to be placed over the top of the hog pen too later on to keep young chickens from flying in there to get anything the hogs are eating. Them hogs just as soon have a biddy as the other mess that's taken to them.

By the way. They have biddy calls too. Sounds a lot like an auctioneer at a backer warehouse. When they get ready to put the cracked corn in the biddy pens they go out and start calling, "biddy, biddy, biddy, biddy, biddy, biddy, biddy" seven times and it's a chant and there's an inflection of the voice on the seventh "biddy." And those little rascals come running from everywhere in the fields.

In the same manner, when they want to call up the grown birds they do the same thing but distinguish between biddies and chickens by calling "chicky, chicky, chicky..." as if the fowl knew the difference.

But they're pretty, a whole conglomeration of colors and builds and the mixing of colors. Makes raising biddies exciting as well as a source of food and money from the eggs. Poor folks in the country couldn't get along without eggs to use in the place of money. But it works out just as well, for the surplus of eggs will feed the people in town who don't have hens to lay their eggs. But the men at the stores sure have a lot of counting to do when they sell the eggs.   □

The Art Of Running Rows

The "old man" is speaking.

"Boy, with all that sap you got in you and seeing as how you're growing like a stackpole and combing your hair different and all that, it's time to git out of them boyish ways and take on a man's job.

"Now you've helped break up this land, but that's boys' work, just following the mules and keeping the plow in the ground. But I'm going to put you on a man's job for the first time. You're going to run the rows in this field this year. And you know I don't have no messing about running rows. They've got to be straight and if they ain't, there'll be hell to pay, boy.

"I've put a coat of red paint on the top part of these stakes, so it will show from a distance, and the white stripe under it just sets it off, and you got good eyes, boy, so there won't be no excuse for not seeing that stake in the distance. So you take these eight stakes and distribute them about evenly down the length of the field. Line them up so that when you look back you can see just one stake. Then you know they're in a straight line.

"After you do that, come back here and I'll git you started on running a row.

"When you plow up to where a stake is standing, mark off the next row by the notch cut in the stake and put that stake in the ground. Do that all the way down so that when you start back on the next row there'll be another straight line to follow."

"Let me put an eye on them stakes down that row. Lord God! He's got one way out of line on down the field. He's going to come back here with a crooked row and he'll have to start all over agin.

"Boy, I told you how to set them stakes, and look what you've done. Now you go back and line up every stake agin, and this is your last chance. You see this plow line boy? I want it to stay tied to that mule's bridle, but I'll take it off if I need to.

"Let me put another eye on that row of stakes just to see what that young upstart is doing. Yep, he's got 'em lined up this time and he'll come back here with a straight row. That'll please him, for he'll be doing a man's job — something that he has to pay attention to — and he won't have to git that plow line on his behind. He'll be gitting off lighter than I did when the old man put me to running rows. I got tore all to pieces. But he started me when I was 10 and I had hard enough job holding up the plow, to say nothing of running straight to a stake.

"Seems like they always start these rip-snorters that are feeling their oats off by putting them to running rows. That's where flub-ups show right now. Of course they'll straddle tier poles in backer barns this summer and learn what it's like in that hot, dark hell where there ain't no light and no air. They'll be standing on their heads in them backer patches too, crapping off them sand lugs in the heat of the day and that'll separate the men from the boys. God almighty! That is a job that'll kill you.

"Tell you right now though, I'm depending on these boys. Oldest are out on their own now and without the young ones coming along, tending a big farm would be out for me. Can't do that hard work no more.

"Ain't no stopping these boys though. They're on their way and nobody ain't going to hold 'em back. Best I can do is to try to instill in them some of the things that were passed on to me. Try to keep 'em settled down while they're growing into men and keep 'em on an even course. They may hate my guts for what I've put 'em through to git 'em this far, but they'll look back someday and know it had to be done in order to git 'em conditioned for the kind of life they face. Course that might not be in my lifetime, but whether dead or alive, they'll know what I meant, and they'll understand.

"When the young'uns were little, used to wonder how I could do a better job by them than was done by me. And I'd a done it too if there had been a way. I love all them young'uns, but I reckon they never knowed it. I had to be the tough one. Couldn't let up. Wolf was at the door all the time and I had to spend my time puzzling over what I could do just to keep us going.

"Ain't been a whole lot of pleasure in my life. Too little money and too many mouths to feed. Walking through the fields in growing season with the old lady on a Sunday evening and seeing the crops almost shouting as they waved in the sunshine was kind of nice.

"Liked to go to preaching to hear the Word, but as soon as I got settled down in the Amen Corner I started to nodding and the brothers had to shake me to git me awake. Then I'd go right back to nodding agin. I nodded through most of the sermons unless somebody got to shouting and talking in unknown tongues.

"Enjoyed quarterly meeting too. An all-day affair at the church with bread and wine in observance of the Lord's supper, but I had a twinge of conscience when it came foot-washing time. The sisters washed each others' feet and the brothers did likewise. I never minded washing a brother's foot, but mine were always cracked and skint up and didn't look clean at best, so I actually felt ashamed when the brother had to git down there and wash my feet in the white tin basin.

"Gitting away from myself. Let me see what that boy's doing with them rows. Be durn if he ain't doing a man's job. Them rows are straight and I wish I could do something for that boy, but it wouldn't do to praise him. I'll just have to tell him they'll do when I know that I've never seen a straighter set of rows from any man, including me.   □

Hand-Transplanting Backer

Y ou people who may not know anything about modern farming needn't ask me. I haven't the faintest idea how farming operations are conducted today. The Agricultural Extension Service could be invaluable to inquirers. So our ASCS officials are there to answer questions about farming today.

I am of the old school and the things that I know about farming are as quaint as the past about which I write. And many ASCS officials are a lot younger than that period and only know about antiquated farming methods from old farm journals or by word-of-mouth passed on from one generation to another.

But if there was one thing we did in those days, it was farm. It was farming, period. And it's time to set out tobacco.

"All right, everybody, let's git going for them backer plants are shouting and almost gitting too big," the old man says, "so we got to bear down and git the job done. It'll take at least two women on the plant beds to pull the plants and you'll freeze half to death out there. Don't know why, but it's always cool when you git on a backer bed to pulling plants. And the sun never shines on them in early morning. That dew seems as cold as frost and you git wet up to your straddle.

"Two young'uns can straighten the plants and pull off the "yaller" bottom leaves. Then dip them in a bucket of water and wash the dirt off the roots and git them to the field.

"You, boy, go down to the branch with a backer truck and the wooden barrel and fill it with water and fetch it to the field.

"And you, boy, hitch up the other mule and knock off them backer rows so there'll be a flat surface for putting the plants in the ground. Ought to be enough pegs for everybody. Some are on the plate of the shelter and some more have been made from "lidard" roots.

"And don't start bellyaching about the few folks who have these new-fangled transplanters that you ride on instid of punching the holes with a peg. If we had the money we'd have one too. We can't even afford these hand jobs that you punch down in the ground that release the plant and the water too when the lever is pulled. All it does to think about that is to aggravate everybody more.

"You'll have to find all the buckets around the place for everybody's got to tote a bucket of water and the plants too. May have to use the water bucket and the milk pail if you can't find enough otherwise. They can be boiled out and cleaned if we have to use them.

"And this business about the peg hurting the palm of your hands, forget it. The hands have always been blistered and bruised when backer pegs were used when backer was set out. Ain't no way to keep it from hurting. Try a pocket handkerchief or a rag on top of the peg if you have to. And I don't want to see nobody trying to git by with a shallow hole. You got to punch down in that ground hard and may have to twist the peg to git the hole deep enough. And if the dirt runs back in the hole, do it over.

"And something else. Don't put them plants crooked on that ridge. Put them in the middle of the row so there'll be a straight line of backer plants when you look back. And put plenty of water to the roots. If you don't they'll just lie there and die in the hot sun and it'll all be to do over again. God only knows how many times backer will have to be replanted nohow.

"And I'm warning you young'uns that will be toting plants to the fields that I ain't having no messing around, and them plants better be straight and cleaned off good. The best way is to git the shuck basket in the barn and tote them in that.

"Now let's everybody git going and go out to the plant bed and pull a few plants to start. That'll give everybody a chance to git wet and cold but it won't be long until that sun will warm you up and the damp places will feel good.

"I seen 'em using a transplanter across the way the other day and it's a fine way to set out backer. The setters are right there at ground level and all they got to do is to have that plant ready and when the "gizmo" clicks, it puts water down there and after the plant is set out it packs the dirt around it and that backer looks pretty when it's first set out. It's standing straight and green in them rows.

"I know one thing. You sure have to tie up them breeches legs around the ankle or a stalk would run up your legs and scratch you all to pieces. Saw a transplanter on an open railroad car a while back and it was passing by fairly fast and I was on the wagon and had to watch the mules while the train was passing, but I think there was a picture of a tiger on one end of the barrel that holds the water for transplanting, and I saw the word "Bemis." I reckon it was the brand name. If it won't "Bemis" it was something close to it.

"Just look at that crowd, acting like them buckets of water are too heavy to tote. They're even spattering it out when they cross the rows after gitting a new supply from the barrel on the truck.

"Let me take a hand and try pulling up a plant by one leaf. That one's pretty tight. Next row ain't that tight. Hey, young'uns, mash that peg harder around them backer plants! If you don't git the dirt solid around them they can't take root.

"Plants are about out, but yonder comes the young'uns lugging that basket and acting like it weighs a ton. Look at 'em. They'll tote it a few yards and set it down. Them young'uns are big enough to tote that basket without all that carrying on.

"Now here this crowd is, already complaining about pegs hurting their hands. Well it's just beginning and they'll get sorer before it's all over. Won't have time for the hands to toughen up for backer's got to be set out when the plants are right.

"There goes the dinner bell. Twelve o'clock already? Seems like we just got started. But I reckon this pack of young'uns wants a few minutes of rest, and I could use a few myself. It'll be a long time til sundown.   □

A Tribute To Mothers

As soft as a baby's skin," the commercial says, and lovely, manicured hands are shown on the TV screen detailing the virtues of the softening agent. Beautiful hands of mothers that match their babies' softness! Beautiful faces, showing little of the aging process! Lovely coiffures that show the modern mother as being the ultimate in femininity that she deserves to be! We pay tribute to the modern mothers who are carrying on the tradition of fashioning the lives of their little ones handed down from generations past.

But in many respects, mothers of today have little in common with mothers 50 years ago or more. Looking backward, I don't know how those old-fashioned mothers bore the brunt of all the things they were exposed to. It was Ma this and Ma that from the time the roosters crowed in the morning until the feet were washed at night unless a young'un slipped to bed without so much as touching those nasty little feet.

Throughout the day there was a constant tugging at Ma's coattail from some aggravating young'un wanting something to eat or to go play with some other young'un across the way. And whatever happened it was a constant cry for Ma — if a toe was stumped, if one young'un had hit another, if a child was scared by man or beast — all the livelong day.

And our Mamas' hands would never have gone into a beauty commercial, nor any other part of our Mamas for that matter, for they were a different breed in those days. There was always a roughness about their hands which was a perfectly natural thing as a result of their lifestyles. Their hands were in lard every day, making panfuls of biscuits to feed their offspring. They were in dish water, cleaning up after the pack. They were in the washtub scrubbing the nasty clothes for a big family and sometimes the middle joints of the fingers would become sore where lye had eaten the skin away from the strong wash water.

Wisps of hair would gather around their faces and they'd blow it aside when it got in their way and sometimes they'd have to take down their hair and twist it and get the ball back in place on the tops of their heads. They had a time. They looked old and wrinkled and haggard, but somehow we didn't pay that much attention. They were our "Ma's" all right, and we could never forget it.

Who was it that made the rounds in the dead of night when the world was frozen stiff and when you walked on the floors they pure creaked and sounded like they were frozen? You know who. In her old flannel nightgown with a cap on her head, she'd walk through every room and stop at every bed carrying the oil lamp to check and see that all the young'uns were warm and that nobody was uncovered, the small ones and the grown ones.

And Ma didn't look like no haint meandering through those rooms. Ma looked like an angel, and when she saw a young'uns eyes open she would smile in the dimness and you just knew that everything in God's world was right. She'd put an arm or a leg under the cover and tuck the quilts under the feather bed, place a hand on the forehead momentarily, and move quietly through the rooms.

Whose hand was there when a young'un woke up at night sick at the stomach and had to throw up? It was Ma's hand that held the forehead while the child's head was over a chamber.

Whose arms were there to comfort a sick young'un? It was Ma who took the child into her arms and the warmness of her bosom and rocked them in that old, old rocking chair until they were asleep and then carried them to their beds for restful sleep again.

Somehow, those hands never seemed rough or wrinkled. That touch was different from all others. It was solid, soothing and more comforting than I can describe. Somehow, the look was right for Ma. Oh, if it could be today they could fix her up and make her look modern and give her a dignity she didn't have in that era. But I doubt that mothers of that era who have passed away would be comfortable with so great a change in appearance today.

Our mamas nourished us from their own bodies and rocked the cradles that soothed us; cooked, washed, ironed, sewed, cleaned up for us; shed tears for our sorrows and laughed with us when the world was bright; molded character by everyday living and saw something in us that nobody else on earth ever saw.

Artists paint beautiful pictures of all manner of subjects, mothers included. But have you ever seen a picture of a mother and child that wasn't touching, whether in the past or present? There's something about the look of the mother holding the child and the way both show absolute adoration that speaks a universal language. Is there any other love on this earth so pure?

We used to run over to "Miss Nancy's" house nearby early on Mothers Day to get red roses to wear to church. Miss Nancy had a red rosebush that pure covered her privy and it was loaded down with blooms on Mothers Day. We had a white rosebush that twisted around an end post to the clothesline, but we didn't want no white roses on Mothers Day for our Ma's were alive and we wanted the world to know it.

But there were those who wore white roses on Mothers Day even then and it made pure chills run down our spines to think about homes without mamas. We felt sad for those who didn't have mamas, 'specially young'uns.

In this column we refer to the "old man" and the "old lady" so nonchalantly as to imply they have no real place in our lives. But every such reference is an unspoken honor and we know that our readers are aware that they represented the Rock of Gibraltar to us. They were our guiding force and however lightly I may dismiss them, they were life's greatest realities.

Our Master has the greatest name in all the languages — Lord — but in the human element, the word that is regarded as the most beautiful and the most revered in all the world is Mother.   □

Scalding For Chinches

N o school today, girls and boys. Just the little ones will be walking the road to the schoolhouse," Ma says. "The sun's shining bright and no sign of rain, so we are going to 'scald' this house today.

"You boys take two hog gambols to tote the pots with and go and borrow at least three washpots. If any neighbor is washing, just go to another one until you find washpots not being used today.

"Fill every pot to the brim and be careful in drawing that water from the well close to the stables for the curbing is half-rotten and don't go leaning up to the edges. Then rake up all the chips you can find around the pots and git a fire going. Put the pots close together so the fire will help heat every pot.

"That water has got to be rolling when it's dipped into the buckets, for I want scalding water to dash on the walls and ceilings. It takes that to kill bedbugs. And even that might not kill 'em, for I think they just run back in the cracks and wait for the wood to cool and they're right back in the cracks waiting to come out of there and crawl to a bed.

"All the furniture has to be toted to the yard for water will be splashing everywhere, so take down the beds and put the mattresses anywhere you can find to keep them off the ground. They've got to be gone over with a squirt can filled with kerosene and every tuft has to be pushed up and sprayed, for chinches just love to harbor there.

"Put the bedsteads against trees so they can be gone over too. Where the sides of the bed fit into the stead, plenty of kerosene needs to be squirted there. That's one of the places chinches dearly love.

"Put the bureaus and tables and chairs somewhere that the sun won't beat down on them too much, or it might cause the colors to fade. They look bad enough now without adding splotches to make 'em worse. And be careful and don't ruin the ferns sitting on the tables. Take them and put them in the yard first. And don't mess up the "dollies" on the tables. That white crocheting just brightens things up and makes 'em look better.

"Somebody better go to the store and buy a gallon of kerosene and another box of lye. It'll take plenty of both before the day's over. I've got a quarter here in my backer sack. Last quarter to my name.

"That water's rolling in them pots, so let's go dip all the buckets full and git in them rooms and start to dashing water everywhere. Lord! Some young'un has left a "pixture" of their grandmammy and grandpappy on the wall. And there's the clock on the mantel. Sit the clock somewhere level and git the pendulum to swinging again or we won't know nothing about the time of day. And turn that "pixture" upside down and in a safe place.

"Now stand off a little distance from the wall so you won't git burned and dip the gourds down and dash that scalding water on the walls as hard as you can. Try to git it through all the cracks. Do the ceilings the same way. And when every crack and corner is scalded, take the scouring broom and add some lye to the water and scour the floors. There's already plenty of water on the floors.

"Keep filling up them pots, boys and you girls be careful when you go to dip water. Put your coattails between your legs to keep them away from the fire. Can't be too careful around an open fire. Chips are all burned up so go to the backer barn and git some wood to put around the pots.

"No, there won't be no dinner today. Everybody'll have to find some kind of left-over ... a tater or something. No time to cook and scald a house too.

"Lord! I hope scalding will git rid of them chinches. Tired of seeing bloody splotches on the sheets where them things have bit us. Makes my flesh crawl to think about them gouging on us while we are asleep.

"Let me git out there with the squirt can and work on them bedsteads and mattresses while you young'uns scald the rooms. Now just look at the back of these bedsteads. Rosin and sweet gum stuck everywhere. I'll bet you young'uns have chewed that mess a hundred times at least. Never seen anything to beat it. Ain't easy to scrape off either.

"Look at them rascals crawling out of the crevices in the bedsteads when that kerosene hits 'em. Only time a chinch looks good is when it's dead. There's another one and I'll squirt you good, you old sucker.

"A lot of trouble raising up every tuft on them mattresses, but it has to be done. At least its a consolation to know you've done the best you can to git rid of them.

"Springs and slats have got to be scalded too, then we'll be through with the hot water. But there's a lot of mess out in the yard and putting it back in place will be a job.

"One thing about it though, ain't no smell cleaner than a scalded house. Scouring the floors leaves a clean smell, but when a whole room is scalded down, it just seems like everything smells clean. Smells a lot better than hospitals with ether and Lysol the first things you smell when you walk in the door. They're enough to make a person sick if they weren't.

"Lord! What a day it's been. The day I dread most in the whole year. But after it's all done and things are put back in place, it just settles the nerves and makes people feel like they're human beings at least. And if bedbugs still pester us, it's not because of nastiness. I just hate them rascals, right along with head lice. Seems like folks ought not to have to put up with such things."

Incidentally, we called kerosene "careseen," bedsteads "bedstids," lye "potash," get "git," chairs "churs," fire "far," but the list could go on and on. □

Fish Every Saturday!

T he "chaney ball" trees are green and their purple flowers give off an
odor of lilac. The yard is swept clean and tubs of water are warming
in the sun for Saturday baths. The old place is looking good for
Sunday. A clean-swept yard does more to spark up the place than anything;
that and floors scoured clean and smelling fresh from lye soap, the shuck
broom and elbow grease.

It's Saturday morning and time for the fish man. He comes every Saturday
morning except during the winter months when people are gobbling down
freshes from hog-killings and feasting on cracklings and sweet taters, liver
pudding, liver hash, crackling bread, sweet tater biscuits, and sausage.
(Maybe yours came on Friday. What's the difference)?

The old Model T pulls up in the yard and parks close to the "umbrella
chaney ball" tree for its foliage is thick and it gives plenty of shade and there
are even one or two old chairs sitting around.

Three or four grown-ups run out to see what the week's fish fare is. On a
good week there are speckled and gray trout, butterfish, sea mullets and
red-fin croakers.

First choice is speckled trout, but they're 25 cents a pound. Six pounds at 25
cents comes to $1.50. Not enough money for them.

"How about the sea mullets? But they're sort of small. Butterfish too, and
everybody don't like them. Easy to dress though. Not many entrails and no
splitting in two. Just slash them several times on the sides and fry them
whole.

Croakers are right pretty and the fins really red. Gills red too. Look like
they were just caught. But croaker is considered low-class fish.

Have to be careful in dressing them rascals or they have a rank taste to 'em.
Cutting off the two fins nearest the head helps, and scraping the backbone
good and gitting out the blood on the backbone helps too. How much are them
croakers? Ten cents a pound is nearer in the price range. Still croakers are
croakers.

Go see if your Mammy has any extra eggs. If she's got three dozen or so
eggs, the dollar added to the egg money will be enough to git the speckled
trout. Them trout are right pretty.

Run and fetch the dishpan. Won't take but about four of them to make six
pounds. Don't worry about your Mammy wanting to set the eggs. There'll be
more eggs as fertile as them. Three dozen eggs at 15 cents comes to 45 cents.
Maybe there's a nickel at the bottom of this old pocket book. That and the
dollar will pay for the fish. Shore won't be pocket change for young'uns this
week.

Not much to scaling speckled trout. Don't have the hard scales like croakers. Clean them good and if they have eggs in them git them out to go with eggs for breakfast. Save the heads too for fish stew. Push out the eyeballs and cut out the whole mouth and git out the gills. Them heads make as good stewed fish as any other kind of fish.

Stew them down good. Go to the garden and there's a little patch of parsley growing up close to the fence. Pull off a right good little bit. Pull up three or four onions too that have good sized roots. Onions and parsley and a boiled egg or two in thickened gravy makes stewed fish fit for a king. Sopping that gravy with plenty of black pepper on it is about as good as fried fish.

Don't cut the backbone out of the fish either. Most of the young'uns like the backbone piece the best. 'Specially the tail end. And leave that tail on. Meal it good and fry it crisp and it's a pure delicacy. Fry all the fish good and brown and cook plenty of cornbread and make biscuits to go with the stewed fish.

Tote the insides and the water and scales to the hog pen and pour it into the trough but you'd better be careful and fast too, for them hogs act like they've never had a mouthful to eat. They go after fish entrails like they do when they kill a chicken.

The grown-ups take turns at getting their baths for they'll beat a way to town whether they have any money or not. Maybe a buddy has an extra quarter so they can at least go to the show, and the buddy will need a quarter at some other time.

But they'll be back before dark to set themselves around the table for the feast on fish. Get the vinegar cruet and put the pure tin box of black pepper on the table. Some love to saturate the fish in vinegar, then cover it with black pepper. Fix plenty of tea too for nothing's better with fish than iced tea. If a fish aint' salted it ain't fit to eat.

Then there's a yearning for water and folks make trips to the water bucket and swill it down. One will pass the dipper on to the other and it's a pure sight to see the crowd standing in line. But they love that salt, 'specially on fish.

The whole house smells like a seafood restaurant with the fish sizzling in that grease, 'specially if a pan gits too hot and the smoke rises up in the kitchen. Then there's a burnt part and the skin is stripped off and the fish put back in the pan to brown again. Everybody hates burnt fish.

But courting-age girls almost rather do without the seafood than to tackle the greasy frying pans and plates and bones after the feast. It ain't easy washing a passel of dishes after a fish-fry. The fish grease is kept in a separate can and it has to be drained off, leaving all the brown accumulation at the bottom, and it's just a mess to git all the grease cleaned from the pans and the dish water is gitting cold and the girls are expecting "company" and Ma will half-kill them if those pans have a greasy feel when she uses them for cooking again. But they love fish as much as the rest of the crowd.

Course there are fish down at the store too, and some people git them there, 'specially if there is no money to pay cash for them. The storekeeper will put it on the books and let them pay later. Then when the bill gits to mounting from all kinds of purchases, they wonder whether they've been cheated.

But the fish at the store don't look as fresh, and when a gill is opened it looks pale instead of the bright red of the fish the "peddler" brings around.

Everything considered, the fish man's visit is one of the highlights of the week and a young'un may reach in the box and git a small piece of ice and run to the water bucket and rinse it off and let it melt in his mouth. It's the coolest of cools on a hot day.   □

Making Soap In An Old Wash Pot

Geese, Chair Bottoms, Soap

T he things that we did routinely around our homes 50 years ago would bring out the television crews today and they'd go into great detail about the age-old practices. Can't you see the TV crews with their lights and power lines and microphones inside a mule stable? But that's where they would have had to be to capture the story for that's where we rounded up the geese for "picking."

Geese are so stupid! And maybe we were more stupid to keep them. Anyway, the idea was for them to eat the grass in the cotton patch so there wouldn't be so much chopping to do, but if it ever helped I didn't know anything about it. I do know that those stupid geese waddled all over the place and messed up the yard something terrible.

Anyhow, whenever the season came to "pick" the geese we would round them up and waddle them into the mule stable when the old plugs were out working in the fields. And I can't recall the exact time of year except that it wasn't in cold weather.

We'd take a barrel like the flour barrel we kept in the pantry and carry it into the stable to put feathers in. We'd take old chairs out to use in picking the geese and one would be grabbed from the pile in the corner and turned bottom-upward and the head placed under the wing and we'd put them on our laps and go to town pulling out those feathers. The feathers were caught between the index finger and the middle one. Those old stupid geese were as still as a mouse unless we got to the quick and then they would let out a "yak." The down was all picked from the under side from the area of the cloaca to the breast bone. When one was "picked" it was turned back out in the yard and they would "yak" occasionally until all the group was back together.

But goose down from those old birds so many years ago is still good in the pillows that I sleep on.

Shuck Scouring Brooms

And how about making those shuck scouring brooms! They wouldn't believe it today. But only the oldsters know about them so there's some explaining to do. You know, those floors in many tenant houses were made from rough lumber, and just imagine taking a modern mop and running over all those splinters. There wouldn't be a string left in them nor sponge in these modern contraptions. But a shuck broom worked fine in those old houses and also accomplished the job. They were tough.

A heavy wooden block about 12-14 inches long and 8-10 inches wide and about 1½ inches thick was used and holes about an inch in diameter were bored in them at regular intervals. And a hole was bored for a handle on a slant that allowed the broom (as it was called) to sit evenly on the floor.

Now about putting the shucks in the brooms.

Ma would take hot water and have her a pile of clean shucks at her side (out in the yard) and she would put whole shucks into the hot water. When they became soft she would take a couple and wring out the water. Then she would pull the top end of the shucks through the holes until they were tight. The bottom of the shuck that was hard and that held the ear of corn, served as the scrubbing surface.

This was continued until all the holes were filled with shucks and the soft ends stood up on the top side of the broom. I never knew why those shucks never came out of those holes, for they weren't nailed in. They just stayed and a new shuck broom would last perhaps two years.

Bottoming Chairs

There were too many old ladder-back chairs with worn straw bottoms at our house to get all of them reseated, for the straw was breaking all the time, but Ma also made some new chair bottoms with shucks. And they were professional looking and made excellent seats. She only used the soft portion of the shucks for this, and only clean, white shucks were used. They were also placed in hot water, and she'd take several pieces and twist them together and do her fastening at the bottom and all the knots and things were on the under side. But the top had a pattern in it. It was a slow process, but sure. Those bottoms didn't travel.

Soap Making

Then there was soap-making. And let me say right here that there would have been no way for us to have survived back then without Red Devil Lye. It was an absolute necessity in our everyday lives. There wouldn't have been those spotlessly white clothes without that lye. Floors wouldn't have been clean. And lye was a requisite to making soap. Whatever we may not have known about life as youngsters, we knew all about what the devil looked like on those boxes. It was always on the light of the moon when soap was made. Make it on dark nights and it would shrink up to almost nothing. And that's the truth.

Anyway, Ma would get out the scales, bring her meat scraps out to the washpot, sit those cans of lye down beside her, and weigh out the scraps and put in lye according to the amount of scraps. And of course there was some water added, but I'm not giving a recipe for making soap (for I don't know it). It didn't take too long to make the soap and after it was good and cold a long butcher knife was used to cut it into squares and it was taken out of the pot and put in the smokehouse to dry out for a few weeks.

Making Hominy

Then there was hominy-making, and here comes the box lye again. Only the best ears of corn were used and it was shelled and placed in a wooden tub with enough water added to allow for the kernels to swell and still be under water. Then lye was added to the corn, for that's what ate off the outside skin and the end of the kernels. I don't know how much lye was used, but it had to be quite a bit for the skin and ends of a kernel of corn are pretty tough. The corn would remain in the tub until it was free of the skins and the kernels swollen and white.

Then it was removed from the lye water and fresh water put in and it was rinsed several times and put back in the tub and more water added and it stayed in that water a day or two. When it was finally ready to be cooked, the washpot was utilized again and the hominy was cooked until it was tender and bowls of hominy were sent to the neighbors and there was enough at home to last for days. But hominy never did much for me. There would be more when other women cooked a batch and we'd get a bowl from them.

Wouldn't the television crews just love to get in on something like that? But no more. Those days are gone. In fact, those things happened half-a-century ago. □

Cuts, Bruises, Stings, Etc.

T here is no way today's generation could survive if youngsters were exposed to all the things we were 50 years ago. First, nobody would take the chances that parents took with their children then, and second, I really don't believe children today are as tough as we were.

All of us of that era can remember terrible cuts and bruises and rusty nails sticking in our feet and encounters with pitch forks and rakes and broken glass. We paid the price in pain for the privilege of going barefoot in summer. But it was worth it for nobody that I knew died from their injuries.

Most all children got one or both of their big toes stumped during the barefoot season — May through September — and wore rag bandages on them for most of the summer. And even after cool weather brought out shoes, it wasn't unusual to see cutouts in shoes for those sore toes, proud flesh and all that.

It seemed that our feet were magnets for old nails. Sometimes they would actually go all the way through the foot, or nearly so. And it was torture to get the nail out. But if you think we were taken to a doctor for a tetanus shot you have another thought coming. No sir, they doctored us at home, although we knew about lockjaw.

The first thing was to try to clean off the dirty foot with the child screaming and warning that it couldn't be touched. But those feet were really dirty and a semblance of washing was necessary. Then the youngster would hold the wounded foot out so it was beyond the porch, and the kerosene can was brought and oil poured over the foot.

But we wouldn't have made it without the rag bags. Next, a ragged sheet or some other sizable white rag was pulled from the sack and a long strip torn off and also narrow strips to tie around the foot after the bandage was applied. But that wasn't all.

Treatment may have varied from area to area, but around home peach tree leaves were plucked from the trees and bruised with the hammer and placed over the wound as a poultice. Then the bandage was applied. Next, an old bucket that wasn't any good for carrying water was found — an old well bucket with holes rusted through; an old utensil used to gather Irish potatoes when they were scratched from the hills before the spuds were ready to dig, or some other worn-out utensil — and rags were placed in the bucket and set afire and the foot was held over the smoke.

Don't ask me what the medicinal value was or why the foot was smoked. I just know that was the way we did it. Maybe peach tree leaves, like some herbs and other plants, have healing powers, too.

I also remember that sometimes pine boughs were placed over the rags and wounds smoked with them. I suppose turpentine was the objective in using the pine. I know that the odor from smoking rags was terrible, especially with a throbbing foot. The odor would spread over the neighborhood and people would get a sniff and go check out their houses to see if something was on fire.

We were bad for getting splinters or long briers or shivers of glass in our feet also. We'd walk around on the ball of a foot sometimes, or on the side, depending on the area involved, and a grown-up would make a search of the machine drawers until a needle was found and begin exploratory surgery. It seemed like that needle would be pushed its full length into the foot. In fact, it was quite a job to pick through the tough skin on the foot — especially the heel — and by the time the "surgeon" was ready to do the dirty work the foot was already sore.

That needle would go a little deeper and the foot would be jerked away instantly. Then the grown-up would get angry and grab the foot again and resume the exploration. This time the needle would strike something that brought excruciating pain and screaming and beating fists, and the grown-up would give up in disgust.

But that didn't solve a thing and the child would continue limping and hopping around and a kernel would form in the groin sometimes and there might even be fever (but the temperature wasn't tested with a thermometer). Who had thermometers in those days?

Mothers would resort to fat (raw) meat and place it over the sore place to "draw" out the foreign object. They also sometimes broke an egg and took the skin from the eggshell and used it instead of the meat. The bandage would stay on overnight and the wound "mashed" the next day to see whether the object had come closer to the surface. If not, the procedure was carried out again and eventually a splinter, a brier or a piece of glass would pop out with the pus, and what a relief!

Those foreign objects had been in the feet for weeks sometimes and once they were removed those barefoot kids resumed a normal way of walking and exposed their feet to the same torture all over.

Fat meat was used in most cases where there were risings and carbuncles. And it usually brought them to a head, too!

And all we oldsters can remember those mustard plasters with the mustard-vinegar smell that they placed on our chests when we had such deep colds it sounded like we were dying. They'd warm them by the fire but by the time they got to the bed with them those plasters would be cold to the chest and the mustard would leave wrinkles in the cloth and the smell was sickening. But they helped.

Then we'd sprain an ankle and a search would begin for a dirt-dauber's nest to make another poultice to bind on the ankle. This was made from the mud used in making the nest, and vinegar. If there were insects around the nest they were smoked away with paper tied around a stick set afire and placed over the nest. Somebody got stung sometimes, too.

I have no explanation as to why mud from a dirt-dauber's nest would aid sprains any more than mud taken from a ditch. Nobody ever told me and I never asked. I just know that's what they did.

Irish potato poultices were used also on some sores. They scraped the potato and put it directly on the sore and I think they sometimes wrapped a collard leaf around the wound on top of the potato and then put on the rag bandage.

When men became galded from plowing, flour would be parched and rubbed on the raw places, and it was as soothing as if it had been a medicated powder. If there was any talcum powder around in those days we didn't have any.

But the way we jumped from haylofts with plows, rakes, plowpoints, fenders, single trees and other farm tools all over the place it's a wonder we didn't get our teeth knocked out, all our limbs broken and cuts too deep to heal without stitches. But I don't recall any broken bones until I was grown except from cranking Model T's or anybody having to be sewn up. I do remember a very few times when the doctor had to come out, but very few.

They gave us the home treatment and didn't seem to worry too much about us. I guess they placed their trust in God. One thing is for sure: He looked after us. No doubt about that.   □

Buryings Of Long Ago

A country "burying" half a century or more ago was a ritual we would not want to see repeated today. Just an ordinary funeral and burial then and now is one of the best ways to look back and see how far we have come.

On wind-swept hills and in dismal back-field graveyards, they took their dead for burial in places that seemed forgotten by time. Places where buzzards soared above the lonely pines and rabbits meandered through brier patches and where loneliness dominated the scene.

When a person died, some of the men or women of the neighborhood went and "laid out" the corpse, depending on the sex. They would fold the hands, remove pillows or bolsters to allow the head to lie flat and have the corpse straight on the bed.

If the mouth or eyes were open they would attempt to close them by placing coins over the eyes after pulling the lids together and tying a cloth around the chin and the head. They would take a pan of water and a washrag and wash the body thoroughly and dress it in its "Sunday" clothes. They would comb the hair in its natural fashion.

After this was finished the body would be left perfectly straight on the bed and the sheet pulled up to the headboard. It was usually several hours before the coffin was brought out, for the dead weren't taken to the funeral home in those days. But this was in the late 20s and early 30s.

When the gray casket arrived, a place was made for it to rest in the front room and in most cases the bed used by the deceased person was taken down and put outside to air. The corpse was placed in the casket and the lid left open for viewing.

Caskets then looked smaller than they do today with less padding, although they did have the white satin interiors. There were no sprays of flowers on the casket. The dark gray of the casket stood stark in its drabness. There were no wreaths, no potted plants, no stands. If it were summer there might be a vase of gardenias in the room, and these flowers became associated with "buryings" of long ago, much in the way carnations are associated with funerals today. We called gardenias "cape jasmine" in those days.

News of a death would spread across the community within an hour or two and people would immediately plan to go to the "sitting up." They sat up with the corpse all night and there were plenty of volunteers for it was a place for the courting-age population to go and parents were so strict on their girls they seldom let them out of their sight, and if a boy came courting he and the girl had to sit in the parlor with the door open, and bedtime was 10 p.m. sharp.

A "sitting up" offered a logical excuse for the youth of the community to get away from home as well as doing a good deed, for the old folks just couldn't sit up all night. However, those that did sit up all night were required to work next day with no consideration given to going without sleep.

The funeral was preached either at the house or at the church, and a lot of the community attended, even children. I never knew why children were exposed to this unless it was the fact that there were no babysitters in those days and practically everyone that didn't attend the funeral was at work in the fields. And everyone viewed the corpse.

They didn't embalm poor folks in those days and when the weather was hot the body had begun to decompose and the stench of death was heavy in the air, coupled with the scent of the cape jasmine. Sometimes the eyes and mouth were partially open despite attempts to close them and their ghostly white faces and sometimes a snag of a tooth protruding from the mouth would send a chill up the spine.

Not only that. Sometimes the body purged from the mouth and nostrils and flies would buzz around the casket. Sometimes wet places could be seen on the side of the casket.

Interment might be at the church cemetery or in family graveyards far off the main road and the corpse would be taken to the burial site in a mule-drawn wagon. Then there was a good bit of walking for the pallbearers over gullies and across small ditches overgrown by brushes and weeds. Sometimes a place had to be cleared at the graveyard where briers, bushes and weeds had overtaken the burial plots before the grave could be dug.

There were no vaults used in the burials that I remember as a boy. Only a wooden box was lowered into the grave and the casket placed in the box and the wooden lid fitted over the coffin.

In those days of my earliest recollection a lot of travel was by buggy. The days of the buggy, the Model T and the Model A Fords seem to merge and to form a part of the whole mode of transportation in that era, although I know the Model T's came before the Model A's.

If burial was in a family graveyard the buggies would follow the wagon to the burial site. "Buryings" in those days took up about half a day. Funerals were long, with the preachers extolling the virtues of the deceased. Then there was the viewing as those attending lined up and passed the casket. Finally, the family gathered to mourn the loved one for the last time. There would be wailing and crying and people would hover over the corpse and express words of love to the departed as those in attendance watched.

By the time the ritual was all over, the sun was getting low in the west and darkness seemed to appear especially early after a "burying." A child exposed to all that carried the image of the corpse in his mind and sleep didn't come easily and there were bad dreams, and upon awakening the darkness would seem totally emcompassing and filled with evil.

In retrospect, I know that such an early exposure to death had no permanent psychological effect on the young of that era. We learned all the realities of life early and in that respect it helped us to be able to cope with the problems of that time in history.

I am also aware that the cheap burials that were the custom in those days were no discredit to the deceased and that even today the expensive rituals carried out in burials is for the living, not for the dead.   □

A Pauper Wears A Crown

In my boyhood I knew an old man (who became old before his time by disease) that I felt was the most curious of the curious. There seemed to be a childishness about him out of all proportion to a man of his age. He had all kinds of "isms" and mannerisms and it was hard to picture him as ever having been a "real" man who thought, spoke and acted as a man.

This old man, (he was only in his 50s when it began), was a victim of rheumatoid arthritis. Before he was 60 he was confined to a wheelchair, and his condition was often compared with Job in the Bible. His legs grew in a sitting position and his knee joints were red and inflamed looking and appeared to have been glazed over with shellac. And before it was all over his hands were clasped tightly together and when he died mold was growing in the area where the hands were closed and there was no way to remove it. That is an indication of the extent of his infirmities.

His gray eyes appeared to have a skim over them and it seemed that he had to stare very hard in order to see objects about him, and this was possibly due to cataracts. But if that had been the case they weren't removing cataracts in my area in those days.

But this old man was a character. After he became crippled, he had to live among his children, for the poor house was out for people like him who had to have a lot of care. He'd stay at one place for a month or two and move on to another, and the family tried to do a good job by him, but it was always a problem for he had a lot of spunk and actually liked to be "cranky" a lot of the time.

He had a mouth full of "solid" teeth, but even had them pulled to see whether that might help his condition. Then he had to "gum" his food and he was a laughing stock for the small children. They poked fun at his eating, what he ate and how he ate. He'd strew his food on himself and on the floor about him and it really was a little disgusting. But what were they to do?

When nighttime came, they'd get him settled in his bed, and on good nights there was no word from him. But there were other nights when all hell broke loose and he awakened everybody in the family. He might have nightmares and scream out and someone would go to his bed and he'd be sweating and turning and trying to slash out with his arms.

The family would become a little angry at his carrying-ons and give him a few words of warning. But that did no good at such times. He'd call out for any of his children, or his dead wife or parents, and he'd raise his head off the pillow in anticipation of their answering. But nobody would come to his rescue.

And then in the dead of night, I was told, he would come out with songs that would pierce the hearts of the household and bring tears to the eyes of the entire family.

What a friend we have in Jesus, all our sins and griefs to bear
What a privilege to carry, everything to God in prayer.
Oh, what joys we often forfeit, oh, what needless pain we bear
All because we do not carry, everything to God in prayer.

And they said he didn't normally have a voice for singing, but that it was resonant and in perfect tune when he sang the hymns at night. It seemed that there was something special about those songs of suffering and supplication.

Then he would come out with another:

At the cross, at the cross, where I first saw the light
And the burdens of my heart rolled away
It was there by faith I received my sight
And now I am happy all the day.

Or:

Rock of ages, cleft for me,
Let me hide myself in thee . . .

The old man was desperately sick and the family thought he was just an old "kook" trying to upset everybody's rest. They weren't even aware that he was "out of his mind" and knew nothing about what he was doing.

He was tortured by day and by night, season after season, year after year. He bore excruciating pain — a stiff neck, stiff elbows, stiff hands, stiff knees, large, open sores on his shins, swollen, stiff feet. Aspirin was his strongest medicine. Morphine wouldn't have killed all his pain. He suffered unmercifully, still he was thought of as an oddity.

In the cold of winter he almost froze in those old open houses, for his legs remained in a sitting position and ice would accumulate in the water bucket on the bureau.

In the heat of the summer he practically suffocated, for there was no electricity and no fans. He couldn't even fan himself, and at night he just lay and sweated in a hot bedroom because there was no way to cool it off. But he was just an "old man."

If they had only known! He too had dreamed the dreams of youth, had had visions of a good life. He had been handsome, agile, smart, a hard worker and a good father. And behind those misty blue eyes there was a wisdom that belied his condition. And only having lived life and being able to look back upon it all in a different light, can those involved at that time fully appreciate the real man beneath the mask of sickness.

He had said, "Ain't but one way to do things, and that's the right way. Do them right and when it's all over won't be no regrets. Do them wrong and they'll always come back at you.

"Build a solid foundation and when everything seems to be falling around you and there don't seem to be no place to go, just stand on that foundation and all hell can't tear you down.

"Only thing a poor man's got to stand on is his word," he said. "A man that's any 'count will always tell the truth and if it hurts him at first, it will prevail and he'll be the winner in the long run."

So the old man died and went on to his reward, never knowing the comforts of life we enjoy today. They weren't available to him, or any poor person of that era. Few really grieved at his passing, for they felt he was better off dead than in a living hell.

After his death, when a normal pattern of life returned to the family involved, I was told that they saw this old man in an entirely new light. He had touched their lives and made such an impact on them they only then realized they had had a king among them. He died a pauper but he wore a crown in the hearts of a family.

This is a tribute to one old man of long ago, as well as to all fathers on this Father's Day.   □

Toting Backer To Be Hung In Barn

Backer Barning Season

L ord, Lord! It's time to git ready for backer-barning season. Time has slipped up and not much time to git everything ready.

Around the barns has got to be cleaned up. Hard weeds as thick as hair on a cow's back. Pope bushes growing at the end of the looping shelter. Cow witch vines twisted around corner posts. Them hoes'll have to be sharpened and them young'uns put to work flat-weeding this mess.

Backer barns' got to be cleaned out. Old baskets and piles of trash backer still in there and rotten ish taters and all kinds of mess. Some of the boards on the looping racks got to be replaced too. And green limbs cut and hauled to put on top of the looping shelter for shade. Them old gum trees got thick leaves and they are good to use. Plenty of them too without going up in the hot woods.

Looping horses' got to be checked out and some 1 by 4's cut to make some of them solid. Backer sticks' got to be hauled from the shelter to the backer barns. Have to watch out for wasp nests too. Them rascals nest close to backer sticks under them shelters and they'll pop you 'fore you can turn around if you don't watch 'em.

Curtains for the backer trucks got to be rounded up from the hayloft. May have to make another one or two from guano sacks. Rounds got to be made for the backer trucks too. Young'uns throw about every one away in the pastures when they use 'em for baseball bats. That won't be no job though. Cut down a few oak saplings about the size you need, take a sharp ax and cut them a little bit "calli-biars" and trim off the bottom to fit the steel pieces nailed on the side of the trucks to hold the rounds, drive a nail in the top and you've got as good a set of truck rounds as you need.

Got to turn them old trucks bottom-upwards too and git off the wheels and grease the axles good and check on the bedding of the trucks. Might have to drive a 20-penny nail or two into them to make them good and solid. Them old trucks take a lot of punishment during puttin'-in-backer season.

All the flues in the backer barns' got to be checked out too. The bottom of the flues that's close to the ground can git holes in them 'fore you know it and you got to be careful and try to keep a backer barn from burning down. That better be done right now too, for it will mean a trip to town and time's running short. Seems like elbows are easy to git holes in them too. Reckon that's because that heat turns when it hits them and puts a little more stress on them.

Got to check out the thermometers still hanging in the barns from last year, too. Got to know the right heat when you're curing backer. Lanterns' got to be taken down from their resting place on the nails under the shelter and cleaned up too. The shades are as black as smut and have got to be washed and the wicks checked. May have to buy some wicks too.

But the worst job of all is patching up the backer barn furnaces. Bricks have come loose and some lying on the ground where wood was shoved in the furnaces and no 'tention paid to where it was shoved. Some cracks in the furnaces inside the barns too. And that's a mess when you ain't a brick mason nohow and trying to do something with nothing to do it with.

No telling where the old trowel is. Can't put everything on the plates of the shelters. Ain't seen that thing in God knows when. And if you don't have a trowel you ain't going to do nothing but make a mess. This flat-spoon mess from the kitchen just won't work with mortar.

That old mortar board must be out there among the weeds behind the backer barn. But a new box will have to be made to mix the mortar in, and sand hauled and mortar bought. Might have to git a few bricks too. Just as well go to the boss man right now and git the money to fix up the furnaces and buy some backer twine. Got enough to git started, but not enough to last long.

Forgit everything else for the next six or seven weeks 'cept backer. Everybody is a slave to the damn mess, day and night. At least all the crops are laid by so won't be no rush to git out in the fields with plows 'cept for the late corn and peas and the grass will probably git them.

Forgit the gardens, even, as far as plowing goes. So the boys will have to plow them out good 'fore backer barning starts. Then weeds and grass will be head-high 'fore backer is all put in. But them gardens' got to produce for everybody'll want the good stuff that comes from them in summer.

Anything else got to be done, do it within the next week or so, for once everybody gits in the backer patches, ain't no turning round. Monday morning til Saturday night sometimes, it's backer, backer, backer. Runs everybody to death and whatever else is done it's when a few hours come when the swapper has finished his and 'fore the other party starts putting in. Women folks just as liable to put out a big washing on Saturday evening as any time and scour the floor at bedtime Saturday night. And God knows when any "arning" will git done. Everybody'll be wearing "rough dried" clothes 'cept for the ones they wear to church and they'll be dragging them every which way from the pile on the bed in the "company" room to "arn." God! It'll be a mess and our tails will be dragging from now til the last of August.

Things will git started off pretty good, but 'fore it's all over everybody will be hollering at each other and fussing and carrying on, for all them weeks in the backer patch will wear down the nerves and work on the body too. It's hard work, putting in backer.   ☐

Is That You Trucking Backer, Little Bud?

Old-Timey Way Of "Puttin' In Backer"

Puttin' In Backer

H ank, you and Fuzz got to git out there and crap backer today. After Shine fell out yisdiddy in that hot backer patch, he's got to lie out on the porch in the shade for a day or two until he gits that sick feeling out of his stomach and gits over that dizziness," the "old man" says.

"You can carry one row apiece and keep up with the grown crappers. And you've got to watch and crap the leaves that show some yaller. Don't be picking that gourd-green backer.

"Here, everybody take a sweat rag from this old sheet. You'll be needing it in a little while. God! It's already hot as fire out here and the sun's just rose.

"Little Bud, you can drive trucks. Now just look at you smiling all behind your ears just because you're gitting to haul the backer to the looping shelter. But you be careful, boy. Don't you go turning over no trucks and "momicking" up that backer.

"Git that mule and truck in the truck row, Little Bud, and less hurry and git a truck of backer to the looping shelter. Must be 700 or 800 sticks of backer to be looped and hung up. Then I'll git up to the shelter and see that them young'uns git to stringing that backer right. They'll worry the grown folks at the looping bench crazy I reckon, but they got to do their share and young'uns have to make hands in putting in backer. First year Sarah's made a hand and she'll have to be watched.

"Here comes the backer trucks so everybody git ready to work. Lizzie Mae you ain't even got no sticks at your looping horse. Git a pile of sticks and stand them up behind you in the looping racks. And let me say right here that I don't want nobody wrapping string around that stick twice and using a hand of backer to hold the string on the stick. Pull that thread far enough up from the stick so you can take a hand and twist it and then take the string that's broke and hold it and pull and you've got a loop.

"Hey, whoa right now! You're wrapping one side of that backer Lizzie Mae. I seen you wrap that string around that backer and just slide it down on your side of the horse. I ain't having none of that. That's the best way in the world to burn up a barn of backer. You know you've got to work that hand of backer so that when it is on the stick it is looped.

"Sarah, you pay 'tention to what you're doing. You ain't handing that backer right. You're holding it half-way down the stems. Now you take that backer like this with your hand above the backer so Lizzie Mae can take it from you without all that trouble. And if you don't watch what you're doing and hand it so she can git to it, she can just snatch that hand til you learn where you're supposed to put that backer.

"Grown folks can tote the sticks to the looping racks and put them on the two top racks and you young'uns can hang yourn on the bottom two.

"And don't you young'uns be running out to that old apple tree and picking up the faulty apples lying on the ground. Ever one of them has got a worm in it and you ain't got time to be running out there nohow. We catch up between trucks I'll cut that old big watermelon under the shelter.

"Here comes Little Bud with another truck of backer. Look at him just a smiling standing on the back of that truck. Anyhow, you've about got the first truck load finished. Better pick up speed though, for if you don't them trucks'll be piling up on you and there won't be no catching up then. When that backer gits good and dry and it gits to wilting in the sun, it'll lay so close together on that truck it will seem like you won't never git to the bottom.

"Lizzie Mae, you take that round out of that truck so Sis can git to that backer better. Pull that curtain out of the way so them young'uns can find that backer right quick. Ain't you wrapping one side of that backer agin Lizzie Mae? Shore looked like it to me. You better not do that, girl.

"Fuzz and Hank are all right out there in that backer patch. They're faring better than the men. Them boys don't even know what hot is.

"Push that backer tight in them racks, for they're filling up fast. Going to have to make a pile side of the backer barn before it's all over anyhow.

"Lord! Lord! Time flies. There goes that old dinner bell. Everybody quit right where you are. Time for some belly-feeding now with them good old butterbeans, corn, collards, sliced cucumbers and maters and boiled meat and cornbread and all that stuff. Take the kerosene can and run some oil over your hands and it'll cut that gum right off. Course the stain will still be there. I reckon it'll be next fall 'fore all that brown stain gits from around the fingernails. Anybody rather have a green mater to cut off the gum, there's plenty in the garden.

"Look at that Fuzz and Hank eat. They can eat enough for two grown folks and them just strapping 13, 14-year-old boys. You feel like eating, Shine?

"Lord! Dinner times goes by in a hurry. Time to git back to the backer barn. You men tie some rags around your foreheads to keep off some of the sweat. Bending down in that backer row will put the water to rolling. You young'uns' feet would git burnt up if it weren't for the shade from them backer leaves.

"There's a whole extra truck waiting to be looped at the shelter and everybody's got to bear down. Looping racks are full. Start that pile close to the backer barn door and pile it straight. Don't just throw it up there.

"Watch what you're doing Sarah, and hand that backer like you ought to. You wrapping one side of that backer now, Lizzie Mae? And let me put a nail in that shackly looping horse or it'll be falling down. I thought them boys had done all that stuff 'fore we started to putting in backer.

"Here comes the crappers and the last truck load of backer. It will be sunset 'fore it's all looped and then its got to be hung in the barns.

"You men go on in the barn and we will start toting the backer to you while the others finish stringing. Little Bud, Fuzz, Hank and me can be toting backer. It'll be pure dark 'fore we git through.

"Young'uns can't tote but one stick apiece, but they're faster'n us grown folks. You men will just have to feel in the dark to git the backer right on the tiers. And don't stay up there and git too hot and fall out.

"Tote, tote, tote that backer and then we can go home, feed up, wash up, eat and have a few hours of rest 'fore starting the same thing over tomorrow."   □

Barning Backer In The Rain

O ld saying "Rainbow in the morning is a sailor's warning" must be so, for the sun shining against the clouds brings out the rainbow and then the sun's gone and it grows darker and rain starts falling again. No matter about the rain, backer is ripe and it's got to be taken from the fields. Rain can't stop putting in tobacco for there's no extra days to wait. Every day is accounted for and when it's your day to put in, you get out and do it the same as if the sun were shining.

Hitch the mules to the backer trucks and go to the fields. At least you won't burn up but you'll be as soaked as a wet puppy all day long.

Shelter hands can get under a backer barn shelter but there ain't much room under there and they'll get almost as wet as the crappers. That backer's loaded with water and the handers get wet as they pull the leaves from the trucks and the loopers sling the water everywhere in the stringing process.

Water from the backer gets in the eyes and burns and the workers use their coattails or their sleeves to wipe the eyes. The backer is brittle from the rain and it is easy to cut the stems with the wet thread. Looping wet backer makes a rasping sound.

Handers, already wet from the backer on the truck, get wetter when they carry the sticks to the looping racks.

Men in the field are saturated, and the steadily falling rain adds to their misery. They want to smoke but don't have any dry tobacco and the matches in their overalls' bib pockets are only pieces of wood with a slightly pink end. All the phosphorus has been washed away by the rain. Their cigarette papers are turned into mush. Somebody has to go to the store and get a can of Prince

Albert since it's in a tin can, and the cigarette papers slipped inside along with some matches.

Somebody starts singing "Stormy Weather."

Everybody becomes chilled thoroughly as the day wears on. The skin on the inside of the hands and the fingers becomes wrinkled from the water. Rain falls on some heads under the shelter where the tin has rusted through or where nails have come loose from the shelter framing.

Water puddles under the shelter and the handers and loopers stand in mud that squshes between their toes. It's easy for a looper to cut a finger with wet tobacco twine and when that thread cuts into a finger it causes acute pain and a rag is tied around the cut, but that presents a problem too, for it's usually in the bend of a finger and if the thread is tied tight enough to hold it binds the finger.

It's even miserable at dinner time with everybody wet and the pot liquor goes fast for it warms up the insides if it's good and hot. Young'uns find dry tow sacks and pull them up over their bodies and lie on the porch and try to warm up. They ignore the itchiness of the rough material.

An old rooster walks over the yard with his tail feathers touching the ground. The old bird holds his body that way so the water will run off his back without wetting his feathers.

After work is resumed, the rain ceases for a while and the sun comes out and it's hot and humid, but soon a black cloud begins to form and the sky becomes dark and lightning begins to flash and thunder rolls heavy across the heavens. Sometimes it gets so wet in the fields the tobacco has to be toted out in aprons made from tow sacks.

The lightning gets sharper and the thunder louder, and many workers are too far from the house to reach safety there. Some people are barning under the shade of large trees and when the storm strikes they run for the tobacco barns as a place of refuge. But tobacco barns are very dangerous places to be during electrical storms.

The smokestack that rises above the tobacco barn is also made of galvanized tin that runs into the flue system and it goes all around the interior of the barn. This actually invites an electrical charge and sometimes lightning does run down the smokestack and plays on the flues lying just above the ground. People inside the barns stay away from the flues and everybody is scared half to death while the storm is raging.

When the fury of the storm is spent the workers go back to the shelter and the fields and everything is drenched, but that barn of tobacco has to be gotten in.

A steady rain falls again and the land looks flooded after the downpour. The looping racks fill up and the tobacco has to be put in a pile near the tobacco barn door.

Wet children work with their teeth chattering and water runs from their hair down their faces. But no complaints are heard for they know they are expected to make hands just as the grown-ups.

As the sky begins to darken the last load of tobacco is looped and all the hands hasten to get the tobacco hung in the barn before dark.

The crappers climb the tier poles and the other hands begin toting the wet tobacco to the barn. Water runs off the leaves as it is taken to the barn and after it is hung on the tiers there is a steady drip and soon the dirt floor of the barn and the flues become wet.

Children in overalls rolled up to their knees and girls and grown-ups walk through the mud puddles to take the tobacco to the barn. It becomes slick at the little incline at the barn door.

When it is all finished it is twilight and the lamps are showing feeble light from the windows. The boys still have to cut green corn for the mules and since it's so late they cut enough to throw into the hog pen also.

Everybody washes off and gets into dry clothes and by the time supper is finished, it's time for bed, for tomorrow's another work day. Children pull quilts from the closet that have acquired a musty smell during the summer and put them on their beds. They snuggle under the covers as the rain that kept them cold all day becomes a lullaby as it hits softly on the tin roofs and sleep takes them into another world.   □

Janet, Glenda And D.C. — Children Of '30s And '40s

Young'uns In Mulberry Tree

Ma's thinking out loud:

Just look at them young'uns in that mulberry tree. They're acting like a pack of pure monkeys up there. Look at that one, lying on his back on a limb and picking with both hands. If their daddy was to see them up there he'd tear them all to pieces, and they ain't got no business up there, but Lord! What do you do with a pack of young'uns when something's ripening?

Never thought mulberries were fit for humans to eat in the first place, but they do have a right good taste when they're a dark purple. But you can't just chew and eat them like most fruits, for it seems like the stem don't chew up too good. You have to sort of pull them between the teeth and throw away the center.

Seems like ants and other kinds of insects git on them too, and I'd have a fit if I saw them picking them up off the ground and chomping on them. Seems like mulberry trees are in a lot of hog pastures and that's where they should be. Good thing there ain't no sow with little pigs out there or there wouldn't be no young'uns up that tree.

Lordy mercy! They're wild up there. Got to have a dip of snuff to settle my nerves. No toothbrush in my apron pocket so I'll just twist off the lid and fill up my jaw from the box. Ought to holler at them young'uns but if I did that now I'd git that snuff down my windpipe and cough myself half to death. Young'uns probably wouldn't hear me nohow.

One thing about it: The Lord looks after drunks staggering along the roads and he looks after young'uns too or every one of 'em would be dead. No way to keep them protected no matter how hard you might try. If it was not mulberries it would be an apple tree or a peach tree or something.

First faulty plums they see on a tree they grab them like they were the best things in the world. They bite down into them and that rough taste gits in the mouth and they start over and eat just the tiny bit that has turned a mite soft. They have to be careful not to git that worm in there too.

Young'uns will eat anything. I seen 'em grab green 'simmons off of a tree and bite down on them and have their mouths turned almost inside out and that rough taste just stays in the mouth, but even that don't stop 'em. They'll pick pure green peaches with all that fuzz on 'em and eat them right down to the half-formed seeds. Makes the flesh crawl to see them pull their teeth across that fuzz but they think nothing about it. Even seen them bite into big acorns, and everybody knows that's no good taste.

And pecans. They'll shell the green hull off of them as soon as they fall and crack 'em in their mouths and they're pure green with all that bitter mess inside and there ain't no way to pick out the meat, so they just eat the whole mess.

They'll pull pure green grapes from the vine, as hard as a ball almost, and gobble them down too. But there's one thing they back off from after taking one bite. That's a green "chaney ball." That stops 'em dead in their tracks, for they're not only rough, but as bitter as quinine as well. Same with green walnuts. Oh, they'll try 'em, but one time is enough.

Green brierberries are shied away from too, but they'll eat a green apple, even to the core! And young'uns love chufas that they plant for the hogs. They taste right good too.

Reckon all the things they cram into their stomachs is the reason they have to be "cleaned out" several times a year. It's a wonder they don't die with bellyache anyhow but you hardly ever hear a word about their stomachs hurting.

Seems like that's about as good as the way they do when a cake is cooked, though. They stand around and beg for the scrapings from the bowl after the batter is poured into the cake pans. And all that stuff is pure raw. Raw eggs, raw flour, lard, and flavoring. They act like it's as good as the cooked cake. But with four or five standing and waiting for a taste, they don't git enough of that to hurt 'em.

I can just see 'em after the frost strikes and they git a chance to run out in the cotton patches and find ripe maypops that have turned yellow and swiveled and popping them open and getting that sweet juice out of them. Can't eat the seeds, but that juice around them is almost as sweet as honey. They play with 'em all summer, gathering them and cutting them into shapes like furniture and putting them in playhouses and even taking the purple blossoms and shaping them for toys too.

And long after watermelons become slick and lose their taste, them young'uns will still bust them and take a few bites and how anybody can take a piece of slick watermelon in their mouths is beyond me.

They're gitting their fill of mulberries now and beginning to come down out of the tree. Their tongues will be as purple as the mulberries and they'll have stain on their hands that won't be off when they go to church Sunday. But that's young'uns for you. They're as free as birds now and as happy as a lark. Let 'em have their good times and something to remember when they're old. I did the same things and I will remember it all when I am old too.

I still say a young'un that didn't grow up out in the country and see the raw facts of life has missed one of life's greatest blessings. It's a pure education if they didn't git a day of schooling. Course they need that too, but everything's not book learning and good common horse sense goes a long way in this world.

Time to finish dinner, but the young'uns won't want a mouthful with all them mulberries packed down their throats. But the old man and them big boys will eat the dishpan if I don't load that table down. □

Curing Backer At Night

I t is night and the lightning bugs are flashing their yellow lights everywhere. The air is oppressive but less so than before darkness fell. Sultry might be a better word. Tobacco barns are running at high heat and there is an almost constant trek from one barn to another and stoking the furnaces with wood, for several barns of tobacco are curing.

Dry wood burns rapidly in the furnaces and this is necessary to keep the heat in the 180-degree range to cook the leaves and the stems that are even harder to dry out thoroughly.

On every visit to the curing barn, the hand-carried lantern with its feeble light is held inside the barn to check the thermometer hanging fairly close to the door on a nail driven into a bottom tier. The eyes also scan the interior of the barn to check on any sticks of tobacco that may have fallen on the flue system that goes all the way around the barn.

Falling sticks while barns are running at high heat are the major cause of tobacco barns burning. There is this ever-present danger when curing tobacco. In hanging green tobacco in the barn, the process is carried out by feel rather than sight, for it is dark inside the barns, so a stick might not be placed evenly between the two tiers. In such a case, the next course of tobacco might dislodge the stick and when the tobacco withers sufficiently it allows the stick of tobacco to fall from the tiers.

A burning tobacco barn is an awesome sight and always a potential danger to other nearby buildings. It also represents a sizable loss to the farmer. And once a barn starts burning it is a total loss for there is no fire protection for any rural building. Fire is a dreaded word in the country.

Wood for curing is stacked near each barn in four-foot lengths, maybe 25 feet long and six feet high. Three or four pieces of wood are usually required to fill the furnace.

In the early evening, there is always company around the tobacco barns. Neighborhood boys who are not curing tobacco themselves come by for a while and tell jokes and carry on in the usual manner of the young. But bedtime comes soon and the tobacco curer is left with his charge for the night, and then loneliness creeps in.

Tobacco curers can't prepare comfortable sleeping quarters, for the inducement to sleep is great at best and a comfortable bunk would defeat the purpose of the curer. He needs to be awake for most of the night. But no matter what kind of bedding there is, sleep still comes sometimes and the wood burns into embers and the temperature in the barns drops.

A wooden bunk is usually built under one of the tobacco shelters, and if there isn't one a tobacco truck serves as a bunk. And rather than indulging in a soft pillow, the head usually rests on a piece of tobacco wood with a quilt draped over it and extending down the bunk.

There are the night sounds. Cats scream and the owls give their cries. A dog barks somewhere in the distance and a cow bell jingles from a nearby stable and all the noises are magnified under the cover of darkness.

Lightning flashes occasionally from a faraway thunderhead that illuminates the cloud and reveals its dark and light structure, and faint thunder accompanies the lightning. Sometimes a star shoots across the sky and leaves a momentary flare in space. There are no lights in neighborhood houses — only the quietness and stillness of a summer night.

The eyes become heavy and there is the urge to lie down on the bunk and forget the tobacco barns, but that urge has to be put aside for it's time to fire the barns again.

Wood is brought from the pile and pushed into the furnace again and the interior of the barn checked. Then the other barns are attended. A lizard or scorpion scuttles from the pile of wood into the night. Lizards and scorpions seem to have an affinity for those stacks of tobacco wood.

A dog appears at the shelter from out of the night and the reflection from the fire makes its eyes luminous. The dog stays for only a moment and retreats into the shadows as suddenly as it came.

All the barns are attended and the tobacco curer finally rests on the bunk. There is no intention of going to sleep and he tries to concentrate on things to keep him awake, but sleep comes anyway and there is the usual one to one-and-one-half hours of sleep before replenishing the fires.

He is awakened by loud thunder and lightning flashing around him and a heavy cloud is rapidly approaching. Curtains made from tobacco sacks are quickly hung around the shelter to help keep out the rain.

A quick trip is made to each of the barns and the furnaces stuffed with wood. The thunder becomes deafening and lightning is blinding as it streaks from the sky. Rain begins to fall before all the barns are attended and the tobacco curer hastens to return to the protection of the shelter.

The rain comes down in sheets and begins to form puddles under the shelter and actually runs into the furnace until dirt is banked around the entrance. The curtains provide some protection but the quilt becomes damp and drops of rain lie on the exterior as if the quilt has a rain-proof surface.

Thunder still rumbles and lightning plays across the sky as the cloud begins to break apart and the rain falls at a steady pace rather than a downpour.

The barns are attended again, with a tow sack draped over the shoulders of the tobacco curer and the overalls' legs rolled up as he walks through the puddles of water. The rain is letting up and the thunder becomes a soft rumble that seems to roll all across the heavens. Lightning is no longer sharp with only faint flashes from the disappearing clouds and the heavens become docile again.

Temperatures in the curing barns are rising toward the 180-degree level again despite the wet exteriors and most of the water that stood in puddles during the height of the storm has soaked into the soil.

Stars appear in the sky again and the Milky Way and the Big Dipper seem brighter than before the storm. The air is cool and there is another period of sleep. Dawn is approaching upon awakening and there is another trip to the barns.

The roosters are crowing and lights are appearing in windows around the neighborhood. Just about everybody "swaps" putting in tobacco, so it's a five or six-day ritual for at least six weeks to get all the tobacco housed.

And curing tobacco at night doesn't give the curer the daylight hours to sleep. Someone will relieve him in the morning so that he can make a regular workhand the next day. But the next night he will be able to sleep in his own bed and another family member will take over the curing chores.   □

'Bugger' A Victim Of Times

B ugger" was his nickname. And he was a cute little bugger. Eyes as blue as a gander's. Skin white as a lily. Dimpled, rosy cheeks and a double chin. He was the pride of the whole bunch. Last of 10 children. Came about during the change of life when everybody thought there would be no more babies.

Spoiled rotten, "Bugger" took advantage of the entire family and squealed with delight at all the attention. They toted him on their backs and tickled him under his ribs and he screamed with delight and wiggled and twisted and carried on the whole livelong day.

"Bugger's mammy made him rompers of light blue that set off those blue eyes and fair skin and dark hair that curled up in the back and made him all the more appealing.

At 20 months, "Bugger" was well into the vocabulary, having been taught by nine other children, and not all of it was proper at that. He'd come out with a no-no and his mama would say some young'un had been putting the wrong words in his mouth.

"Bugger's" mama and papa were crazy about that young'un. They had fretted and worried when they knew another baby was on the way. It had been a hard struggle and they were getting on in years. They allowed that they'd never live to see him grown. Then they reasoned that maybe it was the will of God to send them a child late on to help them in their old age.

His mama was careful about what he ate. No fresh "ish taters" for "Bugger." They might do him harm. No corn that might have had soda put to it. Oh, he'd want all that stuff, but when it came to his safety, Mama did everything she could to protect him.

If the young'uns had him on a backer truck when they were hauling up green corn for the mules or watermelons in season, Ma would holler to the top of her voice to look out for "Bugger." If he went anywhere near the well curb somebody was dashing after him, for "Bugger" was into everything. He even scampered over the backer beds one time after they had been covered.

"Bugger's" fat little feet would get gommed up in the yard and a brother or sister would run and clean it off for him and everybody wondered whether he'd ever amount to a hill of beans the way they kowtowed to him.

So went the happy months with "Bugger."

Then one day the little fellow didn't feel too good, and his mammy thought he might need "cleaning out" so she gave him a good dose of castoria. But "Bugger" still felt bad the next day and Ma felt under his clothing and said he was hot. There was sweat on the little fellow's forehead, and everybody in the house became concerned. Ma told the "old man" to hitch up the wagon and go to town and tell the doctor to come out. But it was the next day before the doctor could come, and by then "Bugger" was sick bad. His bowels were running off and there was a lot of slimy stuff in his stools and they were becoming watery.

"Bugger" didn't pay anybody much attention and young'uns and the old folks too were watery-eyed and the sun wasn't shining anymore. They dreaded to hear the doctor's verdict, but everybody felt sure "Bugger" had colitis. Everybody knew that too many babies had already become victims of that dreaded disease among babies.

The prognosis was colitis, and the doctor took drugs from his satchel, gave him a dose of calomel, and wrote down instructions for dispensing the drugs. Doc said he would be back the next day. And he did have an old car to make calls in.

The old brown cradle that had been used in a back bedroom to store clothing and such items in, was brought out and "Bugger" placed in the front room and there was an around-the-clock vigil for him. Nobody could sleep anyway and nobody wanted anything to eat. Lumps were in the throats of all the family. They'd pass by and kiss him on his forehead and Ma just sat there, wiping his face and forehead and fanning him with a newspaper. She was praying, too.

Neighbors came in and did all the house work and men went to the fields to work, for the family was "done in" and nothing seemed real, or important, except "Bugger."

Everything available was tried, but nothing worked, and the fat cheeks sank in and the little body became emaciated and the eyes looked into the nowhere. "Bugger" just slipped away in the middle of a hot night. And a family mourned unashamedly. They cradled his lifeless form in their arms and tears fell to the floor.

The neighbors were notified and they came in droves while the night was still far from over. They laid out "Bugger" and put one of the light blue pairs of rompers on him and covered the little body with a sheet.

When it was morning, women brought vases of roses, still wet with dew, zinnias and cape jasmine and bunches of sweet Betsys from their yards and the bureau was filled with flowers. The little casket was brought in and placed at a window and "Bugger" looked like he was sleeping among the silky interior of the casket. That night the house was filled to overflowing at the "sitting up" and the next day they had his funeral at the house and the casket was taken to the burial ground back in the field near the house where a weeping willow grew over the burial site to keep sentinel over the body.

It was over. A life that had hardly begun was snatched from earth as if it had been intended. The disease was merciless in its grasp, taking away the brighest it seemed. Here was a star that shone so brightly he might even have become president of the United States. A victim of a time in our history when we were lacking in the medical knowledge to cure ailing bodies of diseases that for the most part are controllable today. Yes, "Bugger" was a victim of the times in which he lived.   □

Taking Out Backer

T en o'clock Sunday night. Hot, humid. No air stirring. Windows raised high but the underwear is moist. Body sticks to the bed sheets. Skeeter buzzes around the face. A hand hits at the insect in the dark. If the skeeter don't bite, a chinch will. What's the difference? Sleep's coming on despite the heat and the bugs.

Three o'clock Monday morning. The heat of the night is past and a little air comes in the windows and the wet places caused by perspiration make the bed feel cool. Something is bothering the sleeper, as if a hand were on the shoulder, shaking and trying to rouse him into consciousness. There's a shrug of the shoulder and a quick turn-over on the bed and arms outstretched over the bolster. Beautiful, heavenly sleep!

Something is really bothering the sleeper. "Git up," he's told. "Time to take out backer." It doesn't sink in. Sleep has too great a hold on the boy. He's shaken again and warned this time. He rises from the bed, stretches, yawns and shivers from the coolness and finally falls back on the bed, but quickly realizes this is reality and not a dream. He fumbles for his shirt and overalls in the darkness, and in another room the older boys are also driven out of bed.

Not a word is spoken. What is there to say? Any word uttered would be a cuss word. There are plenty of groans and yawns and deep breathing. And soon there's a rush outside to relieve the kidneys and then a walk to the stable to bridle a mule at such an ungodly hour. The lantern is lit in order to find the gear to hitch the mule to the tobacco truck.

A shiver runs down the spine for there is heavy dew and a little fog and the whole world seems quiet except for a frog croaking somewhere nearby and a cricket chirping in a secluded place. Everything on earth seems peaceful except the participants involved in taking out tobacco.

The tobacco truck is driven to the tobacco barn door and the single tree removed from the hook on the truck. If the mule is left hitched to the truck he will move, so he is left to wander back of the tobacco barn where hardweeds grow thick and he feeds on the weeds while the boys work.

Sand lugs are hanging in the barns, and that's the worst you can do in taking out tobacco. They're named right, for they're literally full of sand. And it seems that every grain falls when the sticks of cured tobacco are removed from the tiers. The person taking the sticks from the man on the tier poles (me) wears his broad-brimmed straw hat but that sand seeps through that straw like water. And if the head is raised the eyes are filled with the stuff and with that tobacco juice seeped into it and dried while curing, it burns the eyes terribly.

That sand gets into the clothing and even in the mouth, and try a gritty mouth with a bitter taste to begin with and that bitterness from the tobacco added as an extra insult.

The tobacco is in good order, due to the dew and dampness in the air and that's the only way sand lugs can be loaded on a truck. If they are dry, with short leaves, they make so much bulk only a few sticks can be hauled at one time. So the truck is loaded and (I) have to go out in the weeds and dew, with the stubbles from hoeing the area in getting ready to put in tobacco ready to prick the feet, and getting wet up to my thighs in retrieving the mule and untangling the harness and getting the mule hitched to the truck. But I will get a little rest spell for the other boys will take the tobacco to the packhouse and unload it.

The sides of the furnace are still warm from coals that remained after the tobacco was killed out, and being wet and chilly and sleepy and feeling like a suck-egg dog, that furnace feels like the most comforting place on earth. Piling down beside that furnace seems as comforting as a warm bed in winter. Wiping the mouth with the shirt sleeve helps a little in getting the grit off the lips, but it doesn't feel so good when the jaw is moved and the sand in the mouth grits against the teeth.

But sleep overtakes you immediately and it is so short-lived! In no time the other boys are back with the truck and it begins all over again until all the tobacco is taken from the barn in preparation for putting in more tobacco today. And by the time the leaf is packed down in the packhouse, signs of dawn are appearing and there is a light in the kitchen where Ma is preparing breakfast.

But breakfast is only the beginning for Ma, for there are tobacco hands to be fed at dinner time and she has to start the pots boiling early and get busy in preparing vegetables to be cooked. It takes a long time to get collards and corn and butterbeans and okra and things like that ready for the pot. Worms have to be removed from the collards and the corn has to be picked for silks and the greens have to be washed in several waters. There's no end to it, either in the kitchen or in the field. It's constant work. The next thing to look forward to is next Saturday night and Sunday, for the entire week will be spent in the tobacco fields, either ours or neighbors that we "swap" putting in tobacco with.

When it is fully light, old Boss, our "sooner" dog who has slept through the ritual at the tobacco barn, comes to life, raises up and stretches himself and goes to a wagon wheel where he cocks up his leg and growls at a hissing goose with young goslings as they pass by. An old cat is toting a kitten in her mouth, moving it from a nearby shed to the hayloft. The sun is hot, even as it emerges over the trees, and another work day begins for thousands of farmers and their families in eastern North Carolina. □

Suckering Backer; Whew!

O ne day during the week the younger children don't have to work in barning tobacco under the "swap" arrangement, and this day is reserved for suckering tobacco. So the old man speaks to the children at the breakfast table.

"We've got to git out there and sucker that backer today young'uns. There's 15 acres to be suckered. You hear what I said young'uns? Fifteeen acres! And all in one field.

"When we start it won't seem possible to pull all them suckers from between the leaves of backer. And we shore won't git it done today. But it's got to be done and it seems like moving at a snail's pace suckering backer.

"If they finish up barning Saturday morning, everybody in the house will git out there and sucker backer Saturday evening. We let them suckers overtake us, they'll pure grow up and take over the backer stalks.

"That backer was topped 10 days ago and them suckers are already three inches long and growing.

"Little Bud, you and Sis can git the bottom half of the stalks and Shine and Fuzz can git the top. Since you young'uns hain't suckered backer before, I'll tell you how to do it. Now you can't knock off them bottom suckers like grown folks, for your feet ain't big enough. So you take your hands and just strip them off when you push down on them.

"We grown folks just use our toes and strip off the bottom suckers. We run the toes around the stalk and the suckers are pushed off while we're breaking off the suckers on up the stalk.

"And look for a sucker between every backer leaf, and if you overlook them they'll be big and tough next time. You don't know it yit, but a field full of tough backer suckers can drive you crazy and ruin your hands too. My hands have been as sore from breaking tough backer suckers as anything I've ever done.

"Them suckers git more like wood than stalks when they git big and tough and when you break them they splinter and them splinters git in the hand and the more you break the sorer that hand gits. Takes a knife sometimes to git 'em.

"Now start down them rows and I'm going to take two rows, so you watch and see how I do it. Just leave the blossoms on the hills of backer that have buttoned out since the backer was topped and I'll break them out like I want them.

"The sun ain't hot enough to burn your feet yit, but it'll scorch them after a while and you'll have to stand in the shade of a backer leaf to keep that dirt from cooking them feet.

"And if you git a sick feeling in the pit of your stomach from smelling them rank green suckers, I know all about that. After all, your noses are right there among them stalks of backer and sometimes you may throw up.

"I consider suckering backer one of the worst jobs the farmer has to tackle. With crapping it and gitting it in the barns most every day, that suckering is always hanging over you. If it won't for them suckers, there just might be a day every once in a while to sort of let up and take it easy, like sitting under the shade of that "underbrella" chaney ball tree and gitting a piece of ice and three or four lemons and making a bucketful of lemonade and swilling to our hearts' content. And I'd like that as much as you.

"But I can't afford a dollar a day for a backer suckerer. If I had ten dollars to spare though, and I could git ten suckerers, I'd put them in this field right now.

"Them other young'uns will chew their tongues when I tell 'em they've got to sucker backer Saturday evening, and they'll hate my guts for it and in a way I can't blame 'em. They'll be having fits to go to town to see them moving "pixtures" and I can just see 'em making faces behind my back.

"It ain't easy being in my shoes, young'uns, but I'm splinter barefooted talking about shoes. Ain't never nothing to me but the odd one, always ruining everybody's pleasure. If they only knowed. And here I am talking to you little ones as if you could understand.

"Little Bud, you're leaving suckers. Look on that stalk behind you, I see two without even trying to find them. Sis, you be careful too."

"Lord! That sun's gitting hot and I'm feeling weak in the stomach. A meat and biscuit would taste good now. Sis, how about you running to the house and asking your mammy to fix us a meat and biscuit apiece. Some was left from breakfast. And how about drawing up a cool bucket of water and fetching us a half gallon. When you git back we'll git under the shade of that cherry tree a little further up and rest for a few minutes and eat our biscuits. I'm jaded. Hey Sis, bring us some paper or something to hold our biscuits. With all this backer gum on our hands, them biscuits'll taste like gall if we don't have something to hold 'em in.

"Hey Fuzz, watch what you're doing boy. I see suckers behind you. That's all right. Next time around you'll be twisting and turning to break out them foot-long suckers.

"Well look here! A little partridge's nest under a hill of backer. Ten little partridge eggs. We'll show it to Sis when she gits back.

"Lord, this meat and biscuit tastes good. Sort of settles down that squeamish feeling in the pit of the stomach after smelling that rank backer. Shore wish there was a cool watermelon for us to bust and git into. But they'd be so hot in that sun they'd really make us sick. Sis, come and look at this little partridge's nest.

"This hot ground's burning up my feet but it's late in the day now and will soon be time to quit.

"Reckon we've suckered 'bout three or four acres of this 15-acre field of backer. That will help when the whole crowd gits out here Saturday evening. Yep, I really hate to have to tell 'em we've got to stay in that backer field til dark Saturday night. But I don't have no choice. It's got to be done. □

Time To Worm Backer

My God! Them worms are pure eating up this backer. Just be quiet and listen. You can hear 'em chewing on the leaves. Already shredded some leaves, leaving nothing but the stems. Light nights in July and August bring 'em out full-force. At the rate they are going won't be long til there's no backer in the field," Pa says.

"Put them young'uns in there one time and wormed that backer. They had them a time picking off them rascals and slinging them on the ground and seeing them come apart. Some young'uns are scared of worms, but not my crowd. They not only mess with backer worms, they like to catch caterpillars and fishing worms and play with them like they were some kind of animal. Crazy pack of young'uns.

"Got to git a pile of Paris Green and git that sprayer in this field right away. They got any Paris green at the store, I'll try to git some on credit and pay 'em the first of the month. Ain't got time to go to town on the wagon. That'll take a day.

"Next thing is to check on that sprayer. Seems like them nozzles are always stopping up and I'll bet a dollar that Paris Green won't flushed out when spraying was done last year. Ain't no way to keep up with everything and young'uns don't have no foresight. They'll git through with something and leave it just like they finish with it. Even to hoes. They'll chop and git through and leave them hoes gommed up with wet dirt and mud and that mess gits as hard as cement and gitting them cleaned off makes you mad enough to string up a pack of young'uns.

"Same way with backer sticks. Caution the young'uns all you want to to clean off them sticks when they take off backer, but just turn your back and what happens? They leave them strings on the ends of the sticks and just throw the sticks out every which a way and it looks like piling up wood to build a far. A man may think he controls his own young'uns, but they're showing him all the time they got minds of their own and they know he ain't going but so far.

"It'll take a lot of Paris Green to spray 15 acres of backer. Don't know whether the little amount of money I got to run us on will even pay for it. Got to have it though, if I have to go to the boss man. It's his backer as much as mine. He don't want them worms to eat all of his profits either.

"Git them nozzles to working and check on the pumping system. Fill up the barrel with water and add that Paris Green and start painting that backer white. Pumping that pump up and down a row makes the arm muscles tard, but it's got to be done. And the mess gits on the clothes too. Backer truck's the only thing in the world just right for spraying backer. Git in a truck row, put them nozzles on four rows, and let that Paris Green fly.

"But putting "pison" on backer causes a mess. Oh, it kills the worms all right. I mean it kills 'em. They pure smell in the fields sometimes after a big crop of 'em is killed. And some of 'em up on the under side of the leaf stick right there and they go in the barn and are cooked to a black piece of nothing. But I bet a million of them rascals have been ground up in smoking backer and cigarettes. They ain't nothing but backer nohow 'cept for their skins, them horns and bald heads.

"Wondered about all that Paris Green on the cured backer leaves too. Ain't no way to git it off of a backer leaf, and that "pison" is right on there when that backer is processed at the factories. Reckon don't that hurt people when they smoke it? Must not though, for nothing like that is ever mentioned about backer hurting nobody.

"Reckon if Paris Green hurt anything it would be ish taters after loading down them tater vines to kill the lady bugs. Looks like that "pison" would go down to the root system. But I ain't never heard tell of nobody gitting hurt from "pisoning" tater vines. Just watch out for the soda that's put on vegetables and you won't git hurt from what's put down there to protect them.

"Pack of chickens are good backer wormers too. Course they don't go all over the field but where backer's planted around the house they'll go out and jump up and pull them old worms from a leaf of backer and gobble them down like they was something special. No wonder they have to pen them old chickens up in the summertime to clean them out from eating all them backer worms. Don't think much about a chicken eating these little bugs that fly around and the worms they scratch from the ground. But fill 'em up with old green backer worms, and that's another matter. Chicken's as nasty as a buzzard and will eat anything on God's green earth.

"And young'uns are so crazy. Dare 'em to do something and they'll do it as sure as heck. I seen young'uns offered a nickel to bite off a backer worm's head, and fore you knot it, that worm's bit in two and squirming on the ground. Now I can't go for putting a nasty old backer worm in my mouth and that's not saying I'm one of these nice-nasties. They's just some things I take to be a little too fur out for me.

"I might wear my old work socks til they're stiff on the bottom and the old lady shore complains about 'em stinking, but I been told that you wear work socks till you can throw them on a wall and they'll stick there. Then it's time to wash 'em. I might go to bed some nights with my feet not as clean as they should be. I might not brush my teeth and things like that, but I'm still not going to bite off no backer worm's head.

"Just look at all them white splotches on the hills of backer, 'specially at the top where the "pison" hits first. But I guarantee you one thing. In a day or so there'll be plenty of old dead backer worms out there and we'll save many a pound of backer we wouldn't of had. □

Tobacco In Warehouse Ready To Be Sold

Backer Markets Open

I t is total excitement on "opening day." That is when the tobacco markets in eastern North Carolina begin their sales season. It was fairly well into August when they opened 50 years ago.

The excitement almost built to a crescendo as farmers approached the warehouses in the towns. There was a hustle and bustle almost akin to Christmas and many people were on the streets in the warehouse districts.

If a young'un accompanied his daddy to the opening, his first reaction was to the onion smell coming from the hotdog stands. His mouth watered by the time he entered the warehouse district. And the odor of parched peanuts added to his hunger.

They came in carts, on wagons, Ford or Chevrolet trucks, and all entered the warehouse from the same entrance. There was a place to tether the mules after the tobacco was unloaded, and warehouse workers were busily removing the tobacco from the vehicles.

And it was a different look in those days. That tobacco had been hand-tied, stuck up, placed in a straight pile, pressed with a heavy board, and had a starched appearance when it was placed in the baskets. It was a beautiful sight, but there is no way that process could be carried out today at the cost of labor and the time involved in the process.

Many farmers were in overalls, with their white Sunday shirts and Stetson hats. Others wore pincheck britches and galluces. And they all congregated on the warehouse floor and formed circles and talked about tobacco and crops in general, as well as news of the area. But once sales began, they followed the crowd up and down several rows to get the trend of prices being paid.

Many shook their heads as they saw piles of good tobacco going for from 10 to 15 cents a pound. And the sweat began to roll from the heat bearing down on the warehouse roof. The auctioneer would sing his chant: "Nine-dollar, nine-dollar, nine-dollar" while looking for a bidder, then "10-dollar-ollar-ollar, 10-dollar, 11-dollar, 11-dollar, 11-dollar, 12-dollar, 13-dollar, 14-dollar, 15-dollar, sold American" said so rapidly it was almost indistinguishable to the audience.

The best sold for around 15 cents and the lower grades and trash from two or three cents to eight or nine. But that was in the thirties, during the Great Depression.

People were running about and flocking to the latrines that had an odor all their own, even at the outset of the selling season. There was the sweet smell of cured tobacco along with horse dung and perspiration that gave warehouses their uniqueness.

Farmers agreed that they'd never pay out with such prices for tobacco. But even with the gloomy outlook, they spent the day in a carnival atmosphere and flocked to the hotdog stands for the 10-cent delights. They'd eat three or four, burp and wipe the mustard that had accumulated around their mouths off with their hands, then take another swipe on their shirt sleeves. They'd get sodas too. Young'uns fortunate enough to attend were in a seventh heaven.

And even after filling up on hot dogs, it wasn't long before another bag of hot peanuts was purchased and they'd stand up against buildings, prop one leg back against the wall, shell those "ground peas" as many called them, and throw the shells on the streets. Then it was a trip to the water coolers in the warehouses where chunks of ice in the coolers made the cold water all the more appealing.

Despite depression, despite low prices and no prospects of paying out of debt, the opening of the tobacco market was one of the highlights of the year. It meant that a little money was flowing; that a few meager pleasures were possible for a short period of time. After going for so long without an extra dime except for absolute essentials, it gave the sharecroppers a little self-esteem. And it was an unwritten code, but landlords just knew that the first tobacco that was sold would not go on debts, unless a large amount was auctioned off on opening day, and that was very seldom the case.

Young'uns were threadbare. Pantries were almost empty. School was just around the corner. People were tired of the same old diets day after day, with pickings slim in the gardens. There just had to be a little change.

After sales were over, farmers began to leave the warehouses and head homeward. But there was a stop at the general store first. The crowd back home would be expecting something good to eat after tobacco was sold. There was the keg of salt mullets, large fish with the black fat showing where they were slashed open. Everybody would want salt fish and cornbread for breakfast.

There were the round hoops of "rat" cheese and three or four-pound slices were cut off and taken home for a hungry pack of young'uns.

There were the links of smoked sausages, (pure meat) that satisfied the taste buds. Fill up a crowd of young'uns on salt fish, then make biscuits and fit them around a chunk of cheese and cook them with the melted cheese oozing out the edges, and add smoked sausage to the menu, and you never saw young'uns eat so much. They were happier with the fare than they'd have been at the Waldorf Astoria.

There was also a long discussion about tobacco prices and prospects for paying out of debt and having anything left. But nobody really expected that. Heck, what was the difference? It had been about the same in years past. They'd made it before. They'd make it again. Life really wasn't all that bad. □

Putting Soda To Corn

I t's July and dogs are hassling in the shade. June bugs are singing and people are sweating. There ain't a cloud in the sky and folks are looking skyward and hoping for rain. It's beginning to get dry. However, crops haven't reached the burning stage as yet and corn stands head high and is beginning to tassel. The blades of corn meet in the middles, and it's time to soda that corn.

Every young'un from age 10 up knows all about sowing soda. It has to be put down beside cotton, backer and corn and it is a hard job at best, but sowing the nitrogen in corn fields is by far the worst, for the corn cuts off the wind and it's stifling in the heat of the day.

A mule is hitched to a backer truck and loaded down with bags of soda. A tow sheet is placed on top of the bags as well as the ax and buckets are rounded up and rags found and tied around the handles to keep them from cutting into the hands. Then the young'uns head for the "mash" where the dirt is black and the heat bears down.

A muzzle has to be put on the old mule or he'll eat hisself half to death. Mules love to bite off half-stalks of corn or whole cotton plants.

The soda has been stacked under the shelter for a few weeks and when the bags are opened there are some large lumps that have to be beaten up before being sown. The cream-colored nitrogen is not in pellets but rather more like pebbles, and it is easily melted.

With 30 or 40 acres of corn sometimes, it requires a lot of steps to get all the soda sown and the more young'uns to drop the nitrogen, the less burden it will be on all the workers.

Forget about a sore-free hand when you start sowing soda. Such a thing never existed. It will be a blister, a cut or a scratch on the hand. It might be so minute you never noticed it, but you'll find out immediately after you start sowing soda. It burns any wound, and it's constant as long as the hand is in contact with the nitrogen.

The buckets are heavy when the sowers start down a row and the buckets have to be toted by the handles. When the burden becomes lighter the sowers will take them and place them under an arm and dispense the soda in that manner.

The top sides of blades of corn are rough and the edges sharp, and those sowing soda run into the blades as they lap in the middles and pollen or debris from the tassels falls on the head and around the neck.

And those "bram broo" briars grow lush in corn fields and lay low on the ground. Now it doesn't matter whether the proper name might have been "bamboo" briar, or whatever, we called them "bram broo" briars, and who cares 50 years later? Anyone who might care could connect up with one between the big toe and the next one and let it slide about a foot, gathering all those thorns while it was sliding, and he wouldn't care either.

Well, we connected up with them and there was the mess of blood and briar leaves (or what was left of leaves) around the toes and we'd sit down between the corn rows with the temperature about 100 and our necks itching from that mess on the tassels and the cuts and scratches on our hands burning and the soda melted, feeling heavy and liquidy on the hands and we were in a mess.

We'd have to grab up a handful of that black dirt and rub it over our hands to get the soda off before we could spread the toes apart to see how much meat had been gouged out. Then we had to limp the rest of the day and hope that we wouldn't get a piece of decayed stalk between the toes to open up the wound again.

And why didn't we wear shoes in the fields? Because we didn't have any except our Sunday shoes and besides, there were too many other sore places on our feet to wear shoes.

We'd get going again after checking on our wounds, filling up those heavy buckets and lugging that soda up and down those rows, and after a while some young'un would run into one of those bunchy briars and I think we called them "Pepper" briars. Good name. They burned like pepper. Strike one of them and there would be six or eight little thorns on the underside of the foot. Sit down right quick and grab a hunk of dirt and get that soda off the hand and cup that foot in your lap sitting flat on the ground and pull out each little thorn (very carefully) then run a finger over the area to see if one was left. If there was, you knew it immediately.

Unless you had already hurt your foot with a "bram broo" briar, it didn't hurt to get tangled up in a maypop vine. They just slid between the toes and stripped off the maypops as they went.

One other thing could be a problem. If you'd eaten one or two 'lasses biscuits and a piece of side meat with a little bit of grease on it, you might get heartburn down in that "mash" a mile and a half from home and if you burped up grease, Lord, help you! It burned the throat and there was the hot water that rose in the throat and that burning in the chest.

And we loved those 'lasses biscuits. We'd run a finger into the biscuit, then gouge around a little to make more room for 'lasses. But it sure did give us heartburn and when the dinner bell rang and we climbed on that backer truck to ride home, we'd spit out that hot water that rose in our throats and as soon as we got home, we'd go to that Arm & Hammer soda box and get us a big teaspoonful and stir it in water and drink it down before we even washed our faces and hands. But we were ready for a full meal.

But crazy young'uns that we were, we'd run around the house and play at dinner time stid of getting us a quilt and rolling it up for a pillow and lying on the front porch for a nap like the grown-ups did.

Then it was back to the "mash" with another truck load of soda and more beating to be done because moisture had accumulated in the bags while lying under the shelter and that caused the nitrogen to lump.

The Lord only knows how many steps we made up and down those corn rows. But one thing is for sure. We knew the discomfort of those burning hands and the itching and burning caused by those blades of corn hitting us in the face and around the neck. And briars and maypops were a natural part of sowing soda.

Once in a while we'd run up on a citron vine that grew wild in the fields and there would be small citrons on the vine. In the fall when Ma wanted some citrons to make preserves, we'd go to the fields where we knew they grew and take them to the house and they were good after they were preserved, solid and yellow with a lemon flavor. What a time in life!

Today they have the mechanical might and the brain power to accomplish things like sowing soda and make it child's play. Fifty years ago we had manpower and little brain power as far as farming goes. And we made a lot less on our land, but we accomplished the same results. That soda got put to the corn, if it was by a pack of young'uns.   □

Soda Was Stored In Old Barns

Column One Year Old

L ooking Backward" has passed its first milestone and begins its second year today as a Saturday column in The Wilson Daily Times. Perhaps it is time to pause and reflect back on its first year.

It has been a great learning experience for me, and a year filled with surprises. Before beginning the column, I was aware it was different from anything I have seen in newspapers or magazines, and because of that fact I was a little skeptical about its reception.

The first real surprise for me was in learning that many people who never lived the simple lifestyles I depict found interest in reading about that era in our history. I expected that only the farming class who grew up during that period would be interested. Farmers have expressed interest, but college professors, writers, bankers, lawyers, the clergy, doctors, businessmen, teachers, students, out-of-staters, and others have also been complimentary.

Another surprise has been in learning that most rural people throughout eastern North Carolina lived almost the exact lifestyle that I tell about. People have said, "Man, you must have lived next door to me," when in actuality I grew up 50 miles or more from them.

Yet another surprise has been in realizing that people much younger than me as well as those a good deal older can associate with those days. Many people in the 40-year age range lived essentially as I did in the days about which I write.

I have made every effort to picture us exactly as we were — simple, plain, ordinary proud people — striving to exist during a turbulent period in our history that we can now look back upon with nostalgia. I have tried to give vivid details about our lives close-up, so there could be no doubt as to the true picture of poor people before and during the Depression era. We are a part of our history that didn't make the history books and having it recorded offers an insight into our lives that the public hasn't had access to heretofore.

I was aware that "Looking Backward" had to be factual if it were to maintain credibility; therefore I have written strictly from memory.

People have said that I had to have lived that life to tell it as I have. Therein lies the secret, in telling a story first-hand rather than having it written by the second party. The fine details are missing if the writer hasn't experienced what is being written about. I was there.

During the first year, I took events in chronological order to give an entire year's perspective on farming operations. It began when the tobacco stalks were bare except for the suckers left after the crop was harvested, on through Indian summer, fall and gathering the crops, Christmas and the winter months and the new year through tobacco harvesting season. We have now covered the yearly cycle and there will be no attempt in the future to place events in chronological order.

This year we will get a closer look into our personal lives at eyeball-to-eyeball range. We did many things besides farm in those days and there was a family way of life inside the homes and there are many recollections about those days.

For me at least, there is much nostalgia associated with our customs and the way we did things and the more comical part of our lives. Looking backward into the simplicity of our lives at that time should provide many laughs as well as a certain sadness associated with that period.

With an entire year's farming operations detailed, we can now reflect on the lighter moments in our past. I feel the best is yet to come.

I found it hard to accept the fact that a true story told so simply, without glowing language and without the benefit of heroes or heroines, could merit the interest of the public. If there is one redeeming grace for "Looking Backward," it is the fact that it speaks of truth, which is often stranger than fiction. The central theme is of very poor people, striving to survive through their own ingenuity. The fact that we did survive with all the odds stacked against us is the remarkable part of the story.

I have been the greatest beneficiary of "Looking Backward." To have looked back upon our past and shared those experiences that come from the depths of my heart has been a personal reward I can't adequately describe. Every word, every line has been written with genuine pleasure, for with a distance of 50 years or more separating those events from today, there is a halo over that era that wasn't there at the time the events were a reality.

In retrospect, I have concluded that we were a far more ingenious people during that period in our history than we are today, considering the advantages we have today as compared with the hardships of those days. We were far more intelligent than we have been given credit for, or chaos would have reigned and we would have given up the fight.

It is my hope that "Looking Backward" has given a little stature to the hard-working men, women and children of that era who fought long battles and won in the final analysis by their perseverance.

Those who were not there can never know the real story of the Depression and life on the farm, but we can tell them of those days and leave it for history to look back upon us and judge us as we were.

But to see it all with beauty is another matter. I believe that all of us who remember those days see so much beauty and nostalgia about that era that the sacrifices and hardships become secondary.

I can only feel gratitude for every person who has found a pleasure in reading about those golden days of our past. □

This Picture Tells The Story Of An Era

A Feast On Barbecue

I t is late August and the end of "puttin' in backer" season. The "tips" have been pulled from the mass of suckers at the top of the backer stalks and the spindly, small leaves put in the barns to cure. They look gourd-green and spotted as they go in the barns, and they'll probably come out more a green color than anything else.

All the signs point to late summer. In the gardens the collards are showing holes where the terrapin bugs have attacked them and grass has grown tall and seeded out at the ends of the rows. Okra stalks have run up and a few blossoms are at the top of the stalks. Butterflies are flitting around in abundance and hardweeds have grown tall with their small, yellow flowers too insignificant to add beauty to the scene.

Stripped of their leaves, the backer stalks look forlorn in the fields and corn is brown.

But a hard task has been completed when the backer season is finished, and farmers celebrate by holding a barbecue. Those who swap among each other all join in and pay for the pig and each family cooks good things and everybody congregates at one of the houses and they all have a feast.

The barbecue is usually held on a Saturday and it means a whole day of resting and messing around and just doing nothing but stuffing the belly and belching and drinking lemonade and sitting around in the shade and it seems like heaven after seven or eight weeks in the backer fields crapping and looping and hanging and curing backer and getting up every morning in the dark and some mornings soon after midnight when backer has to be taken out.

But the process begins late Friday afternoon. The men kill the pig and get him ready for the pit about sunset, for with no way to refrigerate it, a minimum of hours is allowed for the pig to stay fresh. All the innards are thrown away and the whole mess buried and a cloth is draped over the pig and it is placed on the side table in the kitchen until about 4 o'clock Saturday morning when it is put on the coals.

The pit is usually dug under a backer barn shelter or some place around the backer barns and cleaned out smooth and oak saplings cut and brought up and placed in a pile. The iron rods are taken from the back of the shelter and placed over the pit and everything placed in readiness for cooking the pig.

The large end of the pile of oak wood is set afire in early morning and when there is an accumulation of coals they are put in the pit with the shovel and the entire bottom has to be filled. Then the pig is placed over the coals with the skin side up and soon the grease starts a slow drip, causing little ripples of smoke to rise from the pit.

That green oak is kept burning and some dry chips added if necessary, for it requires a lot of live coals to cook a pig. A jar of vinegar with red pepper cut up in it will be needed later on to saturate the meat when the pig is turned over. The vinegar is sopped over the meat with a rag tied to a stick.

There is one thing the young'uns have to do Saturday morning, and that's sweep the yard clean and burn the trash. The yellow chaney balls that have fallen from the trees have to be taken to a trash pile in the field. But the yard is swept early before the sun gets hot and the tobacco trucks pulled in the yard to serve as tables for the food. They're lined up end on end and placed at the shadiest spot in the yard.

A wooden tub is scrubbed out good and then scalded, for there'll be a tubful of lemonade so everybody can swill down every drop they can drink. There'll even be freezers of homemade ice cream.

While that pig is cooking and the smell filling the neighborhood, the women are flouring those chickens and putting them in hot grease to fry and baking cakes and cooking chocolate syrup to slur over them.

Fresh cucumbers have been split long ways a day or so earlier and salt and red pepper added so they'll be saturated for the feast. And eggs are boiled and deviled and hoecakes of bread cooked to go with the barbecue and collards and butterbeans and all the other good things.

Where I lived, slaw was not a part of the menu when barbecue was served half a century ago. And neither was cornbread fried in grease as is done today. It was either cooked in a hoecake on top of the stove or baked inside the stove.

That pig is turned over and it's golden brown and sumptuous amounts of vinegar are daubed on the pork and it fries as it hits the cooked meat. Menfolks standing around begin to pull off ribs to taste the delicacy and somebody pulls out the tongue and feasts on it.

The crowd begins to gather at noon and those backer trucks are overlaid with white cloths and the food is placed on the tables and they start fanning flies (just as they do today even without the stables and henhouses and hog pens) and the flies are fanned throughout the meal.

When the skin is good and crisp, the pig is placed in a wood tub and brought to the house for chopping up. The hatchet has been sharpened and the oilcloth removed from the side table and the boards on the table serve as a cutting board. They show marks from former barbecues already. That pig is chopped up fine and toted out to the backer trucks in dishpans and they start loading down the plates.

It's just too good to be true. All that good food and no more backer to "put in" either. Everybody's in a good mood with clean clothes and washed hair and looking good except for the hands that still carry the stain gathered over the barning period. And Saturday night and Sunday coming up too. What a great world! □

It's Revival Time

T he annual revival was a very special time in the community. With few social activities, the two-week affair was one of the highlights of the year. For 14 nights the people of the area turned out in droves to hear the evangelists brought in to minister to the public. There was also a 11 a.m. service each day for the old folks while the younger ones carried on the daily tasks.

Revival in our community always came at the end of the summer when we were busy getting up fodder that had been pulled and bundled and placed on broken corn stalks to cure. Of all the no-nos in farming, pulling fodder had to be the pits. But we did it, every year. And getting it up and stacked was not one of its best features.

As the sun began to get low in the west, we would take to the fields to gather the fodder to take it to the stack. We would gather as many bundles as we could carry on our backs and start toward the stackpole near the center of the field. Fodder is slick and scratchy, and it is easy to lose the grip on the cured blades of corn.

In bare feet, we would start our journey, knowing that there were obstacles in our path — maypop vines, briars that had run over the ground, cowwitch vines, and tall hills of grass. The worst obstacles were the briars, for they somehow fitted between our big toes and the toes next to them. The briars would tear the flesh as the vine slipped between the toes and we would fall, losing all the fodder besides being hurt. So we would gather up the bundles again and start the process all over with a bloody foot.

Once we reached the pole on which the fodder was stacked, we had to throw it up to the stacker after the pile began to build. And he had to be very careful on that stack or he would slip to the ground and getting back on top wasn't an easy task. There was a lot of cussing in those fodder fields 50 years ago. And if a cloud was coming up we had to be very fast or that cured corn would get wet in the fields and it was essential to stack it so the water would run off it as it does a duck's back.

But we survived that, for we knew that it would soon be revival time and we would have some place to go that night.

And revivals had two meanings for two different groups in those days. To the "old folks" it meant renewing their faith for another year, a rededication of their lives to Christ, and bringing sinners into the fold.

But for the young folks it meant going out early and doing a little courting in the "tin lizzies" that were parked on the church grounds along with a sizable number of mules, wagons, and buggies. We boys would have it arranged so that the girls would sit toward the back of the church, and if the boys went in, they were all the way at the back. And when the sermon was in full swing and testimonials had been given and the preacher was warning of the penalties of sin, we sinners would make our exits and those "brazen" girls would leave the church as unobtrusively as possible.

Sometimes a mother would see a wayward daughter leave the church and follow her outside and get her back into the fold. But every mother didn't attend every night, and those girls got away with special freedoms on those nights. And it was pure pleasure. A hot night, a hazy sky, or moonlight reflecting on tin roofs and dark shadows from nearby buildings, a boy and a girl secluded for a little spell and everything in God's world seemed right.

But there were some recriminations at altar call, for the evangelist always warned that the wages of sin is death and he exhorted the young sinners to come to Christ or risk death and eternal hell. They were pretty tough words for young people who felt all the instincts of youth and whose thoughts were on love rather than the Bible.

Revival time was also a season of good eating. The women saved their best for company and the preachers that visited the homes during the revival. Nothing was too good for the preachers, even to the last country ham that was saved for that very special occasion. And the last jar of grape preserves. Even late summer frying chickens were penned up to get the tobacco worms and other insects out of them so they could add to the menu for company.

And when company came the children waited and got the leftovers, (and they didn't complain about it in those days either). Company got the best pieces of chicken, the leanest slices of ham, and the juiciest part of pies and dumplings. Children ate a lot of chicken backs and necks and even feet in those days. And yes, they did clean the feet and even they were good. When they scalded the chickens, they put the legs into the boiling water, and the scaly skin slipped off with ease. They cut off the toenails and floured those feet and fried them like the rest of the chicken, and they were especially good if flour was put into the pan after frying the chicken, browned and thickened and the bony parts of the chicken placed back in the gravy.

And that bed in the parlor was gone over thoroughly for chinches. It would have been a disgrace for preachers and other company to be bitten by bedbugs. The squirt can filled with kerosene was put to use and all those tufts that held the mattress together were searched and squirted with oil and all the crevices in the bedsteads as well.

Some preachers even then spent their venom on the sins of using tobacco, and smokers and dippers were chastised for their indulgences, but nobody failed to note that the preachers took every penny they could get from the sale of tobacco. And the amount given for preaching the word was small enough at best. Sometimes they were pounded with hams and canned stuff and anything else in the pantries to help them make ends meet.

So revival came and went and it left a loneliness over the neighborhood and there was a void in people's lives for a little while. New converts were baptized and many born-again Christians started out on a new path, but after the altar calls were forgotten and there was no constant reminder of the sins of the people, there were many backsliders, at least until the next revival. □

A Long-Ago County Fair

N ot too long after the late-summer revival and before the beginning of school the latter part of September, the annual county fair comes to town. And talking about excitement! The fair really gets a pack of young folks up in the air. Now you can keep a young'un behind those piney woods most of the time, but you can't keep him there all the time, and when the fair comes everything that's big enough to fend for himself is hell-bent on attending.

Sometimes the "old man" will take the younger children on the wagon for a day at the fair, but many refuse to assume that responsibility and a lot of the smaller children are denied the pleasures of the fair. But those 15, 16, 17-year-old young bucks determine to be a part of the annual event.

They pick them a day the latter part of the week, say Thursday or Friday, and let in on the "old man" to let them off for an afternoon and he may hum and haw, but the boys never let up, and the "old man" has to give in. Not only that, he has to find a little folding money. He may come out with a dollar for each boy, but they say that is not enough, and somehow or other, he has to find a couple of dollars for each one.

So they set off in early afternoon loaded down with sweaters or coats they don't need at that time of day, but their mammy says they have to have a coat if they are going to be there after the sun goes down. And Ma asks them if they've put on clean drawers, for no telling what might happen.

And they'll have to beat a way to town and God only knows how they'll get back home. They may even have to walk the seven or eight miles back. With more traffic to town than usual because the fair is going on, they will eventually find a ride with somebody.

Once they catch a ride to town, they are put out on the outskirts and they have to walk over a number of back streets and across small fields to get to the fairgrounds. The blare of the music is heard blocks before reaching the grounds and the boys almost bust their britches with excitement.

Inside the grounds, the activities are going on at such a fierce pace the boys stare in wonder at it all. People are everywhere and dust particles are in the air from the stomp of feet over the dry soil. The ferris wheel is running and they stare at the top but determine that they will ride on the high monster. Swings are slinging young folks around and they're screaming either with delight or from fear and there's a contraption that turns the riders on their heads, slings them sideways and darts off at a high speed.

But the smell of onions and hot dogs and mustard overcomes them and they hunt out the stands and buy two hot dogs apiece, all the way, and a cup of grape juice in ice to drench them down. They ain't even half full from the two dogs, but they'll wait a while before another round. Two dogs and a drink costs them a quarter apiece, so they can't go but so far in the eating line. They've got to get on the rides to tickle their stomachs.

There is the mooing of cows and the squeal of pigs and the bleating of goats and the crowing of roosters over in the livestock building, but the boys will never go in that place. Can't nobody tell them about the livestock. They're already pros in that category.

The midget on the stand fascinates them as he begs the crowd to go in and see the two-headed snake, the half-man, half-woman, the biggest man on earth and the fire-eaters. All for 15 cents. The boys take him up on it.

Then there's all them women on the next stand with their faces painted up and dancing a jig and the crowd is invited in to see the "girlie" show. Those boys are excited at the prospects and line up at the window to get tickets, but a smiling attendant tells the two younger boys they are too young, so the 17-year-old goes inside for his eye-opener and that's worth the trip to him if there were nothing else at the fair. He'll tell the other boys about it later.

The sun goes down and the lights come on and the glare is so bright the boys shade their eyes for a moment. There's a big difference in a kerosene lamp and hundreds of electric bulbs giving off their bright light. And the colors amaze them. There are the balloons, the shiny costumes of the men and women who are a part of the fair and the brightly painted rides on the midway.

Their coats feel good now after sweating throughout the afternoon with water accumulating on their foreheads and around the bands of their caps. They stop by the gambling places and watch people throwing at the pins lined up as the targets. They don't try their luck, knowing they could knock down all the pins but they can't tote all the stuffed animals and baby dolls around and have no way to get them home if they did.

They run up with other boys and girls they know and all of them tackle the rides and holler and scream when the tubs are slinging them around and then they try the thing-a-ma-jig that turns them bottom upwards and when it's over they're as sick as buzzards and feel disoriented for a little while and their heads are swimming and they feel like they've about had it. But the feeling passes and they gom down another hot dog.

The firecrackers light up the sky and everybody pauses to watch the spectacle. Afterward the crowd begins to thin out and the boys head for home. They have to walk a few miles before a neighbor spots them on the side of the road and gives them a ride in his Model T. Then it's back beyond the pines and routine again, but it's a diversion, a glimpse at another world, a few hours away from the hard work on the farm and they'll have something to talk about for weeks.

That's a county fair for you from 50 years ago. □

Sweltering Summers

My, how times have changed! Ain't hardly nobody today but what's got an air conditioner to switch on and cool a hot summer day (or night) down til it feels like the middle of October. Man, you ought to have been around 50 years ago (and many were that can vouch for what I'm saying.) We burned down!

We actually fared worse when the weather was real hot than we did when it was real cold. We could at least heat brick bats and flat irons and wrap them up and take them to cold beds with us in winter and with plenty of cover we were snug and warm. But we didn't have anything to cool us off in summer. Nothing 'cept newspapers folded up and a few fans made out of pasteboard with a wooden handle that we got occasionally from a funeral home or a furniture store or somewhere like that. But fans were "scace." There were a few fans presumably made from bamboo, and those that opened up that the women used when they went to church.

Most windows in those tenant houses were small, 'specially in the shed rooms that opened onto a porch and were separated from the rest of the house. The shed room window was usually higher than the others also and they were good places to sweat yourself half to death. We'd tie the old curtains up so they wouldn't knock off any of the wind, but that didn't help, for there was no wind.

But I hope you don't think we just lay there and melted. We took to the porch with our quilts and slept on pallets on the hard floor. Skeeter bites were better than suffocating, so many a night we lay on those pallets, and the grown-ups took to the floor also. We slept any place where there was any air moving.

Little boys used to sleep stark naked in the summer, and you could see them scratching skeeter bites in their sleep and never know what was going on. They might moan and groan and flip over a dozen times, but as soon as the sun came up, they were up and raring to go again.

Grown-ups would roll up the newspaper or take the fan and swish them around their face until their arms became tired. And most all of the girls retired to their beds rather than piling down on the floor. In the first place, they weren't as hot-natured as the boys, and it was a little beneath their dignity to lie on the floor.

And those that did lie on beds usually became saturated with sweat and their clothes were pure wet. It don't feel so comfortable lying on a wet bed. Yeah, I've seen wet sheets where people's bodies lay at night.

It seems like it used to get a lot hotter in summer and a lot colder in winter than it does today. But that is easily understandable when we realize all the things we have to make us comfortable that weren't around 50 years ago.

It could be sultry at sunrise in summer and it seemed like the humidity was bearing down on you and buddy, you could look out before the day was over. Every crop would be wilted down and unless one of those ungodly thunderstorms of those days came up, you felt like a wet dishrag before the day ended. Then you had another night of heat to look forward to.

We had to be careful about the livestock too. If there were any hogs around with any weight on them, there'd better be a mudhole around for them to get into or the heat would get them. Of course there weren't mudholes around in dry weather, but we'd have to draw water from the well and fix a cool place for them. A fat hog in the summer heat is like a snowball in hell.

And you'd a thought those old dogs were going to hassle themselves to death. They'd lie in the shade and pant and sweat would drop from their tongues. They sweat through their tongues and the pads of their feet, you know. A dog shut up in a hot place in summer is in for trouble. 'Course we didn't have that big a problem with them in the old days, for they must have been wiser then than they are today. Anyhow, you couldn't fix a place tight enough to keep a dog, 'specially if it was a bitch in season. I believe they'd have come through a brick wall. Never knew anybody to keep them from getting out.

Anybody remember how those old chickens would get in a hole scratched under a canna bush or a popeberry bush (or any kind of bush) and lie with their wings outstretched and hassle in the hot sun?

Those old mules would sweat too. You could pure see where they sweated through their coats and when you took off their collars they were wet on the under side and any person who ever plowed them can remember the smell of a sweaty mule. And when the weather got too hot we had to let them rest for a spell when they were plowing the fields. They had to have plenty of water too.

Can anybody today imagine how hot it was in those old kitchens 50 years ago with a wood range going full blast and steam coming out of those pots and the odor of collards boiling and a peck of "ish taters" simmering on a back eye? Those womenfolks looked like blood would pop out of their faces sometimes and they were constantly picking up their aprons and wiping perspiration from their faces. They were actually hotter than those working in the fields, for there might be a wisp of air moving about sometimes, whereas in the kitchen, nothing was felt but heat.

I'll tell you something, buddy. By the time we got through puttin' in backer we were ready for the "September gust" as Pa called it. That was usually the storm that sort of broke up summer and brought some relief from the heat. We had about had it by the time the storm came. And when that air turned cool and we didn't sweat our heads off, we felt like new people. It was really something to be able to go from a pallet in a hallway or a porch to a bed with a mattress and a quilt to make things comfortable.

Yeah, we had it tough folks, but still it was a good life. A real good life. Heck, we ain't living like that now, and that makes all the difference.   □

A Typical Privy From The '30s Era

All Those Farm Smells

H ardweeds grow tall behind barns and around hog pens and dog fennel takes over along wire fences. Pope bushes grow rank around privies and cowwitch vines climb to the top of the outhouses and creep slowly across them with their long, red-orange blossoms shining among the dark green vine.

"Back House" lilies come up early and their profusion of flowers decorate weed-filled back lots where chickens spread their wings and sun themselves when the weather is hot. And if there are mud holes in the lots the hogs take to the water, saturate their bodies in mud and spend their days grunting in the coolness of the water.

And there must have been some form of status symbol associated with the privies of those days, for they weren't all built alike. It seemed that the higher up the ladder a family's standing was in the community, the better the privy.

And privies in those days were not professionally built and moved to the site as the trend became later. They were built on the spot, some straddling ditches, some built over pits dug for that purpose, and some just sitting on top of the ground.

The deluxe models were three-seaters with hinged tops that could be raised and lowered and doors that hooked, but these were rare indeed, and all of them were built over pits. They were at the better houses too. But even they were supplied with newspapers and discarded catalogs, for toilet paper was non-existent in the rural area.

Next down the ladder was the two-seater, also with a door, and this was the most popular privy of the late 1920s and early '30s. It was equipped with a stumpy broom used in tidying up the tiny structure and there were no tops for the seats.

Last was the "back house" that never had had a door, only the place cut out where the door should be, with tow sacks serving in place of the door. They were attached to nails driven on each side of the cut-out, and a lot of this type had either a pasteboard box or a nail keg on the floor where hens went to lay. Many a baby chick saw its first light of day in a rural North Carolina "back house." And this kind usually just sat on top of the ground.

I never saw a painted privy in those days (but few other buildings were painted either.) In the case of the privies, it might have been intentional in not painting them, instead allowing them to weather down and blend in with the surroundings rather than accentuating them with paint.

And there were well-worn paths to the privies that usually sat back a little further than the back yard. Cotton or corn or potatoes might be planted in front of the "out houses" and it would take months to wear down the rows so the ground would be smooth.

Odors were as much a part of the farm scene in eastern North Carolina 50 years ago as were the sights and sounds of country life. I can't imagine country living without them and although they were "accepted" rather than "appreciated" they helped to form the total rural setting.

There was the mule lot, always a source of odor for the soil was torn up by the mules' hooves, and they stayed moist and a lot of the time wet from the rains.

There were the chicken houses where the chickens roosted at night and their droppings piled up in straight rows from the roosts above.

There were the mule stables and cow stables with their accumulation of dung over a full year.

Hog pens were also a source of pungent odors for they are filthy animals and clean habits are not a part of their make-up.

Then there were the toilets that gave off their odors as well, made worse if live things invaded the refuse. In those cases, lye would be used to clean the area, and sometimes lime was also used.

Chickens that roamed over the yards were also a source of odors as well as aggravation. A bunch of chickens is as filthy as hogs. Bare feet often came in contact with their droppings and it wasn't unusual to see anyone in bare feet walking on a side of a foot or a heel while searching for a sizable hill of grass to pull between the big toe and the next one, or rubbing the foot vigorously over the grass to be "cleaned."

Add to this the small animals that died in the lush summer growth and were undetected until the odor of death filled the air. These had to be tracked down with the sense of smell and the decayed bodies buried, for this odor differed from all the others and could not be tolerated.

If this sounds like a gross topic that should be omitted in recalling our lifestyles half-a-century ago, it is gross, but all of us who remember know that the sense of smell was ever present in those days, and to evade it would not give a true impression of us as we really were.

But there were two sides to the coin, and there were also the sweet smells of cape jasmine, honeysuckle, and fruit trees in blossom. I don't know how "cape jasmine" became "gardenia" with the passing of time, for the aroma is the same and "cape jasmine" certainly sounds as romantic as "gardenia." But cape jasmine grew in many yards and their sweet smell perfumed the air and seemed to purify everything.

Honeysuckles grew wild on fences and along ditch banks and its fragrance never ceased to elicit remarks about its perfume as well as the humming birds that gathered the nectar from its flowers.

When the air was sultry and steaming from the summer sun, the heat waves actually seemed to be visible in looking across fields of corn with its blades rolled, wilted tobacco patches, drooped collard leaves and pope bushes almost appearing lifeless in the sweltering heat.

It was at such times that all the odors that were so much a part of rural life were at their peak. People said we needed an electrical storm to purify the air and get things back to normal again. But they needn't have specified "electrical" storm, for as surely as those black clouds rose in summer, heavy thunder and sharp lightning accompanied the storm, often with strong, damaging winds.

And sure enough after the summer storms, the air cleared for a while, crops drank up the rains and showed new growth, and the air became more bearable for a spell.

Oh. Another word about those privies. In general they were considered to be the women's domain and many of the men left their use up to the female gender. I never knew whether this was early signs of male chauvinism or whether men felt it a little below their dignity to use facilities that they felt reflected on their manhood. I just know that's the way it was.   □

Memories Of Fall Day

A fall day that lingers in the memory.

The old swimming hole is deserted except for a drake and his dull-coated mate slowly moving across the tranquil waters. At the edges of the pond the gums, sourwoods and other trees reflect bottom-upwards in the water. Colors of yellow and gold mingle with a tint of pink.

There is still evidence of the equinox storm that turned corn stalks criss-cross in the fields, leaving the heavily-fruited stalks almost touching the ground from their burden. Cane stalks were also blown to the ground but they have already been cut and taken to the mill and the juice cooked into syrup. The equinox storm comes at summer's end to mark the change in seasons. The storm has caused tobacco to come into high order and mold gathers on the edges of the leaves in the packhouse.

Cotton patches are white, with the green and brown of the leaves attesting to a change in seasons. Farmers are awaiting the first frost to strip the leaves from the stalks, making picking cotton easier.

Morning glories are still prominent in the corn fields and they bloom profusely in early morning as if they are aware their days are numbered. Hot peppers, hidden and protected by the tall grass that seeded out and spread its foliage over them, are pulled from the stalks, some already red; others red and green mingled, taken to the house and strung for drying by piercing each stem with a needle and tobacco twine to form the "string." They are then hung on a wall somewhere near the kitchen stove to be used for seasoning sausage as well as other foods during winter.

Husk is heavy on the corn and squirrels in the oak thickets are already gathering acorns, and the old folks say this portends a bitter winter ahead.

Wasps remain close to their nests; a few late apples hang precariously onto their high place in the trees; the grapevines are shedding their leaves and children search for the few remaining grapes that have acquired a sugar-sweetness.

Looking toward Mr. Sempse's place, everything is bright with color — scarlet, yellow, gold, pink, purple, orange — all mingling into a brilliant picture. It is like that at any place, but Mr. Sempse's is the nearest viewpoint from the pond.

Changing. Always changing. The eternal plan — conception, birth, fulfillment, death. Winter gives way to spring when life flourishes and reaches its fulfillment during the hot days of summer, growing the grain and fiber and food for harvesting when the growing pains are over and another cycle in the plan is completed.

October! How bright the skies! Is there a heavenly blue? The name sounds appropriate for the season glorified by deep blue skies with autumn colors more sedate than the breathtaking spectacle of summer — mellowed, softer, in harmony with the browning landscape. The orange of the pumpkins on the vine; the soft tan of mown hayfields and the still-sweet smell of the cured hay stacked neatly around poles in the fields; the ash-white foliage of the reed beds as they go into hibernation; yellow broom sage waving in the breeze. Beautiful October!

Savor the beauty now, while it is a reality, for so soon it will become a memory. The leaves will shine their brightest just before they give up all life and return to their origin, the earth from which it all began. They become playthings for the autumn winds that toss them about aimlessly, leaving only a mass of debris after a brief moment of glory.

Gashes in the earth speak of the harvest season. The sweet potatoes are harvested, the late white potatoes, the peanuts, leaving the fields bare and forlorn looking. Partridges fly overhead, then land in the corn fields to feed on the grain. And black walnuts fall heavily from the trees, still encased in their green-brown shells that will dry out with time.

In the gardens where greens have blossomed out, butterflies congregate with their show of color in a ritual as old as time itself.

Quilts in the closets have acquired a musky smell during the summer and they are hung on clotheslines and fences for several days to air, and the feather beds are fluffed up and placed on porches for the tranquilty of fall will fade and the winds of winter will blow and warmth will be needed in the open houses.

Pink, wine, yellow, and white, the chrysanthemums bloom in small, obscure places, adding to the beauty of the season. They, too, will become victims of the first killing frost. And the pine needles are thick beneath the towering trees. Always the pines. Always a part of the rural landscape. Always forming the circle that designates home.

On light nights, moonbeams reflect on unpainted tin roofs and they sparkle and shine and the neighborhood becomes a silhouette of buildings and trees and paths that are discernible, giving a romantic appearance to antiquated surroundings.

The cows savor the last grass of the season, now becoming scarce in the pastures and the mules hang their heads over the lots and nibble at hardweeds grown tall from the rich soil. They seem content to rest and swish their tails at the flies that always plague them, after months of labor tilling the fields. Another evidence of fall is the conglomeration of cockleburrs that have matted their tails.

October's bright blue skies! October's splash of color! October's crisp, cool air when the humidity is low and warmth from the sun soothes rather than irritates. It is a moment in time when things seem ideal for a little while. It is a time of pause, a time of reaping, a time of assessment. The fruits of a year's labor are there for the harvest. The golden harvest will be over and the landscape will become barren, replaced by a new season, always changing in a predetermined pattern that needs no edict from man. Irreversible, inevitable, infallible.   □

Halloween In Name Only

H alloween in the '30s was different in one respect. We didn't "trick or treat" in the open spaces for "treats" would have been hard to come by. But we knew about Halloween and our teachers of that era can be credited with keeping us up to date with tradition. Drawing paper was very popular in the schoolroom then and when special occasions came the appropriate colors were used to decorate blackboards and windows.

At Halloween there were witches on broomsticks cut from black paper, showing a silhouette that was pasted on the windows, orange pumpkins made into jack o'lanterns, and other symbols of the season. But if witches and goblins and ghosts were symbols of Halloween, then we celebrated that season almost year-round. The ghost tales of those days were almost unbelievable.

In my neighborhood there was supposedly a little black dog that traveled up and down one road at night and many people told of seeing it, especially when they were curing tobacco and were isolated and everything was quiet. It would be late at night when it passed by and it is strange that it could be seen so easily when the animal was as black as the night.

Lights from the graveyards would go straight up into the sky for an interval, then turn and float across the area and finally disappear. Some people said it was phosphorescence from dead bodies that caused the lights. But I personally never saw any of those lights or the little black dog, for I never looked toward the graveyards at night if I could help it, especially if I were by myself, and the dog just didn't happen to pass by when I was traversing that road. I'm glad he didn't.

There was one tale told to me that outdated my time. But this woman said that when she was young there was a woman who lived in her neighborhood that people called a witch. She looked like a witch, was a loner, and didn't associate with the people of the neighborhood. But apparently the hunters were able to have at least some rapport with her. They would take their hounds and go hunting for rabbits but couldn't get the dogs to go into the thickets, scent the rabbits and get them out into the open. They consulted with the witch and she told them if they would tie one certain dog they would be able to get a good supply of rabbits. They did this, and subsequently got a lot of hares, according to the tale.

There was also a house in the neighborhood in which this woman grew up that she said could not be locked and kept locked throughout the night. They had holes bored in the doors of houses then and holes also bored in the door facing, and heavy chains were run through the holes and secured with locks. But she said that they would be unlocked every morning.

There were the legendary "Raw Head and Bloody Bones" that lurked in every unfinished loft, particularly in those dark, gloomy houses that were poorly lit. That was the tale that got small children's eyes closed very quickly when they were reminded that those feared characters were watching down on them. "Raw Head and Bloody Bones" were about the greatest terror that very young children faced.

And there were many "hainted" houses. We didn't pronounce them "haunted" houses. "Haints" dressed in white floated around certain houses and strange noises reportedly could be heard at midnight.

There were also many superstitions and some of them persist today. We couldn't take a rake or an ax or a hoe through the house. It was bad luck. We couldn't enter the front door of a house we were visiting and exit through the back. A black cat crossing the road in front of you was always bad luck. Breaking a mirror was very bad luck. If a rooster crowed in the doorway there was supposed to be a death in the family. Washing clothes between Christmases was also bad luck. (In remembering I believe that the bad luck came if bed clothes were washed, and not wearing apparel.)

When we were young'uns and company came to spend bedtime, we'd get in a back room (for young'uns didn't sit in the same room with the old folks all the time except when the weather was cold) and there were always ghost stories. And some older boy would find a sheet and drape it over his body and make an entry while the story was in progress and young'uns would scream like they were dying. But the old folks didn't run in to see about them. They knew it was just a pack of young'uns carrying on.

Sometimes a pack of young'uns would get brave and decide to go to a graveyard at night. But it was a touchy situation and if one made a funny noise the others would start running and carrying on like you wouldn't believe. Once at the graveyard, we'd walk among the tombstones lightly and then run all the way back home. If a young'un got left behind, too bad. It was everybody on his own. We especially liked it if girls who were brave enough to participate in a boys' world were left behind to scream in the night. But in our hearts we were as scared as they were.

And somewhere near Halloween there would be a hayride. It was always on a night that wasn't too cool and usually when there was a moon. A mule would be hitched to a wagon and bales of hay or loose hay placed in the wagon and the young folks would climb aboard and sing and carry on and have a barrel of fun. We'd ride for miles along the roads that meandered through the back country and that was another occasion when young people got a chance to court away from the prying eyes of parents.

Halloween was celebrated in name only fifty years ago out in the country. □

Just A Simple Party

I t was just a simple party in a quaint setting, but it might have been a gala in a formal garden for all that it seemed to be.

It was in a clean-swept yard on a summer night and there was the aroma of cape jasmine and the faint fragrance of honeysuckle from a fence across the field.

There was a silvery moon and stars with their brightness dimmed by moonglow, but the fireflies were close-up as they performed their nightly ritual for the benefit of children who plucked them from the air at dusk and crammed them into jars. And there was romance.

Pecan and oak trees on the perimeter of the yard served as a backdrop and moonlight filtering through the foliage cast specks of light on the ground beneath the trees.

There was a guitar. There were love songs. But it might have been a performer in a symphony orchestra and a baritone soloist of international renown for all that it seemed to be.

So soon removed from childhood and adolescence and carefree days when they roamed the countryside and found all manner of mischief to partake in, the youth of the neighborhood congregated as young men and women with a new perception of life.

It was a complete transformation, as has been the case in every generation throughout history. The only distinction in this case is that it was the generation of the 1930s, the last before the world turned modern.

Simple, plain country boys and girls with no pretentiousness and no false illusions about themselves, they were happy to be a part of the life experience.

Those skinny, giggly girls of a year or two earlier were suddenly like young goddesses with soft curves, radiant smiles and eyes that pierced the soul. How could they be so blue, like the blue of the sky; so gray with long lashes that spoke of intrigue and passion; green like growing grass or so brown they were impenetrable?

These were the same girls who had pestered the boys and whose arms and legs had been twisted until they screamed in pain. As a result, many of those rambunctious boys had had their rear ends torn up by irate fathers.

And those gangly boys who had roamed the fields and streams throughout childhood were also transformed. Some had had their heads shaved in summer, accentuating their large ears. And an accumulation of dust on the heavy down on their faces had made them more unappealing. No more.

They had ransacked girls' playhouses with their homemade carts, tearing down the stobs and tobacco twine that separated the rooms of the young housekeepers and sending their mud pies and jars of red pope berry juice onto the swept area of the make-believe domains.

Faces that had held no distinguishing features in childhood had suddenly become beautiful with blood-red lipstick accentuating sensuous lips and white teeth that showed no signs of neglect. They were the same girls of yesteryear.

Those once-shaven heads and down-covered faces had also gone through the molting process and emerged as handsome young farmers. With the smell of brilliantine about them, the hair was well-groomed and smoothed down in keeping with the style of the day. Tanned by work in the fields and with muscular builds from manual labor, they bore no resemblance to the boys they had been.

It could have been at any other place under the stars, and in any other setting, but none could have been more magnificent for all that it seemed to be.

There were the usual games — pocket handkerchief, post-office, turn-the-bottle — that ended in kisses and a boy-girl closeness not customary at other times. This, accentuated by moonlight and shadows and the fragrance of the rare perfume of summer, gave the feeling of being in another world rather than in the midst of tobacco-cotton country in semi-isolation.

There was ice cream — chocolate and vanilla — made in freezers at the edge of the yard, hand-turned by the boys who took the ice that had been stored in the smokehouse, chipped it up into small pieces and packed it tightly around the freezer, using plenty of salt taken from the pile left over after meat was cured.

There were cakes with thick icing served with ice cream on tobacco trucks overlaid with white clothes, lighted by lanterns used in tending tobacco barns.

There was laughter. There was gaiety. There was no evidence of a care in the world, although it was at one of the most critical times in the history of our nation. We didn't even know about drugs except those our parents had forced us to take. One or two boys might have had a drink of whisky before the party but they had control of themselves.

It wasn't a group "washed" in purity. It was only a general representation of youth at that time in history, with the same emotions of the young in any generation. It was a generation standing on the threshold of the world of reality, not sure about the future or even their goals, but confident that everything would be all right.

Soft lips met on this enchanted evening and there was a quickening of pulsebeats and the stars became diamonds in the sky and they felt all the passions of young love.

There was the long walk home afterward down a country road that became a pathway to heaven, for all that it seemed to be. There was soft laughter from the couples savoring this rare moment in time. Hands met and clasped in the moonlight and it was so insignificant and happened so long ago.

It was only a neighborhood party, but oh, what it seemed to be!   □

I Went To The Show At The Carolina

'Sad'dy' Evening In Town

L iving supposedly dull lives in the sticks half-a-century ago, there are many people who may wonder how we ever managed out there behind the pines. But we did pretty well, at that. And besides, it wasn't all dullness. There was Saturday evening to look forward to most every week of the year, 'cept those times when Pa made us do some job in the fields that we could have done just as well on Monday.

And there were no "afternoons" for us then. There were morning, evening, and night. And "Sad'dy" evening was when we went to town. And we looked forward to "Sad'dy" evening almost like Christmas.

There were the "pixture" shows, and if we missed a week we were left hanging for there were serials running every Saturday and a stagecoach was always falling from a high cliff or an Indian ambushing the hero, or something and we just had to find out what happened from week to week.

Ken Maynard, Johnny Mack Brown, John Wayne, Bob Steele, Gene Autry and many other western stars were our heroes and the subjects of long conversations.

Since we didn't have a "mobile" of our own, we boys had to catch rides to town and there were too many of us to try to get a ride in one car, so we'd spread out on our own. But first we had to confront the "old man" for a little pocket change, and that was like pulling eye teeth, not because he didn't want to give us the money, but because he simply didn't have it.

Pa carried his pocket change and a dollar or two in an old snap-open leather pocketbook in his front pocket, and when we lined up he'd close his eyes tight and run his hand into the pocket, retrieve the pocketbook and see if he could find a quarter for each of us. There might be some fumbling with nickels to see whether they might be quarters. And when we got that quarter in our hands we were as proud as children with $50 of their own today.

There was the quick "washing-all-over" in the washtub, if you can "wash all over" in a washtub, clean overalls and white shirts, hair plastered down with brilliantine that sometimes ended up in little droplets on the back of the neck. Then we made our rounds to Ma. Sometimes she might have a dime or 15 cents for us from egg money that she kept in a Golden Grain sack pinned to her slip. That was pure gravy if Ma had some extra change, and she was proud when she could add to our spending money. She'd smile and pat us on the head as she gave it to us. And you'd better believe we loved Ma.

Then we were off to the big city with each of us fanning out in different directions in search of rides. But strangely enough, all of us seemed to get into town at about the same time. We would congregate with other neighborhood boys in front of the theater. They had different names in different towns, so I'll call ours "The Carolina," for that was its name.

If we had more than a quarter, most of us would buy a box of popcorn, but if not we'd forgo popcorn for ice cream and a pop later on. And there's no way to describe the joy of watching the action on the silver screen and we wished the show would last forever.

But town was total excitement for us anyway and the main drag was to us what Fifth Avenue was to New Yorkers. And we thought those young doods living in town really had it made until we'd see many of them going out to the country to try to find work and something to eat. Then we realized they were worse off than us.

Anybody remember the Israelites that used to congregate on the streets on Saturday evening? They'd hold religious services and would always draw a crowd and sing and beat on their tambourines. I remember they had long hair (a monstrosity in those days) and dressed and looked strange, but I don't have a clear picture of them in mind. However, they were a part of the town scene in my boyhood.

Why is it that a blind accordion player's melodies are somehow sweeter than others? They used to play on the streets and the songs they played were always the latest and the tunes haunting so that they lingered in the memory. Pennies and nickels were dropped into the tin cups attached to the straps that held the instruments around their necks in the days when money was almost nonexistent.

And there were the blind and handicapped that had their pencils for sale. Some were deformed so severely they even brought sadness to the heart of a child. There were those who had to walk on their hands and feet in a horizontal position as well as the blind who seldom wore glasses and their eyes appeared to have receded in the sockets and only a tiny part of the useless eyes were showing, just a tiny white speck at the corners.

There was the instant picture stand where you could get one of those perfectly horrible "pixtures" made for a quarter.

And the streets were filled with people. For the youth, the dime stores were the most popular places, especially Woolworth's. It was like a beehive in the dime stores on "Sad'dy" evening. Boys and girls crowded the front of the stores and half-way courted, those that were old enough, and made plans for that night. And people flocked there to buy items for the home — dippers, egg-beaters, lampshades, flesh forks, shoestrings and many other things.

The drug store was especially nice. There were fans attached to the high ceiling that turned slowly, although we didn't feel any cool air from them. And behind the counter there was a large mirror and fancy woodwork that was a part of the soda fountain equipment. And there was ice cream! Tutti frutti, chocolate, vanilla, black walnut. We boys would buy a nickel cone and lick it until it got down to the cone, then take small bites to make it last longer. And the cone was as good as the ice cream. Of course we asked for a glass of ice water to go with the ice cream.

If we had another nickel in our overalls pocket, we'd buy a fountain "Co-Cola." We didn't pronounce the "Coca" as it was pronounced later, before the word became "Coke." The "Co-Colas" were delightful served in fragile Coca-Cola glasses, small at the bottom and widening at the top with the brand name on each glass. There'd be shivers of ice and plenty of fizz and we felt we'd stepped up a notch when we drank from glasses that were the nearest to crystal of anything we'd been in contact with. But I'm not saying we knew anything about crystal, or what the word even meant at that time.

By this time the day was waning and we started looking for somebody to ride home with. There was no desire to linger on in town, for "Sad'dy" night was coming up and there was always something to do in the country. Half-a-day was long enough for us in town. We began to feel crowded in after making the rounds and taking in the street sights. We started thinking about fried fish that would be on the table when we got home.

If memories could hang in galleries, I'd love to preserve for posterity some scenes from that world that I knew and loved, such as the busy streets on Saturday afternoon. I would provide all the detail that I remember for generations yet unborn so that they might see, rather than hear of a world that so many know nothing about.

But that can only be for those who were there, who saw and lived that life. In our hearts there are moments that have acquired the luster of waxed wood, mellowed and more treasured with the passing of time. Only the wanderings of the mind can bring them back in full clarity as if they had occurred yesterday. They glow and warm the heart and bring smiles to the face as well as tears to the eyes sometimes.   □

Fighting Filthy Flies

T he old country ditty, "Chicken in the Bread Tray Scratching Out Dough" was a lot more applicable to our past than might be expected. Those old chickens came into the house sometimes and they just loved to walk over back porches. It was a common sight to see a woman with a broom and a dipper of water walking behind those chickens and cleaning up after them.

"Open house" is viewed in a different light today than it was many years ago. We held "open house" all summer. The doors were wide open and there were no screens either and the influx of flies was unbelievable. And no wonder. They had ample breeding grounds in the stables, the lots, the hen houses and the hog pens. And boy, they swarmed by the million and made life miserable for everybody.

Oh, we tried to control them. Every time anybody went to town a bunch of sticky fly catchers was bought and they were pulled out and attached to the ceilings and flies would almost instantly get themselves caught on the syrupy, gommy surface and soon there was no sticky surface left to catch them.

Women would make their own fly traps by taking jars and almost filling them with water and cutting pieces of cardboard and making a hole in the center and putting syrup on the inside. Flies would go for that syrup and land up in the water. But it was an effort in futility. With so large an army working against you, there is no way to win.

And if there are those who feel that housekeepers were lax in those days, they are dead wrong. The exact opposite was true. Women did everything in their power to have clean houses and they fought flies as they would the plague. They made miniature brooms from broom sage and used them at the tables when the family was eating. They also made fly chasers from a piece of cloth torn into thin pieces and attached to a straight limb.

When a meal was prepared the flies were swished away and a cloth placed over the food and the fly chasers were put into use when the family was eating. People would eat and fan flies and blow at them when they pitched on their faces.

And those little pudgy fat babies had the hardest time you ever saw. They'd fall asleep with a piece of biscuit or other food in their hands and around their mouths the flies would take over. Fly specks would be on their faces and they'd fight at them in their sleep. Mothers would take pieces of tobacco cloth and drape over the cradles to keep the flies out, but in summer heat tobacco cloth is hot also, so it was miserable for the little ones.

But it wasn't long before somebody thought about building "kiddy coops" for the babies, and what a relief that must have been for those cute little rascals that had borne the brunt of the fly invasion. The "kiddy coops" were large enough to allow the babies some freedom, and they were covered with screen wire. They had a top that opened and the babies could sit in comfort in their quarters and the flies could do no more than pitch on the outside of the pens.

Then came the doors covered with wire mesh and it was as revolutionary as a major invention would be today. People got in on the bandwagon to get screen doors to keep the flies out. But there were problems there also. How many of those old tenant houses do you think had standard-sized doors? Not one in 10. And the new screen doors were made to a standard. If height alone was a factor, the doors could be cut off, but hardly none of them were squared off and some were too wide for the standard doors. Some had to be made by hand.

But the screen doors were a start at controlling the flies. And half-screens came on the market that could be placed in windows and extended to fit and people got in on that one too, and that helped to keep the flies out further.

Of course the flies congregated on the outside of the doors and a pack of young'uns running in and out, in and out all the time turned a passel of the flies inside the house. But along about that time Watkins products and Rawleigh products' salesmen were making their rounds through the country and peddling their products door to door. And they had fly spray and hand sprayers, and you'd better believe the womenfolks saved up enough eggs to buy the fly killer.

They'd close up the house and spray every room and in an hour or so they'd sweep up cupfuls of dead flies. That would relieve the situation for a day or two until the young'uns succeeded in turning in another drove of flies and the process was repeated all over. But some people had dusters that sent a cloud of Black Flag over the rooms and that got 'em also.

The Watkins man and the Rawleigh man became popular figures in the back country and if the women didn't have money to pay for all the products they needed the salesmen would charge it until their next visit. They'd buy liniment, flavorings, salves and even pie mixes that were a far cry from those available today. But they did have a good amount of gelatin in them and coconut, lemon and other flavors that at that time were delicious to country hicks.

Over a period of time we worked out of the fly-speck era and looked to further advances to benefit us. But we had one time with those flies. And it seemed that a dead fly just under the surface of a pan of chalky-white milk could look the darkest of anything I remember not to be able to see the actual fly. And no, they didn't throw away that pan of milk. They did what a lot of people would do today. They took a cup and dipped the insect out and tried to forget it. Heck, people have done worse things in years far removed from those days of 50 years ago.   □

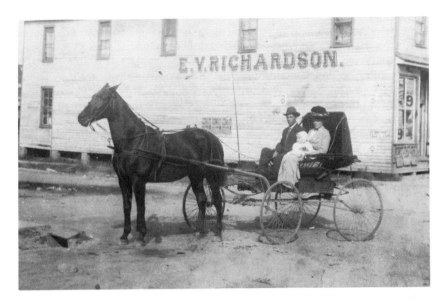

(N.C. Dept. Archives and History)

Buggies Were Still In Use 50 Years Ago

Chicken Stew On Sunday

I t's Sunday morning, about 9:30. Sun's shining. Birds are singing in the trees. Hens are cackling out in the barnyard. Pigs haven't rooted under the fence as yet (but they will before the day is over). Everybody's getting ready for Sunday school and church.

Uh oh! A buggy's coming up the path loaded down with people. Young'uns are even hanging on the sides and standing in the back. Company has come to spend the day!

The buggy is driven up to a tree so the mule can be tethered and the young'uns jump to the ground, followed by the "old man" and "old lady."

Everybody meets at the front door and "howdys" are exchanged and everybody is doing "tollible" and the young'uns scatter over the yard and the old folks go inside and Sunday school and church are forgotten and the whole day's schedule is changed.

Arrival time is important in such Sunday visits, for nobody knows in advance that there will be company. And there is the matter of something to eat. Adding six or seven more mouths at the table makes a difference.

If the cousins that are visiting are the ones that like to do the same things the children at home like to do everything is fine and "a good time is had by all." But if they're the ones that don't want to do anything unless they can do it like they want to or don't want to do this or that, the young'uns at home are as mad as hell and a young'un might be tripped before the day is over, then dared to tell it.

And look out old hen! Your day has come! It's at such times that chicken stew becomes the main dish for you can take a fat hen and have enough broth to make a peck of pastry, and that's what it takes to feed a pack like this.

Ma points out the hen she wants us to run down and it seems like every one that is killed on the spur of the moment has game in them, for they can fly almost like a bird. So we set out to running her down and she takes off about four feet off the ground and flies half the distance of the yard. We want her to go under the shelter so we can hem her up in a corner, but she darts away like a rabbit and heads for the bushes and we're right behind her and she finally goes under the shelter and we get a hand on her and up she flies again over our heads, and she's hassling by then and we are too.

But she's got to be caught so we let in on her again and finally pin her down up against the garden fence and she lets out a yell until a hand is placed around her neck and the neck wrung and then she jumps all over the place until life is gone.

Then she's scalded in a bucket and the smell of wet feathers is sickening. All the feathers slip off with ease except the pinfeathers, and the feet are dipped in the scalding water also and the yellow skin pulls off, leaving white legs and feet underneath. The toenails will be cut off and the feet cooked along with the rest of the chicken. The head is skinned too and the eyes removed and the beak cut off. The head will also go into the boiling pot.

It takes a hen a good two hours to become tender and she is put to boiling as quickly as possible and a plain cake is beaten up and poured into a big pan and placed in the oven. Dough is kneaded for pastry and flour sprinkled on the oilcloth on the side table and the long bottle used as a rolling pin is put to use rolling out the dough to be cut into strips and placed in the broth after the chicken is done. You wouldn't believe the amount of dough that's rolled out. It looks like enough for an army, but every mouthful will be eaten.

There would be a bigger crowd, but only the medium-sized to small young'uns come a visiting. The older ones stay at home. Seems like there ain't the closeness among first cousins that there is between brothers and sisters and that's understandable, and when a young'un gets old enough to rebel, he or she is left at home.

Finally everything's ready and the young'uns wash their hands and gather round the side table and the grown-ups at the dining room table and a saucer is used to dip up the pastry and plates are filled and the yellow broth gathers around the edges of the plate and black pepper is dashed all over it and everybody settles down to eating chicken stew.

A jar of beet pickles has been opened and a jar of peaches to go with the cake, and beets are placed in the plates and the red juice mingles with the yellow broth and it's a pure feast. Good-sized pieces of pastry are taken into the mouth and it's so slick you don't even have to chew it. And all the flavor that only a fat hen can give to pastry, is there to enjoy.

Everybody is stuffed like a hog and burping and almost gasping for breath, especially after eating a big hunk of cake and peaches too, after already being full of pastry.

The girls are put to washing dishes and the old women go to the front of the house and settle down to talking about their biddies or the number of quilts they've quilted, or even about Bible scriptures. The men might stroll down into the fields to see how the crops are growing. The little girls retreat to their "play house" and the boys scatter all over the place. They "rassle" or race or play "hiding" or throw balls and end up throwing horseshoes. But if the "odd" boy is there, they pester him the whole time and would jump on him, but they know Pa would tear them all to pieces if they do that.

The day wanes and it's time to untether the old mule and head back home. Young'uns pile into the buggy and goodbyes are said and a promise is made to repay the visit. It's a once-a-year ritual. Brothers and sisters and the young'uns make the rounds and every few Sundays it's either cooking for company or going to their house and seeing how their chicken stew tastes. It's all right for the old folks, but for the young'uns — blah! □

Sundays In The Sticks

S undays. They were something else to the generation of 50 years ago. They meant no work, no matter how badly cotton needed chopping or tobacco graded or fodder pulled. Sunday was a day of rest, and the only way we ever deviated from that schedule was when the hogs rooted under the fence and started roaming over the neighborhood or the cow crossed the fence, even wearing the yoke placed around her neck to help prevent break-outs. In those cases we had to round them up, do some stabbing down to the fence, and go back to our Sunday schedule of leisure. But the Bible says if the ox gets in the ditch on Sunday, get him out.

But somehow we boys didn't exactly call all of Sunday leisurely, for part of the day was spent at church, and that was torture. And the old folks didn't just send you to church. They took you. So forget about playing hookey.

Nobody of the present generation would believe the length of those sermons. Preaching started at 11 a.m. and church was usually over about 1 to 1:30 p.m., unless they had an altar service that lasted for half an hour or more. And they did just that sometimes. They would have a testimony service sometimes and individual church members would give their personal testimonies and they would get spirit-filled and speak in unknown tongues and there would be shouting all over that old church.

But the length of the service wasn't the worst part about church. The "garb" we boys were forced to wear was the greatest indignity I can imagine for any country boy that ever grew up to be a red-blooded man. I suppose that some boys of my era escaped this indignity, but about all those in my neck of the woods were also involved. We were forced to wear knickers to church. Surely there were suits with long pants then. The only thing I can figure out about it is that our mothers wanted to keep us innocent little boys as long as they could, and they figured keeping us in knickers was the best recourse.

But I have news for those mothers at this belated date. Knickers or not, we were not nearly as innocent as they might have thought.

Anyway, we put on those knickers every Sunday morning and traipsed to Sunday school and church. We'd yank at them and kick the floor to show our rebellion, but we still wore those knickers. And like everything else made of wool in those days, they were hard and had a feeling of fine metal splinters. We wore them summer and winter, spring and fall.

And remember that we had only about a five-month reprieve from wearing long-handled drawers, the kind with flaps in the back. Put a hot-natured boy into a pair of long-handles, add a pair of thick wool knickers, and you'll see a sapling boy with sweat all over his head and an itch from that wool that is tormenting.

To add insult to injury, those knickers were equipped with buttons that fastened just below the knee cap. There were two buttons, one too loose, and one too tight. If the second button was used it bound the leg and felt like it was cutting off circulation and the first one was too loose and this allowed the leg to dangle and it was a mess either way. But we had to undergo this torture in the name of "fashion." Overalls never felt quite as comfortable as they did on Sunday afternoons.

We would snicker in church sometimes and would have become hysterical, but a stern look from the "old man" would calm us down. We used fans supplied by some businesses in town to cool ourselves off as we fidgeted during the service. And we could always find something to laugh about. One or two of the older "sisters" of the church used strings from pieces of cloth to tie around their legs to hold up their stockings, and sometimes the strings would extend beyond their dress hems, and this would really get us going and we'd have to hold our heads down and literally swallow the laughs.

When preaching was finally over, if the preacher didn't come home with us and there was no other company, all of us got to sit down at the table at the same time to have our fair chance at the meaty pieces of chicken. When we waited, too often we got the backs, necks and feet. And canned apples sweetened and a little spice put in them or canned peaches tasted good as dessert.

After dinner, we were home free until time to feed up. If the weather was right, we usually always played baseball on Sunday afternoons. Now there was baseball gear in those days, but we boys out in the sticks were not fortunate enough to have it. So we improvised our own tools of the trade. Somebody would make bats out of a hickory sapling or some other hard wood from the smooth part of limbs and whittle them down to the shape of a baseball bat. We even used tobacco truck rounds sometimes.

We made our baseballs from tobacco twine. First, we found a round piece of rock or something about the size of a bantam egg, and began winding the twine around it until it was the approximate size of a real baseball, pulling the twine as tightly as possible while winding. When the ball was the size we wanted, we'd search for a needle with an eye large enough to accommodate four-ply tobacco twine, and there was a long time in sewing the end of the thread to make the ball solid.

If there were 10 boys, they would be divided equally on each side, with size and age also considered for the two sides. And as is the case today, everybody criticized the umpire. We always accused them of being prejudiced and we did our share of hollering and belly-aching during the games.

We played in back yards or cow pastures or hog pastures, and we handled the ball with our bare hands. Those string balls were not that hard to field so long as they were dry, but when they became saturated with water after falling into mud holes, they could really sting sometimes, and if an off pitch hit a player in the face it would leave red marks from the string. Then the ball would start raveling and little strings would appear on the edges and finally there would be a conglomeration of dirty tobacco twine and a new ball would have to be made.

The games would last until almost sunset and only the fact that the mules, cows and hogs had to be fed ended those Sunday fun times for us.   □

Model T's Made Us Feel Rich

T he poorest of the poor are better off today than we were in the 1920s and 1930s, for if a family's income is below the poverty level today, Social Services provides assistance in most cases and people receive food stamps and other services. No such help was available then, so each family was dependent on its own ingenuity to survive.

There had been better times during World War I when farm prices rose as a result of the war. But I entered the picture in 1918, the year the war ended, and when I was old enough to remember, the only testimony to that better era was an old Overland automobile under our shelter that looked awfully long and large in my eyes, and it was no longer in use. But it was a good place for hens to go to lay their eggs.

In the "front room," as we called the parlor in those days, there was a davenport covered in "pure leather," solid black, that must have been 7 feet wide, and two chairs covered in mohair that almost stuck in you when you sat down in them, and the foot-pedaled organ with its ornate woodwork and oval mirror. There was even a rug on the floor, although it was very worn and faded.

The only other items of value in our house was a washstand with a mirror and a large white pitcher and bowl. The rest of the junk wasn't worth a quarter.

But despite all the poverty and lack of money, there was a Model T Ford (five passenger) in our yard. I don't know whether we bought it new or not. I remember the curtains we hooked around it to close it in in winter. The curtains were made from a black material that had the appearance of leather, but it wasn't and it had a cloth backing.

The windows were made of celluloid and were stitched into the curtains. Celluloid had a yellowish tint, and when looking out the windows the landscape took on a yellowish hue also.

I know one thing about those Model T's. Many a man and boy suffered broken arms from trying to crank those "tin lizzies." On the left, under the steering wheel, was the magneta, and on the right the gas lever. Now if the magneta wasn't set just right and the gas lever was pulled too far down, when the engine ignited it would give a kick to the crank and if you didn't respond almost like lightning the result was a broken arm.

And nobody today can imagine how far up the ladder we climbed when there were Model T Fords parked in our yards. After all the years of having to hitch a mule to a cart, a wagon, or a buggy to go anywhere, it seemed unreal to have a vehicle available that would carry you "rapidly" and without the burden of hitching up the mules and the slowness of the journey.

With really cheap gasoline in those days, 50 cents would buy enough to go courting on or to make a trip to town. And you could always carry along some hay wire in case something came loose. You could usually fix the Model T's with a piece of wire.

And the women folks just loved them. It gave them a status symbol they hadn't known before, and they could take pride in riding to town in a real automobile.

Another advantage was that if it became necessary to lift a wheel off the ground a strong man could easily get the work done. Of course there were those slender, 2-foot high hand pumps used in inflating the tires, and a jack even then to lift the car for changing tires.

The male ego went sky-high when young men had cars to drive. Oh, they would break down and a new set of coils would have to be bought or some other part, and the car might be out of use for a few weeks. But a Model T was a status symbol and got them away from a mule-and-buggy image. The buggy days had been a status symbol in the past also and there was a time when a young man was as proud of a pretty horse and a shiny buggy as the generation of the 1920s and 1930s was proud of the Model T.

There are flashbacks in which I can remember young men of the day all dressed up for dating and going out and cranking the Fords and stepping onto the running board and climbing into those babies and jogging off with a smile on their faces. And although I remember blue serge as the predominant material in men's clothing in those days, it wasn't like that with those young fellows.

I recall hard-brimmed straw hats and thin-lapeled suits and a lot of them plaids with slender legs and it seems there was a lot of green in them and there were string ties. So fashion played a role in our society, as humble as it was, even in the days when we were at our poorest.

As to the young women's apparel in those days, the best recollection I have is of shirtwaists and dark skirts and I know there was some influence on women's clothing from the "Charleston" dance and I can remember a few short dresses with no waistline and it seems they were of sedate colors of tan or gray.

One thing that I regarded as a sign of affluence in those hard times was the matronly women at church who wore stoles made of fox fur. I was intrigued by the heads and the eyes where the garments were snapped together.

Now back to cars. Those Model T's gave way to the Model A's, and we had stepped another notch up the ladder. And young people loved the Model A's. Those models also introduced the rumble seat, and they were a lover's delight!

Oh, but we young upstarts loved those rumble seats. And when Ford came out with its V-8 engine we thought we were in our zenith. It was a much sleeker, longer, streamlined automobile and with its V-shaped motor and eight cylinders, man we had beauty and power too! But all that luxury was in the hands of very few people that I knew. But us poor folks did get to ride in one every once in a while, and boy, they'd take off like a bat out of hell.

Don't hold me up to dates, for that was a very long time ago, and I'm going by memory only, but it seems that the V-8's came out about 1934. And in the era of the V-8 there came out a song entitled "Wahoo." The setting for "Wahoo" was the prairie states, but we coined verses applicable to the V-8 and all the young people were singing it.

Those remembrances are so far removed from all the problems of the world in which we live today, it seems that we were in seventh heaven to look back upon it all. □

Memories Of Christmases

T he war years were long past, and country people were beginning to have better lives. During the war Marines and GI's stationed at Cherry Point, Camp Lejeune, Fort Bragg and Seymour Johnson Air Force Base fell in love with a lot of the southern belles and married them, taking them away to other areas of the nation to live. And change was everywhere.

Ma and Pa had grown old, as had all those born in the last third of the 19th Century. The old house where the children had grown up wasn't the same anymore. It was quiet, with a loneliness about the place. The house almost seemed unoccupied. The stables were empty and all the farm equipment had been moved to some of the boys' homes.

Ma and Pa sat quietly a lot of the time and seemed to have their thoughts elsewhere. They especially liked to sit in their old chairs by the hearth and watch the fire fade into embers, and a smile would come over their faces sometimes as if they were reliving moments from a distant past.

Fall came and with it the harvest, and Ma and Pa watched from their window as the sassafras bushes across the way turned a fiery red and the woods put on their fall coat. They observed as the younger generation picked the cotton and gathered the corn, and they realized they were in the twilight years of their lives.

No one ever knew their real thoughts, for they seemed to get a special pleasure from spinning their own dreams. But it was easy to imagine that their thoughts went back to the times when all the family was together and they wondered whether they'd ever live to see them grown and on their own. They must have wondered what happened to the years and marveled that all had survived.

Things had changed so much since the war, and old folks like Ma and Pa were unable to keep up with it all, so they lived in their own world while the younger generations adapted to the change.

Christmas was approaching again, but for Ma and Pa there would be more sadness than cheer, for several of the children lived hundreds of miles away and couldn't come home for the holidays.

People were decorating their homes inside and outside, with bright lights and Christmas trees and all manner of glitter that had not been a part of earlier celebrations of Christmas. And children already had tricycles, dolls and bicycles, and Santa Claus hadn't even come yet. This was hard for Ma and Pa to accept, for they hadn't hardly been able to get just one toy for each child.

Ma wouldn't be cooking for two or three days for Christmas as she did in the old days. She was too feeble for that now. They would spend Christmas with one of the children nearby. The meals would be delicious, the house would glitter with decorations, and there would be several presents for everybody and the grandchildren would shout and sing. But it wouldn't be the same.

So the old folks gathered the black walnuts under the tree beside the smokehouse, picked up the pecans and stored them in tow bags in the shed, made brooms and swept the leaves from the yard, burning the trash and watching the acorns pop open in the fire, sending little spirals of smoke into the air. They tried to keep busy for a part of each day.

And the trees became bare and the north winds blew and the boys cut wood and took it to the porch for Ma and Pa and they cried at their sons' kindness.

Sometimes Ma and Pa would talk about little events that happened when the children were small and occasionally they would be laughing when one of the children walked in, but no one inquired into their private world.

A few days before Christmas Pa went out and cut a little cedar tree and drug it up to the house and Ma told him to put it in the corner where it had always stood, and Ma went out and found a few boughs of holly with a lot of red berries on it, and a little mistletoe. There were no other decorations in the house, and it was almost eerie in its quietness. And Christmas would come with no one there.

Ma and Pa were taken to a son's house on Christmas Eve and the old folks were cold from the chilly winds. But inside there was warmth and cheer. Heat from floor vents warmed their chilled bones and they thought it had turned warmer. Christmas tree lights twinkled and glowed and all the things Ma and Pa hadn't had were there to speak the messages of Christmas.

And then the phone started ringing and all the families from far away were talking to Ma and Pa and other members of the family and everybody was wishing each other a Merry Christmas and Ma was laughing and crying at the same time and some were telling about snow and catching Ma up on the grandchildren, and one call followed another.

Christmas carols were playing and the wind was up and Pa was beginning to nod. But Ma was all hepped up about talking to the young'uns and Christmas, and she started crying again, saying that she wouldn't even know who her girls were from the way they talked now — like northerners. She wiped her eyes with the corner of her apron and said she didn't know how the young'uns could even think of the way it was when they were little as being like Christmas. There was so near nothing to make it seem like a real Christmas, she said that except for the cooking and feasting and the few dime-store things they could get for the family, it didn't fill children's hearts.

But there are moments in time etched in the memory that linger over a lifetime. And for this family, those Christmases past loomed larger than life and represented a beauty glorified by childhood that outshone all the glitter and decorations on the most eleborate Christmas cards. The humble house along the winding country road that by today's standards would be called a hovel, stood as a castle in the mind, made more magnificent by the love, the sharing and the togetherness of a family.

If Ma could only have known the beauty of those cheap toys in the eyes of a child — the baby dolls, the bright colors of ten-cent tops, the shininess of the little red wagons and tricycles, pocketknives and horns — and the good cooking and the closeness of the occasion, she would have known the true spirit of Christmas more in her old age than she ever knew in those ancient days.

And when Christmas came and the spirit of the season descended on the world, there was reserved in the heart of this family a time more precious in memory than when it was a reality. Each member wanted his or her own family to know that feeling and to feel the joy and see the beauty of it all as it had been. Each only hoped that when their young children could look back upon half a century there would be something there to bring to memory the beauty of Christmases of today to be preserved in their hearts.

Those Christmases were not missing in glitter and glamour. They shone like the star of Bethlehem in the memory. □

Preserve A Part Of Today

I f it's old, it's of value. That is the trend today. For what other reason would crowds flock to flea markets regularly looking for old relics of the past? They are collectors' items today. Most of these items are of little significance except for the fact that they are old and no longer available. They are items that most of us grew up with that had no meaning for us at that time.

Famous restaurants, banking institutions and other places prominently display antiquated farm machinery, old quilts, and even use the exteriors of buildings and some parts of interiors to create a setting of the past. If we oldsters could only have known what the future held, we could have thrown hundreds of small items into a box or an old trunk and capitalized on them half-a-century later.

But for today's generation, let me suggest that you think seriously about the future, for the todays are soon yesterdays and the years pass so swiftly if you are caught up only in the moment, history is being made and you may be leaving behind a part of it you'd like to preserve.

I suggest that every person who has an interest in preserving intimate, minute things in your personal life, start a collection box NOW. Don't wait until tomorrow and don't be unrealistic as to what you want to preserve. Forget the items that would require a lot of space or that would cause problems in keeping. After all, we are thinking about a half a century hence.

Collections could be from any or all members of a family or general household items that have value as keepsakes.

Those insignificant things from the 1930s would be evidence of a life of the past, capable of setting a mood, recalling moments in time, places, events, sounds, smells, thoughts. They would be with you while other treasures of an era were only memories, rotted into nothingness and again a part of the dust of the earth.

If I could go back and have one collector's day in history, I'd take a box and very carefully collect many small items, realizing that I was gathering those things for a world of the future.

The old hatpin with the black bead as adornment that Ma used; the gold (colored) stud that Pa used to attach those stiff collars to his white "Sunday" shirts; the sleeve holder that he used to shorten his sleeves. This was an elastic band worn on the arm.

The contents of one drawer of the old Singer sewing machine; a comb Ma used in her hair; one sock that Ma knitted from tobacco twine; the old snap-open pocketbook Pa carried in his front pocket; one month from a calendar from that period; one Farmer's Almanac; one small catalog of the 1930s;

One edition of the daily paper; the black tin box in the top bureau drawer on the right that Pa kept his papers in (and the papers that were totally without value — no insurance policies, no deeds of land, no stocks, no bonds, no nothing of importance);

One Cloverine Salve container and a color picture that came with the sale of a box of salve; one Rosebud Salve container; one turpentine bottle with the cork stopper intact; one Sloan's Liniment bottle; the shoe last that was used to half-sole our shoes (the kind that worked well on the round of a chair); Ma's wooden butter mold with a fancy flower design; one pair of homemade BVDs; one pair of white overalls made from Smith Douglass fertilizer bags;

A bow tie that my grown-up brothers wore; a pair of men's sock supporters; Pa's old straight razor, the leather strap and the shaving mug; his shaving brush; the hair curlers my sisters used (the kind that were put in the lamp chimney to heat); one buckle from a pair of overalls with the picture of a bird dog (Pointer brand); one pack of Wings cigarettes; one pack of Avalon cigarettes; one Golden Grain tobacco sack; one Prince Albert tobacco can; one Bugler cigarette roller and a pack of Bugler tobacco;

Pa's pocketknife; one of Ma's "horn" hairpins; the old aluminum dipper (the one that got bent up from blowing off the porch so much); one sling shot; one wheel that we rolled; one baseball made from strings that came off of tobacco sticks; one label from a Turkey brand syrup bucket and the labels from Karo and Crown brand syrup buckets;

One hamestring from Zeb and Gray's hitch-up gear; one thermometer that we hung in the tobacco barn while curing to check on the heat; one currycomb and the old coffee grinder in the pantry.

I have searched the old place over foot by foot to collect these items —

rambling through bureau drawers, moving around items in the kitchen, running my hands over the plates of the shelters, walking around the yard, the lot and down the path to the tobacco barns. I wasn't able to come up with any other items I could have preserved.

All of that stuff put together wouldn't be worth a dollar ninety-eight (at that time) but if they were in my possession today they'd be fit for the Smithsonian Institution in my book and I could not place a monetary value on them. Why?

Because they would be tiny bits of my heritage that would in themselves resurrect memories of specific times and places and events in that long walk from so many yesterdays to today. Some would bring laughter, others tears. But they would be tangible reflections on the inconsequential events that in retrospect stand out as the shining hours of my life.

If there is one lesson life teaches, it is that what matters most is not how high the mountain we have climbed or our personal achievements, or our social status. Rather, it is always the little things that touch the heart and place themselves indelibly in the memory. They become a source of sustenance against the present pressures of life.

We are the products of our heritage and our greatest satisfaction comes from recollections of that heritage, usually always with nostalgia and with simpler lifestyles and more fulfilling than those of today.

If you care about the present and wish to preserve a minute part of it, start today. The present will become as antiquated as our past, and it is highly possible that today's generation may become interplanetary travelers of the future. You may need to hold on to the small material things today to keep you within the realm of reality tomorrow.

Don't ever live in the past. Rather, preserve a little part of it. Tomorrow never comes but yesterday is forever. □

Hogs Get Out On Sundays

Ma's up early swishing around in the kitchen, cooking breakfast and preparing dinner before getting ready for church. A young'un is sent to the well to fetch the bucket with the chicken inside that was lowered into the cool water to keep it overnight. The poultry is salted, floured and placed in the big skillet to fry. The taters for "tater salad" are mashed up, onions cut up over the taters, vinegar added, boiled eggs split half in two and the yellw mashed up. But some of the whites are saved to decorate the top. They are sliced off round and placed on top of the bowl in the shape of flowers and a little of the yellow added in the center.

Pa walks down in the fields after breakfast to see how the crops are growing. And the young'uns get to searching for the garb they have to wear to church. It's the same every Sunday, but finding it is the thing.

Finally, about nine o'clock, everything comes together and everybody is in a hustle to get ready for church.

Ma's busy with that old peach-colored corset and all those hooks and eyes and trying to fit it around her plump body. It's a sight to see her holding in her breath and fastening those hooks and it looks like she'll never make it, but finally she has herself "melted down" in it and you thank God you're a boy. And those things look even worse on the clothesline. And big! They're wide and with all the slats in them and the garter belts dangling in the wind, they're a pure monstrosity.

Pa's found his blue serge breeches and the Sunday galluces, but the gold-colored stud to his shirt collar is misplaced and he's going around like a chicken with its head cut off and Ma goes and picks it up on the opposite end of the bureau from where it usually stays and tells him if it had been a snake it would'a bit him. Then she retrieves the white collar from the drawer for him to attach to the shirt.

There's a speck of something on Pa's breeches, besides lint, and he tries spit to get it off but finally resorts to a wet rag. The girls are doing all right with their dressing but the boys, as usual, are snatching at those despicable knickers they have to wear and delay putting them on as long as possible. But they finally manage to don them and those long black ribbed stockings and start tackling those unmanageable cowlicks on their heads when Pa walks to the door to take a peek down the path. Yep, those shoats are running every which a way down in the field and the old sow leading the pack.

The boys are told to go git 'em or they'll eat up folks'es corn and everybody in the neighborhood will be on him for letting them git out. No time to change clothes. Just pull off the shoes and stockings and run 'em back in fast.

So the boys set off with the knickers dangling around their legs (and itching) and let in behind the swine and they try running in the opposite direction and boys are darting in and out of corn rows and jumping over soybean vines and they finally get them headed for the hog pasture. The gate is opened and the hogs are back in, but a search has to be made where they got out and the place stobbed down. So they go and get stove wood, the ax and nails and knock the wood down as far as it will go so that it catches the nail driven near the end of the stob.

But the boys ain't fit to go to church in the shape they're in. Their faces are mottled from sweating and there are black "tater ridges" under their necks and there must be 50,000 of those small weed seeds that latch on to anything that comes along except money, along with a passel of cockleburrs on those knickers. It will take somebody at least an hour to get all that mess off those pants.

This pleases the boys, for it exempts them from church, and they hasten to get out of the knickers and into their overalls. It caught them just right this time so they didn't have time to shed the Sunday clothes and get into work clothing to run the hogs in.

But those piney-woods rooters start the same thing all over again. It's a pure ritual. They run around the wire fence, nudging under the wire to see where there is a weakness. There are already two or three stobs between every post, and they have found about all the weak spots, and undo some that have been stobbed down. They pure squeal sometimes as they congregate at a spot they intend to come through as if they know what they're doing. And hogs ain't even supposed to have any sense.

One of the young'uns can't resist the temptation to "finger" out a piece of chicken from the brown gravy that Ma left in the pan at the back of the stove. Before he even washed his hands! And the other boy threatens to tell Ma and they almost fight, then the guilty one goes to the other, calls him "Shine" to designate brotherliness, puts an arm around his shoulder (that is shrugged off) and tells him that he'll give him his two "steelies" in his marble collection if he will just keep quiet about the hand in the chicken.

There's some thought before the "tattler" decides to take him up on the offer, for "steelies" are hard to come by, seeing as how there ain't many ball bearings rolling around the countryside. So they're real brotherly for a few moments, but the "chicken-dipper" doesn't like the idea of giving up his "steelies" so he runs off a distance and calls the other "tattletale" and they have another long run around and around the house.

Pretty soon the family returns from church and things pick up their normal routine again. And nobody finds out that a nasty hand got into the chicken. But they say what you don't know doesn't hurt you and so it was with the chicken. But that was just one time out of many that the hogs got out, and it seemed like nine-tenths of the time it was on Sunay. And not just the boys, but the whole pack became involved in getting hogs or cows (or something) in. Anything to mess up the quiet of a Sunday long ago.   □

Wanderings Of The Mind

S ometimes at night when all is quiet and sleep won't come, the past returns with a glow brighter than when it was a reality. With all the tragedy, all the hardships, all the trauma of those days erased by time, a shining light appears that illumines those events and transforms the ugly into something of beauty. That is in great part due to viewing life from the eyes of youth. In remembering those days we are seeing them with 20-20 vision rather than with eyes clouded by advancing years.

The mind wanders to a rainy night with a heavy downpour falling on a tin roof and the steady drop of rain on bed linens. The bed is pushed beside another and a bucket placed on the floor to catch the rain. The drops become a symphony as they hit the bucket and occasional lightning lights up the yard and the rumble of distant thunder is heard.

The flimsy curtain is pulled back and lightning reveals a barn door being pushed back and forth from the wind and the top hinge squeaks from the movement of the door that hangs at an angle with the bottom hinge broken.

Or to a dry night when rain frogs croak endlessly in the swamp that has become crusted over with cracks from dry weather. They croak the night away while people sleep but who occasionally awaken and have to pull the slop jar from under the bed to relieve themselves and then return to their slumbers.

Or whippoorwills calling in the wooded area across the road after the sun has faded behind the trees with red clouds illuminating the sky as day ends. At that time between sunset and dark the whippoorwills give their lonely calls.

. . .A neighborhood barber gathering the boys up for their annual "sheepshearing" for summer. A cigar box with a pair of hand clippers with dull blades that sometimes pull rather than cut the hair. A barber's apron made from a flour sack that "holds" the hair rather than letting it slide to the floor. A front porch, a Saturday morning, a straight-back chair with a dishpan placed over the seat to add to the height. Children's heads shorn to the scalp with the white skin of the head accentuating the large ears and the steady buildup of multi-colored hair around the barber's chair.

An accumulation of hair down the back that itches like scabies and gets inside the ears, sticks to the shirts and feels like tiny wires sticking in the skin.

. . .A summer day with early morning fog and dampness hovering near the earth and the sun obscured by the fog. The dampness accentuates the odors of corn silks in fields that almost isolate the old house. Only by looking down the long lane leading to the road can signs of other community life be seen.

. . .The smell of urine strong behind the smokehouse and the lots pungent with their miry accumulation of manure and stale water. The odor of the hog pen permeates the air.

. . .A cow in her stable with a new-born calf still wet from birth and the soft moo from the mother as she licks the wobbly baby dry. The afterbirth still hangs as mute testimony to the birth process.

. . .A Sunday afternoon with a baptizing at the old mill. People gather on the banks and watch the ritual as those being baptized file into the water in a long line and await immersion, causing the lilies to sway from the ripples of the water.

An average-sized preacher with some large members to baptize, requiring an assistant to help bring up the sisters and brothers from the immersion and the gasps from some who get too much water in their mouths during the baptizing and the snickers from bystanders as the stout ones are immersed.

. . .A frosty morning with a sow nursing her just-born babies under a tin-top shelter with pine straw piled high in anticipation of the event. Spotted, white, red, black, a general Duke's mixture of tiny pigs snuggled against the mother's ample udders for future porkers. But scours will get some, others will be mashed by the mother's weight and some survive for the hog killing the next winter.

. . .A heavy cloud when the fury of hell appears to have been released upon the area with lightning flashing and striking trees and buildings and trees almost bending double from the storm. Hail spatters on the ground and the day almost becomes night and scared children find refuge on feather beds that are piled in the closets during the summer months. Others congregate in the halls with all the doors closed but the lightning penetrates the cracks in the doors and thunder sounds as if it will take off the roof of the house.

After the storm water is standing in low places and trenches are dug in the fields to drain off the excess water from crops. Hens with biddies are caught out in the fields foraging for food and some biddies are dead from the drenching while others are alive but beaten down by the rain. They are gathered up and dried off and put in a warm place to dry out, even if a fire has to be built in the kitchen stove.

After the storm children wade in the side ditches along the roads despite warnings that they might get foot itch from the water.

. . .A lonely Sunday afternoon when the little world in which we live looks barren and when the drabness of the setting takes its toll on the human mind. There are times when loneliness sets in and when life seems to hold little for the people; when their plight shows through the exterior veneer. It isn't all peaches and cream.

The wanderings of the mind about insignificant events in a world almost forgotten by time and circumstances.   □

This Is The Way It Was, All Right

(Duke Homestead State Historic Site, Durham)

Golden Grain Was Our Thing In '30s

Dipping, Chewing, Smoking

C ome hell or high water, the women of the 1930s dipped their snuff. They might feel guilty when the preachers preached the sins of tobacco (although the church didn't hesitate to take money from the sale of tobacco), and they might be embarrassed if the pastor caught them with a wad of snuff in their mouths and the telltale signs — a trickle of brown juice down their chins — still they just had to have their snuff.

With so few luxuries in life, they perhaps felt that snuff was the one thing they could enjoy while carrying on their everyday lives.

Salty Galenax, Sweet Lorillard, Tube Rose, Sweet Society, you name it, and they dipped it. And there was a pure art in spitting the juice. If three or four of the older women were spending an afternoon on the porch, they'd load up with snuff and the juice would get to flowing and they'd take the index finger and the middle finger and place them over their lips and spit that juice 10 to 15 feet out in the yard. And if an old chicken ran by at the right time, he'd catch a wad of juice "caddab" on his feathers.

Most of the women used toothbrushes, but not all of them. They'd go up in the woods and find what they called "toothbrush bushes" and pull off a dozen or so of the tiny limbs and take them home, remove the bark an inch or so and chew the wood until it was suitable for a toothbrush. The brush would be dipped into the snuff until it was saturated with the powder, then they'd take the brush into their mouths and turn it over and over to savor all the flavor. I have been told that a toothbrush bush is black gum, or "blaggum" as one reader put its.

Some women chose to take a piece of pasteboard, fold it and fill the mouth from the box, while others just opened their mouths wide, held their heads back and filled a jaw with the brown powder.

Snuff was as much a part of rural life as pipes and roll-your-own cigarettes, as well as chewing tobacco. And dipping snuff became a little more complicated when dipped in the houses. Some women had these dime-store spittoons that didn't turn completely over, but others used tin cans with the top left on them to use as a handle for their spit cups. And the cans were opened with sharp butcher knives, leaving dangerous rough tin that sometimes cut the hands when grasped in the wrong way. And when a little young'un got tangled up with those cans, it was a mess. The kind of mess I mean is a "nasty" mess, for that snuff juice would run out on the floor.

Some women would fill their jaws so full of snuff they looked abscessed. And while it was dry in their mouths they sometimes coughed when the powder went up their noses, and the powder would spurt out of their mouths and they'd start dusting off their clothing. If they tried to speak at such times, their words came out as indistinguishable garble.

And if the women dipped their snuff, the men did their share of chewing and smoking. The corncob pipe had about gone out of style by the time I came along, although some of the real old codgers pulled on them. But that didn't mean that corncobs had no other uses. Wooden pipes were generally smoked by the older men. But cigarettes were the going thing in the early 1930s.

Men were urged to smoke and posters in country stores showed famous movie stars lighting up and the spirals of smoke rising above them. Even women were pictured smoking. And that was almost an unpardonable sin for women to pull on cigarettes in those days.

Of course rural men and boys didn't have the pocket change to purchase a pack of cigarettes daily, so loose tobacco in small sacks with a string at the top to open and close the container was the main source of cigarettes. Oh boy! It was the age of Golden Grain. I'd be willing to bet that 90 percent of men living today who grew up in eastern North Carolina in the Depression era have rolled a Golden Grain at some time in their lives.

The tobacco came with tissue-like paper used to form the cigarette and the paper wasn't gummed either. The paper was held with the thumb and forefinger, the tobacco poured onto the paper, the string to the sack pulled with the teeth and the free hand and the sack returned to the bib of the overalls pocket. If the papers gave out or got wet, brown paper bags were found, cut and used for cigarette papers.

Then the cigarette was rolled and saliva used to hold the paper together with one end pinched up to keep the tobacco from running out. It was lighted with a country match (if it wasn't wet). In summer there was a problem in keeping the matches dry for sweat wet the overalls. Some men kept matches in the exterior narrow band on their straw hats.

Then there was Prince Albert smoking tobacco of about the same consistency of Golden Grain, but a lot of men used that in pipes.

Later on we started using Bugler smoking tobacco and there was a roller that made the tobacco into cigarettes. Bugler was more like the tobacco in the various brands of cigarettes with a string-like texture and it had gummed papers. But if Bugler tobacco was rolled too tight you couldn't draw through it and at best, the cigarette dried out quickly.

I maintain that somewhere in eastern North Carolina a giant monument should have been erected many years ago in honor of Golden Grain tobacco. It should be in an area surrounded by tobacco, cotton and corn, and should bear a replica of a sack of Golden Grain tobacco, maybe standing on one edge with the brand name as well as the sheaf of grain, for it was that low-class tobacco that taught the rural generation of the '30s to really appreciate quality cigarettes.

But on Saturday most of us bought a pack of 10-cent Avalons, and we really thought that was something. It wasn't that we wouldn't have liked Chesterfields or Camels or Lucky Strikes. Rather, it was the fact that they cost 15 or 20 cents a pack if I remember correctly.

When some of the boys would have a pack of cigarettes and the others didn't, there was a little rhyme we used that went like this: Pardon me boy for being so bold, but can I have one of those ready-rolls?

So a pack of Avalons didn't last long and it was right back to Golden Grain again. And that went on for years.

And so we dipped and smoked to our hearts' content in those olden, golden days, never dreaming that we were endangering our health even then, and that habits had been formed that would go with many of us for a lifetime.

I knew one old man that sucked snuff up his nostrils. Picture that when the snuff juice got to flowing.

Snuff and chewing tobacco had a medicinal value also. During cotton-picking time stinging worms would get under cotton leaves and were undetected until a hand came in contact with one. Those stings really burned and whelps welled up instantly. When that happened any picker dipping snuff or chewing tobacco would supply a wad to smear over the wound, and it really worked. Anybody stung by a stinging worm would be happy to git a mouthful of snuff or chewing tobacco on a hand that felt like it was almost paralyzed. □

(From UNC Library Collection)

We Followed The Mules Day After Day

Mules Important In Past

There is no way to disassociate the animal world from our lives on the farm 50 years ago. Animals were as much a part of our everyday lives as the human element. We were dependent upon mules to plow the land that was our source of survival. And chickens were very important as a source of food, as were hogs.

We tried to do a good job by those old mules, for they had to plow every foot of ground we tended. They got regular feedings of corn and hay, and Pa bought bricks of saltpeter to put in their corn troughs.

And when their shoulders were rubbed raw by their collars, we used some kind of black salve (I don't know its name) on them and also made cloth pads to apply over the sores. We really cared about those old mules and it was essential to keep them in shape.

After plowing in the fields for a full day, we'd take their bridles off and sometimes those old mules would go directly to an open place and lie down and wallow in the dirt.

It was a sight to see them moving around and getting themselves saturated in dirt. And they would roll completely over and get dirt everywhere, then rise from the ground and shake their bodies, raising the dust around them. Then we'd take the curry comb and comb them down.

And a pair of young mules was as much a status symbol to some people in those days as a new car is to some people today. A few landlords were especially proud of a new pair of mules and they'd hitch them to a wagon and ride over the neighborhood, catching the eye of the neighbors as they went by. They might be iron grays or blacks with light mouths, or soft browns with black manes and tails. And they were sleek and spirited.

They were also hard to manage. It wasn't unusual to pass a house where there was a young pair of mules and see the owner hanging on to one end of the rope and that rip-snorter of a mule pulling him across the yard. Mules can be stubborn, and when they're young they can present a challenge to the owner. They'd curse sometimes, then plead with the mule to calm down. "Whoa, now" was a familiar phrase during such rituals, and the mule usually gave in and was harnessed. But those young mules were nervous, like some dogs are nervous, and their muscles would quiver and they were alert to every noise.

Neither was it unusual for such a high-spirited team to run away. They might be trotting along at a fairly fast pace, and any noise or other distraction might cause one to jump suddenly, and the other mule would follow suit and they would run totally out of control in any direction and not necessarily along a road. They were oblivious to objects in their path, and often the runaway ended due to the vehicle they were pulling hitting an object and stalling.

I witnessed a tragic accident as a result of runaway mules of the type I have just described. They were fine examples of the mule world and they ran away on the highway after it was paved. There was a large tin sign — maybe eight by 10 feet — along the road where signs are usually positioned. The mules left the highway and hit the sign, dislodging it, and the tin severed one of the mules' feet. It was hanging only by a thread of skin. The owner came and shot the mule on the spot.

But in general, the old mules were docile and could be ridden from the fields when people went to dinner. We could climb up on their backs and save ourselves a mile or more walk to the house.

I grew up with old Zeb and Gray. I don't remember when Pa bought them but they were around as far back as I can remember. Pa must have bought them in more prosperous days, for there certainly wasn't money around to invest in mules in my day. Because we owned our own team, Pa farmed on thirds rather than on halves as sharecroppers farmed. But as far as finances go, we were no better off than they.

Now Zeb and Gray were not a "matched" pair of mules at all. You know Gray's color (sort of light) and Zeb was black and of a slenderer build than Gray. And their personalities were as different as their colors. Zeb was a sort of spirited old rascal but he was usually always easy to manage. But Gray was just plain stubborn. Lots of times when we tried to put the bridle on her she'd sling her head away from us, but would finally come around and accept the bridle. In general, when you go to the stable to bridle a mule it comes up to the door and knows what to expect.

Well sir, about twice a year old Gray would decide that she didn't want any part of work for the day, so she'd turn her head to the back of the stable, leaving those hind legs confronting you if you tried anything. And if we tried getting rough with her she'd lay back those ears and give a kick you wouldn't believe.

The longer this went on the more stubborn old Gray became. She'd finally turn around facing us and start kicking the back of the stable and boards would start flying. She riddled the back of her stable several times during my boyhood. So whatever we had planned for that dumb mule would have to wait for a spell. We'd leave her alone for an hour or two and most of the time she would come up for us to bridle her.

And Gray was literally scared half to death of bridges, and little wonder with the contraptions we called bridges over those lowland ditches. They were no more than hardwood poles lying across the ditch and boards placed over them. They had been nailed down at some time but the boards became shackly and loose.

More than one time Gray would balk at those bridges and we'd have to lash into her to get her to cross. But in quite a few cases we boys landed up in the ditch along with sheets of cotton or hay when Gray would jump across almost and get the wagon off balance.

And even those old mules were rambunctious enough that they'd run away occasionally. Zeb was worse about this than Gray. Old Zeb ran away with me on a tobacco truck one time and when he made the turn from the path into the yard he wrapped me around a "chaney ball" tree, the truck turned bottom upwards and it slowed Zeb down enough that he calmed down. But don't ask me why I didn't get off that empty tobacco truck before I got slung off, for I'll never figure that one out. It seems to me like I had gotten hung up in the plow lines, but I'm not sure about that. It happened a long time ago.

Before there was an old Model T Ford around home, Pa hitched Zeb and Gray to the wagon and drove to town about once a month for supplies. He'd lay a board across the wagon body for a seat. It was an all-day job when he went to town on the wagon. And horseflies would pester them, leaving drops of thick blood where they bit.

Flour, weighed-out coffee and rice, sugar, snuff, and syrup were the usual supplies.

But it was always Pa that had to drive the wagon to town, for even 50 years ago grown-up boys in the family were reluctant to be seen in town on a wagon. And most women chose to stay at home rather than having to sit on the wagon floor with their legs outstretched in order to go to town.

It was a little below the dignity of the young and the women to be seen publicly on wagons except on the farm. This is an indication of the fierce pride of rural Tar Heels of the past.

It wasn't unusual for a woman to ride in a buggy to town in the days when buggies were fashionable but this attitude changed after Model T's became fairly common in the area.

When women really needed to go to town shopping, if they had to ride in wagons, or Hoover carts, many would get off at the edge of town and walk in and return to the wagon when it entered the rural area on the way home.

Mules are considered long-lived animals, but like all other forms of life, they come to their ends also. Sometimes a mule would die in the community, and farmers were not equipped to bury such a large animal, so what did they do?

A trace chain was attached around the dead mule's neck and a pair of mules was hitched to the chain and the dead mule was dragged far up in the woods so the stench would not permeate the community and the body was left there for the buzzards.

It was only a few hours after the body was left in the woods that the buzzards began to circle over the area and this went on until the body was picked clean, leaving a skeleton in the loneliness of the woods for woodcutters and log carts to pass on their way into and out of the woods.   □

Cows Created Problems

I look back upon those old milk cows that plagued our childhood and wonder whether it was worth it to have them around, especially since we were not really a milk-oriented family.

Not a one of us drank milk. Pa said it tasted like a cow smelled, and Ma and her people never had a taste for dairy products and, as a matter of fact wouldn't eat beef. But some of my crowd did like butter (but not all of 'em) and all of us liked buttermilk biscuits.

Of course when Grandma (Ma's mother) came Ma had to make water biscuits for her. I could never figure out how anybody could like biscuits made with water better than those made with buttermilk or clabber. The water biscuits were pale and harder when they were cooked than those made with milk.

It seems to me that we'd have come out a lot better buying buttermilk and butter from neighbors who had surpluses rather than keeping a cow around all the time. We could have sold eggs to buy the milk. In the first place, it wasn't a year-round thing for old Daisy dried up sometimes and there was an interval of months when we didn't have milk anyway.

In the second place, we didn't have first-class dairy feed to give to the cows in the winter months. They fared good when there was plenty of grass in the spring and until dry weather struck in summer. The cottonseed meal that we got when the cotton was ginned didn't last but a few months, and with hay and shucks as their winter diets, milk production was cut drastically.

So we'd have to mess with old Daisy for months with no milk as a reward and we just had to wait until the next "freshening." And we called all our cows "Daisy."

But, as is the case with children, we had no choice, so we had to put up with Daisy, like it or not. And my brother and I were delegated the chore of milking the cow. He'd milk one day and me the next, and he could run rings around me in milking a cow.

I'm double-jointed or something, for when I close my hands tightly my knuckles crack, and every time I pressed on the cow's teats there was that cracking noise and my hands would get tired. Neither could I get the big stream of milk that my brother could. When he'd milk foam would be two inches thick at the top of the bucket, but when I milked there were only a few bubbles at the top.

But that was the easy part of milking when the cow had a young calf. I'll bet that pound-for-pound, a calf is stronger than a baby elephant. And we'd have to turn that calf out so it could nurse the cow until she let her milk down. And you never saw anything any more rambunctious than those little rascals after those teats.

Now some of those old cows were kickers so we had to build a contraption in order to control the cow while milking. It was a frame wide enough to accommodate the bovine and long enough for her body to fit into.

At the back of the frame we could slip a round pole between the cow's hind legs after we positioned her for milking. We always milked from the right side, and we could place the milk pail under the cow. With the pole between her legs there was no way she could raise that right leg.

If we tried to milk those kickers without resorting to our "contraption," we'd sometimes find an old cow's hoof in the milk pail, and that milking was lost.

And cows always have cockleburrs in their tails (year-round) and whenever you milk them they swish those tails and your face is a prime target. Try a burr-filled cow's tail for a facial on a cold morning (or a hot one for that matter).

Once the cow let her milk down, that calf was nursing a mile a minute and gobbling down that milk. I'd grab him by his ears and pull him away and he'd jump like a jackrabbit and sling me around, stomping my feet all the while. He'd "baah" and the old cow would let out a low "moo" and I'd have a heck of a time getting that calf back in the stable.

In other words, it was a mess keeping dairy products before we had ways to refrigerate the mik and butter. Some people had milk safes in the yard under shade trees and pans of milk were placed there for the cream to rise. But after the cream was skimmed from the top of the milk, both the cream and the milk had to be poured into jars and heavy string tied around the jars and they were lowered into the cool well water. Foods would stay fresh overnight in the water. The cream was placed in the earthen churn with a wooden paddle and set on the hearth until churning.

Not only was milk placed in the well, but other perishables as well. If fryers were dressed on Saturday for Sunday dinner they were kept in the well overnight.

Sanitation was also a big problem with milk. In the late 1920s and early '30s a great number of rural houses had no screen doors or window screens, so it is easy to see how flies would swarm by the thousand around food items. Flies were our greatest plague in those days.

Looking backward, I know that we'd have been better off without the succession of "Daisies" that I grew up with, but what the heck. I'm no worse off by the experience and it was just a part of learning about life.

As to beef, we got that only in the fall of the year and that was when someone would kill a yearling and peddle it through the neighborhood. They'd have the meat cut up and wrapped in white sheets or tablecloths and it was displayed in the back of Model T's, and later Model A Fords.

Many people today can recall those bloodstained sheets when the beef man came around. He'd lay the cover back to show a tempting variety of the red meat — large round steaks and squares of stew beef and large hunks of pure lean meat and piles of tallow and fat.

The whole beef process was different in those days, in eastern North Carolina at least. T-bone, porterhouse or ribeye steaks were unheard of out in the sticks.

I was over 21 years old before I even knew there was any kind of steak except round, and it was always tenderized with the edge of a saucer — beaten on both sides — salted, floured and fried in lard until brown, excess grease poured off and flour added and browned and water added to make the gravy and the steak placed back in the pan with the gravy with onions added sometimes.

We had never heard of outside grills to cook on and charcoal was a commodity we were not familiar with. Where cooking with coals was concerned, it was always with oak wood, except that when meat was smoked in the smokehouse, hickory was the choice wood.

And since we were a pack of nuts about milk and butter and beef, we never had stew beef the way it is prepared today.

Ma would buy hunks of that pure lean meat, chop it up and boil it until it was tender — real tender — and shred it, add (lard) for seasoning, with just enough gravy to cover the meat and sage added. Try that one sometime. It's good!

And cows learned to jump over fences just as hogs rooted under them. And we fashioned yokes from hardwood limbs and placed them around the cows' necks, hoping the protruding parts would catch in the meshes of wire and hold them in.

Sometimes the yokes worked, but not always. So the old cows would occasionally sail over the fences and go directly to whatever was green nearby, and we had to hurry, for they could do a lot of damage in a little while.

We'd turn them back toward the fence and they'd head off running with the wooden yoke dangling from side to side until we finally got them back in the pasture. But once a "jumper," we knew they'd do it again.   □

Zack Coor Remembered

Every community has that very special person like Zack. And in my reflections on life in eastern North Carolina half-a-century ago, I am not in general calling any names or designating any particular area. But I know that if Zack were around today he would be happy for me to mention him as one of the memories of those days.

Zack was very special. Now he didn't have quite all his buttons, and he was a roamer. He had a radius of 15 or 20 miles that he traveled, stopping at practically every house for a meal if nothing else. But most of the time he was willing to go out to the woodpile and split wood, get up piles of trash or help feed up. And it wasn't that Zack didn't have any place to go.

Zack was the son of Puss. They were Zack Coor and Puss Coor. But Zack didn't have the inclination to sit around home, and he chose haylofts or piles of cotton under shelters or on porches or tobacco barn shelters for a sleeping place. After a good night's sleep, he would emerge with bits of hay or cotton in his kinky hair, and he always wore a tattered old hat and he went barefoot long after the weather became cool and resorted to shoes only when the frosts came. His feet must have been as tough as leather, for he walked anywhere without harming those feet.

Zack surely never brushed his teeth during his lifetime, and they showed the effects of neglect, especially since he smiled a lot and carried on wherever he was (and chewed tobacco too). He was a teaser and a jokester. He was one of the ageless people. He was perhaps in his 30s during the 1930s, but he was thought of as a youth, really. Nobody knew Zack's age.

Now if you wanted to know what was happening in the community, the real low-down, Zack could give it to you. As I have said, he visited every home, knew all the people and their habits, and got a close-up look at their personal lives.

Zack knew all the gossip, and if everything wasn't just right, he was the first person to become aware of it and when people heard gossip that had no supporting evidence, they would hope for a visit from Zack. If a man and wife were having trouble, they'd better keep it from Zack's ears, or it spread over the community like a contagious disease.

If a man had a whisky still back up in the woods, he'd better be darn sure Zack didn't find out about it. If somebody was running around, look out for Zack to break the news. If an unmarried girl became pregnant, Zack always got word of it and it was public knowledge before the evidence showed for itself.

But Zack didn't just come right out and tell all these things. He had to be coaxed into giving all the information that he kept in his head during his roamings. A little pocket change would help sometimes when somebody wanted to get a juicy bit of information out of Zack.

It is strange how the memory can paint a picture so vividly it is as if the image from so long ago could be as clear as a cloudless day. I get that image of Zack as I recall trivial incidents across the expanse of years.

Zack was honest. He didn't drink and he didn't smoke. He didn't curse. Women were not afraid of him. If he came to the door when the men were away, he was treated the same as if they had been around. He would chat with them and tell of a few recent events in the area. He would draw in his breath deeply and comment on how good something smelled cooking, knowing that he would be an invited guest when the meal was ready.

Zack Coor was a simple man with no real philosophy of life, but a full participant in all that it had to offer. But beyond his simplicity, he was far more intelligent than he was given credit for. His secret to survival was that he loved people. He was unique.

But Zack offers a good example of how times have changed in the past 50 years. It could not be that way today, and he wouldn't be free to roam the community. Those were the days when barns were unlocked and the smokehouse was about the only building that was ever locked. Not even the dwellings were locked in those days. There was a certain amount of stealing then, but on a much smaller scale than today. It was a freer society and women were not afraid to walk the roads at night.

It is better that Zack lived his life in another era, for he would never have been happy with a life of restricted freedom. He would no doubt be victimized by society today if it were possible for him to roam the back roads and the highways in the present generation. His life would be in danger every moment, and there would be no place for him to lay his head after a day of wandering, for all the buildings of value are put under lock and key and roamers are looked upon with suspicion.

Yes, Zack would be proud to know that he is remembered in history and it would be a special honor for him if he could know that he has outlived his time in memory. But his life poses a question for our present society. We have come so very far since those days there is no way to compare the two worlds. We have seen most of the great events that have occurred throughout world history since the 1930s. We who are the products of that age can look back upon it all and only we can know exactly how far we have come.

We have gained most of the material things that we didn't even think about in that age, and nobody would want to revert back to the way of life we knew then. But have we really come so far when we have lost many of our former values? When we can no longer walk the pathways that we remember as children with total freedom and with no fear of tomorrow? Life was ours. The future was ours. There was no fear of manmade weapons that could destroy our entire world. We did have the promise of tomorrow and we were happy in that knowledge. We can't say that today. It isn't the same world. It is well that Zack lived out his lifespan in a simpler era. □

Rabbit Boxes And School

A boy rises early on a cold morning to make the rounds to his rabbit boxes. He runs to the kitchen where his mother already has a fire going and sausage frying, carrying his brogans in his hands. A chair is pulled out from the side table and he slips the shoes on, then places a foot on the chair to tie the strings, then the other. His mother pats him on the head and smiles and he gives her a quick hug and opens the door.

Outside, it is still dark and the stars hang low in the skies. A chill runs down his spine from the slight wind. But there are signs of dawn in the eastern skies.

As the sun comes over the horizon, he is greeted by a white frost that almost appears as snow. Corn and cotton stalks are covered with frost and even debris on the ground is a mass of white.

As he approaches the area where broom sage grows thick, the grass sparkles as the sun's rays play on the tiny specks of ice. It's a good morning to find rabbits in the boxes. Two rabbits from six boxes isn't bad, and he'll have to whet his pocketknife after he gets home from school, give those old bunnies a tap on the back of the head and dress them for smothered rabbit and gravy later on. He'll slit the hide around their feet, those hides will be pulled off up to the head and then the head cut off, the entrails removed and the meat taken to the kitchen where Ma knows just how to prepare the animals for a rabbit feast.

At the house, the other children are preparing for the school day. It means an early start for there is a 2½-mile walk to the six-room schoolhouse. Fingers and toes get cold on a frosty morning and mittens and gloves come in good. Leaving home around 7 o'clock in the morning isn't easy on small children. But first-graders are perhaps the most eager group of schoolchildren.

Once at the schoolhouse, there are the readers for the small fry — Baby Ray, The Little Red Hen, The Hiawatha Primer, and drawings on the blackboard. Was it Baby Ray that had all the first-grade poems in it? Or was Baby Ray a story rather than a book?

— — —

Hi diddle diddle, the cat and the fiddle, the cow jumped over the moon
The little dog laughed to see such sport and the dish ran away with the spoon.

— — —

Ba, ba, black sheep, have you any wool? Yes sir, yes sir, three bags full.
One for the master, one for the dame, one for the little boy that lives down the lane.

— — —

Humpty Dumpty sat on a wall, Hampty Dumpty had a great fall.
All the King's horses and all the king's men, can't put Humpty Dumpty together again.

— — —

There was an old woman who lived in a shoe. She had so many children she didn't know what to do.
She gave them some broth without any bread, and spanking them soundly, put them to bed.

— — —

Little Boy Blue come blow your horn, the sheep's in the meadow and the cow's in the corn.
Where's the little boy that looks after the sheep? Under the haystack, fast asleep.

— — —

Mary had a little lamb, it's fleece was white as snow.
And everywhere that Mary went the lamb was sure to go.
It followed her to school one day which was against the rule.
It made the children laugh and shout to see the lamb at school.

— — —

Maybe a wrong word here and there. So what? Most of the rhymes are intact after 58 years.

In the third or fourth grade I remember a book entitled "Merry Animal Tales" that fascinated me. And there was a weird reading book that I associate with the name "Medusa." I remember there was one story about three sisters that shared one eye and it would be passed from one to another.

Anybody remember that one? Another good book was "Hans Brinker and the Silver Skates."

The largest book we used in grade school was geography. That was wide and longer than the others, and not as thick. There was the thin, smaller spelling book, the arithmetic book, and history.

Along about the third grade they started teaching writing exercises to us. On that rough, lined paper we would make slanted lines in rapid order across the page between the lines without picking up the pencil. And next there would be a continuous circle of O's, then reverting back to the slanted lines. But that was a valuable exercise.

And there were the spitballs on the high ceilings after we got to about the fourth grade.

Anybody else eat parched meal in class? We used to take plenty of that to school in old snuff boxes. And parched meal ain't bad. It's cooked to a golden brown in a heavy frying pan with salt added. But if you get that stuff down your windpipe you'll almost cough yourself to death for it's a dry powder when you put it in the mouth. The teacher always takes that away from us if she catches us eating it in class.

There is the pump where we get our drinking water, and the little collapsible aluminum cups that we use for drinking. Every student is supposed to have his individual cup, but you know how it is. Some of us never had one, so we take a sheet of paper, fold it like you make a dunce's cap to sit on the head, and catch water from the pump in it and use it as a cup.

In the sixth grade we get to go to the 'sylum over at Goldsboro on a Friday. That night they have their weekly dances. The teachers get somebody with a big-bodied truck to take us and one good time is had by all. (The only name we knew for what is now Cherry Hospital and O'Berry Center was the 'sylum, without the "A" pronunciation. And only black people were patients there. And we always referred to them as "crazy" people). And in the seventh grade we get to go all the way to Raleigh to "Dix Hill" and see the "crazy" people there.

We are taken through the entire institution, into some patients' rooms, on down to the kitchen where bread is baking and it makes us so hungry our mouths water. We see the large cooking utensils, and before long it's time for the dance. The dance is held at the 'sylum at Goldsboro.

Diked out in their Sunday best, the patients who have been good that week are allowed to attend the dance and boy, can they ever dance! It is exciting and interesting, and we get to ride in the back of the truck all the way home!

We also get to go to the museum in Raleigh, and the governor's mansion.

There is the large pile of coal at the back of the schoolhouse over which we run and play during recess. And there is a lot more. But it's about time for school to turn out and there are rabbits to dress and feeding up to do after the school day is over.

Iced Tea Habit Formed

S ometime in the late 1920s or early '30s the drinking habits of "tobacco country" Tar Heels changed drastically. Somebody introduced iced tea to we farmers, and we latched on to it like Maggie latched on to Jiggs. It has never been the same since.

I don't know where those tea leaves had been all that time before we learned about them, and maybe the higher echelon of local society (in town) was indulging long before then, but tea just hadn't been our thing.

And at first some people claimed it tasted like Black Draught, the purgative. But it didn't take long for most of us to change our minds. It caught on like wildfire and became a staple in all the homes.

Before iced tea, we drank coffee (if what we drank could be called real coffee), during all the seasons except summer, and then we drank plain water with our meals. But once we got the taste of sweet tea, and cold at that, we'd fight for it at dinner time. We hadn't been used to beverages that were sweet and cooled us off too.

But let's back up and go into a little more detail about coffee. At my house we didn't buy a brand of coffee. Pa bought it at the supply store in town and it was weighed out from a barrel, and it must have been at least one-fourth chicory. And there weren't percolators in my neck of the woods then. Coffee pots had enamel finishes and were made larger at the bottom than the top.

And coffee grounds weren't dumped every day, at least at our house. More coffee would be added to the grounds already in the pot until the pot finally had to be dumped.

Children drank coffee just as the grown-ups did, and we thought saucers were made to drink from, so we'd pour the hot, weak coffee from the cup to the saucer, hold our heads down to the table, blow and then suck the liquid into our mouths. We sounded like some form of suction system at work with all the noise we made.

When the coffee was real weak and a light brown color it was called "taplash," but I haven't the faintest idea where that one came from. I did see black coffee at some people's houses, although I never knew anyone who used milk or cream in their coffee in those days. And even back there I remember seeing Luzianne cans at some places.

But tea changed coffee drinking to a certain extent. And tea called for preparations each day, for a child had to go to the store for ice. This was before refrigerators, remember.

That daily ritual to the store was delegated to any child old enough to be trusted on the road, and if all the children were at work in the fields, one would leave about 45 minutes early to get the ice.

Stores were only able to supply ice after the ice and coal companies in town started furnishing boxes to the local merchants and delivered ice daily. Several blocks were consumed in the neighborhood every day.

It was usually a boy that made the daily trek for ice, and some had to walk a mile or more to the nearest store. Occasionally a girl had to go for ice too. And once in a great while, when the mules weren't busy plowing the fields, a boy got to ride on a tobacco truck to get the ice.

So about a quarter past eleven each day, a child would set out for the store with eggs in a paper bag and an ice sack, usually made from a salt sack.

There was the same admonition each day: "Don't drop them eggs and watch what you're doing. And don't be messing around and killing time along the road or the ice will melt and there won't be enough for dinner.

"Don't be sitting that bag of ice on the ground or you'll git dirt all over the sack. And put on your straw hat. You're brown enough already and the sun's too hot to go bareheaded.

"And hurry now, for dinner will be on the table when you git back. And be careful with them eggs."

What would we have done without hen fruit in those days?

But despite all the admonitions, a child can easily become distracted by other things, and it was the same with the ice-toters. Sometimes they would stop along the road, break dog fennels or speak to other children in the yards along the way, sometimes switching the eggs from one hand to the other and having them drop on the ground occasionally. If they were nearer the store than home, they'd tell the storekeeper the eggs got broken and they would bring others the next day.

Sometimes a toe would get stumped along the road, the ice would slide from the sack onto the dirt, the child would nurse a bloody toe and the ice would start melting and wet a place on the dirt road. But the ice would be retrieved and the journey resumed until the precious parcel was home at last.

There was no use of complaining then, so the ice, getting smaller in size by the moment, was washed and beaten, either by a wooden mallet supplied by the ice man, or the ax or hammer.

Men fresh from the fields would swill down a full glass of tea sometimes without even taking the glass from their lips.

After filling up on vegetables and tea, everyone would retreat to the front porch, some with quilts to roll up and use as pillows, and stretch out full length on the floor. They would usually take a newspaper to fight off the flies during the short siesta.

Some would get a good nap during the dinner hour, even snoring sometimes, and those who didn't want to bother with a newspaper in fighting the flies would place their straw hats over their faces while snoozing.

But the neighborhood bell rang religiously about a quarter past one every day, breaking the reverie, and the field hands rose from the floor, stretched, and those doing the plowing bridled the mules and returned to the fields as did those who were chopping or engaged in other chores.

We drank tea on through the fall, but when winter returned we began sipping that "taplash" with our meals again. But remember this was just before soft drinks and moon pies took the country by storm.

Once the ice boxes were filled with a variety of soft drinks covered in chips of ice, we swilled them to our hearts' content (if we could get a nickel to buy one). And if we had a dime we'd often buy a bag of "ground peas" and pour them into the drink and eat them as we drank the beverage.

Let nobody say we farmers didn't drink our share of "belly-washers" as we called them then, and most of us still have the habit. But it was iced tea that changed our drinking habits and it's equally as popular today.   □

'Run-Away' Marriages

A lot of couples used to "run away" and get married. That was partly due to class distinction, even in the 1930s. In most cases, but not always, a landowner whose daughter fell in love with a tenant on the farm, or a sharecropper on somebody else's farm, refused to let her associate with the lowly boy. And that caused problems. And a few times it was the higher-up boy and the lower-class girl.

Although circumstances were different then than today, romance was the same and there were the same emotions that young lovers experience in all societies.

Sometimes a certain boy was never allowed to visit a girl in the home. So any meeting between boy and girl had to be on the sly. They'd pick their chances and meet at somebody else's house or when the "old man" was gone for the day. What the "old man" apparently didn't know was that love will find a way, despite all opposition.

And girls from such families usually led a little more sheltered lives than the average, although I don't know how they could have been more strict on them than most parents of that era were. Those girls had better wardrobes also, with many more dresses and other wearing apparel than the average girl. So there was a certain distinction between people even during the time when nobody had any money to speak of.

It used to create great excitement among the community when a boy and girl eloped. Of course we never used that word, and it was always "ran away." Everybody wanted to know the details about how the girl escaped and what she was able to take with her. Sometimes she was able to sneak out a suitcase with a supply of clothing. But at other times she would have to leave with nothing but what she was wearing. She usually left in the night after the "old folks" had retired. Sometimes the lovers "ran away" from school.

Somebody would be waiting in a Model T or a Model A Ford to transport them all the way to Dillon, South Carolina where they could get married in a few minutes. And they always felt home-free once they had crossed the North Carolina border into South Carolina. And in those days Dillon was considered a long way from eastern N.C. Nobody from my area ever "ran away" to Virginia.

So the newly married couple would settle down with the boy's parents temporarily, and all hell would be to pay in the home of the girl's parents. They'd rant and rave and swear their daughter would never darken their door again. She would never get her clothes or anything else she owned. She would be left out of the will and the "tramp" she married would never be worth his salt and the daughter would live a life of drudgery.

The parents of the girl would often become angry with the boy's parents and wouldn't speak to them and family feuds might go on for years sometimes.

In a lot of cases, time took care of the situation and the girl's mother would eventually persuade her husband to allow the daughter to return home, although the girl's husband might still be forbidden to visit. But time usually took care of the situation and eventually the son-in-law was accepted as a member of the family, if reluctantly. And by the time the babies started arriving, things were back to normal. But sometimes there was never a reconciliation.

Of course the community always sided with the tenant boy rather than with the father of the more affluent girl. And sometimes to the surprise of the father-in-law, the "tramp" might become an enterprising businessman in later years and gain his full respect.

Boys and girls of their own level fell in love, married and raised families without the hullabaloo created by the more affluent girl and the poorer tenant boy, or vice versa.

It was as it has always been, but in a different setting. The moon was just as bright then, the stars even more brilliant in a pollution-free atmosphere, the magic of love just as enchanting. A country road could be a walkway to heaven, an old pond with a moon shining down and lilies swaying in a gentle breeze could provide as romantic a setting as Lake Louise.

Weddings were simple affairs in those days, and I never remember a church wedding in our neighborhood during my youth. The couple was usually married in the "front room" of the girl's parents and only close family members attended. There were no wedding gowns as such, no floral decorations, no burning tapers, no singing, and few rings out in the sticks. Many couples were married during that era with no sign of engagement or wedding rings, although most of them did get rings in later years when circumstances changed and money was available for such items.

It was a realistic society in those days, and people simply made do with what they had, for there was no other alternative. If they had thrown up their hands and given up, the situation would have been hopeless. But nobody ever said anything about giving up.

So the boys and girls of that era married and settled down to housekeeping, in a tenant house and if the boy had been able to save anything when the crops were sold, there was a new small wardrobe, a new bedstead, mattress and springs, several yellow pine straight-backed chairs, one small rocking chair with no arms, a linoleum rug for the "front room" and kitchen floors, a small cast iron cookstove with no reservoir, sitting on legs four or five inches from the floor, a homemade "eating" table and a smaller side table.

But the greatest prize of all was a new kitchen cabinet, usually in white or green, that had a wood sliding door for closing the cabinet, plus a flour bin-sifter combination and shelves for storing other kitchen items.

With the mamas and papas supplying quilts and a few chickens for eggs, it wasn't too difficult to set up housekeeping in those days. And a lot of the furniture they started off with was retained for many years, and some of it is still in use today.

Boys No Saints In 1930s

When I am writing about events of 50 years ago or more, I am reflecting back on what we senior citizens of today were like when we were children or young adults, and our children and grandchildren can get a close-up look at us as we were in those days. And buddy, we were far from saints! Ain't nothing we wouldn't have done if we'd had the chance, and I might as well tell it like it is. We were held back, but it was due to the bounds of society and hard economic times. This refers to the men in general.

I'm thinking about the country stores again, and all the mess we got into as a result of habitating the joints. You see, the store was the congregating place, the place where the ideas originated. We loved those country stores like Karo loves syrup.

First, we loved the stores for all the goodies that were there. After we got on to Pepsi and RC Cola, we just loved that carbonated taste, and it was pure pleasure to burp and let the gas from the beverage go up our nostrils. Oh, we'd shake those bottles and turn them loose and the foam would go everywhere, but we were swilling it down as fast as we could. And it seems like there was a lot more carbonation to the beverages then.

We tried them all, the big oranges and the strawberries and the chocolate flavors and the root beers along with 10-cent Power Houses that weighed a fourth of a pound; same size Baby Ruths for the same price, Mary Janes in clusters of three for a penny; Bit 'O Honeys, you name it, and we tried it (whenever we had the pocket change).

But we went a lot further than that. When we scallawags got about 17 or 18, a lot of the boys decided to go whole-hog and get stumphole whisky just to show we were men. Saturday nights would see a drove of "hicks" traipsing up and down the roads with two or three fifths of that mess, hollering and yipping and pretending to be painting the countryside red with all manner of crazy fool things.

As you know, some of the things we thought up (and did) will never make a column in a newspaper. It's just that way and that's all there is to it.

But picture us, if you will, walking along the highway that had been paved by then, and along comes someone on an old car and stops for a load of the riffraff. Everybody that can piles in and we head for town. Everybody takes a snort from the bottles and pulls the shoes off and sticks the feet out the rolled-down windows. Those felt hats are turned up at the front and man, we're on our way!

Some of the crowd is as high as a kite and they're laughing and giggling and carrying on in a way you wouldn't believe. We're going to town to hunt for girls! But it's pathetic how few we ever found on such expeditions. It's a wonder the police didn't pick up every one of us, especially in the neighborhoods we habitated in town.

By the time we got back to the store, some of the crowd were plain drunk and pure walleyed. Everybody would stay at the store until they sobered up enough to stagger home and slip in so the old folks wouldn't know what they'd been up to.

Every once in a while we'd decide to do something really mean, and we'd do that right too. Somebody would catch a cat and take a paper sack and saturate it in kerosene and tie it around the cat's tail and set it afire. Anybody meaner than that today? That cat would run off at 90 miles an hour and meowing like you wouldn't believe. But that ain't no worse than taking a bunch of kittens and putting them in a tow sack and dumping them in a creek to git rid of them. Some grown folks did that.

If we got real rambunctious we'd go where cows were pastured and get one by the tail and run it all over that pasture on a moonlit night.

We'd play cards — poker or black jack or setback — and bet a nickel a game if we had any money, or for fun if everybody was broke. And yes, there were dirty jokes by the hundreds then, and every one was told at the country stores.

On Wednesday nights some of the boys went to see their girls, so there weren't as many youths around the stores on that night. And the older generation didn't usually habitate the stores on Saturday nights, when the young crowd got good and drunk. But anybody that took the booze made sure that his "old man" wasn't at the store. Lord have mercy! It would have been a calamity for the "old man" to see his boy in such a shape. And for some strange reason, nobody tattled on those rip-snorters in those days.

We learned the facts of life just by being out in the country, not from the birds and the bees, but from the hogs, cows, dogs, chickens, geese, turkeys, and all the animal world that was a big part of our existence. It was at the country stores that we learned the "fine" details. Country stores were a part of our "basic" education in those days, and not all of it was learned in the proper way. But you didn't get any counseling at home. That's for sure.

I reckon the old folks in my time never really learned all that went on at those stores a long time ago, 'specially the womenfolks. Most of the men knew, but they weren't going home and tell all that mess to the old lady. That would have been their ruination as well as the boys. They enjoyed a lot of that mess that went on as well as the boys and they weren't about to give it up.

But come to think of it, the country stores didn't have all that bad an impact on our lives in the long run. It was merely youth's fling and something they had to get out of their system. Some tried the rough style and decided it wasn't for them. Others didn't do so well in life, but in most cases it wasn't due to the influence of the store. They say youth always has its fling, and so it was in the '30s as well as in any other generation.

But if anybody thinks their pappies and grandpappies were cloaked in purity, in most cases, they can think again. There are exceptions, of course, but the generation of those days was the average of any generation, and as mean as hell.   □

Unwed Mothers Scorned

T his story is given as an example to stress my points on unwed mothers of half-a-century ago. I know of no such actual case, although similar situations did occur. This story is used to indicate the almost paranoid views of the general public concerning unwed mothers in those days.

So, walk with me on a balmy night to a small body of water surrounded by trees and bushes that grow in swampy places. Observe the tranquility of the scene with stars reflecting in the movement of the water and the croak of frogs on the edges of the pond. Everything is quiet and peaceful and it is a secluded world.

Two people are there — a young man and a young woman — and all the necessary ingredients for romance. The young woman has slipped away to be with the man of her dreams against her better judgment. She has been warned by her parents to steer clear of such situations. But love is such an overriding factor it sometimes takes precedence over caution and nothing tugs at the heartstrings more than love between a man and woman.

She is very young, pretty, and a nice girl. He is from a respected family and has a good reputation in a nearby community. He is handsome and she is filled with love for him and he pretends to be as sincere as she. They embrace and one thing leads to another and soon they have gone beyond the bounds of propriety. She is tearful and he is consoling.

But he persuades her to meet him at their rendezvous several more times and she is always tearful and remorseful afterward. She suggests that they marry, and he promises that they will go to the altar eventually. But that day never comes. Men wanted to sow their wild seed, but wanted their brides to be "lily white."

She is pregnant, and her world falls apart. She has no one to turn to, not even her own sisters or her parents, for none of them would understand. She is desperate for the man she loves to do the honorable thing and marry her. But he doesn't come by anymore. She will disgrace a family and hell and damnation will be the sermon she will receive from church, family and friends.

She wants to run away from it all, to go some place where she will never be known and where there might be a hope of beginning life all over. But there is no place to go. There are places that take in unwed mothers, but she knows nothing of the procedures to get into those places. Her plight will become known soon.

When it is finally evident that she is pregnant, there is hell to pay in the household. She is threatened with being strung up and whipped with a rope.

She is called a "hussy" and "bastard" is thrown at her daily. Every member of the household looks upon her with scorn, and only the prevailing love of a mother saves her from even worse treatment.

Everyone looks at her with their spectacles at the ends of their noses, even to the preacher. She is told that the wages of sin is death, and that she has to pay for her mistake, as if she didn't already know. Nobody looks at her the same anymore. She is a marked woman, and nobody is more aware than she that she has erred from the prescribed rules of society. But wasn't there anywhere in the rules that allowed for a second chance?

Under such circumstances there were shotgun weddings sometimes and the guilty man was occasionally brought to trial, but in most cases the woman had her baby and continued living with the family while the man went free. And nobody thought very much about the man's role in creation. After all, it was "natural" with him.

Another new life comes into the world with all the strikes against it in the beginning, although most overcome those strikes and make their marks in the world. In time the new life is accepted into the home and a young mother does more than her share because of her mistake. She never regains the status she held before she erred from the straight-and-narrow. She is always reminded of that misstep.

Such women are turned out of some churches and have no recourse for guidance from the pulpit. In no other area are Christians of the era so unforgiving. The taint of such a woman on a community is so great every member of a family is affected. It lessens prestige. It makes a good family cheap in the eyes of the holier-than-thou citizens. But one thing is for sure: It sometimes happens to those who cast the first stone.

Neither the church, the critics nor the family study the lesson of love and understanding taught in the Bible. If they only stopped to consider that love and forgiveness is the answer to the problems of mankind, lives could be made more livable with richer fulfillment for everyone involved. But we are taught to fear God rather than love Him. The way we are taught He is up there to mete out punishment rather than truly loving all human beings. We must not deviate from that path if we want to reach heaven when we die.

It was a strait-laced society in which we lived half-a-century and more ago. That was in part because of ignorance and moral values that the public placed upon itself. And moral values differed then, from the tobacco patches of North Carolina to Times Square in New York.

And there is still no basis for condoning "free love" as it is known today, but times have changed to the extent that participants are open in their lifestyles and most couldn't care less what the church, the public or families think. This is as extreme as it was 50 years ago, but at least people don't have to face life with blemishes so great they can't be erased.

One of the worst things I can say about our society 50 years ago was the way unwed mothers were treated. In looking backward upon those days, it leaves a feeling of shame for the public to have been so "pure" as to have ignored so great a lesson for mankind — real love for our fellowman — that overcomes all obstacles. None of us from that era can be proud of our record on unwed mothers.   □

Those Packhouse Dances

A nybody that ain't been to a square dance at a packhouse out in the country has missed one of the great joys of being young. Man, we used to have those old buildings shaking when 15 or 20 couples were out there promenading and skipping over the floor. Sometimes it seemed like the plank floor would fall in.

But there was more to it than just having a dance. It had to be at the right time of year. They were usually held in the spring before the weather became hot. It would have been unbearable in a packhouse during the heat of summer. And tobacco was packed down there after it was cured. By the time all the tobacco was graded and sold, cold weather was setting in.

But there were other considerations also. Many girls had to start talking the dance a week or so before it was held. They'd mention something to the old folks about a dance being at "so-and-so's" house, knowing just what to expect.

"No sirree, you ain't going to no such place," was the "old man's" first comment. And the "old lady" would put in her two-cents worth. "Them places ain't nothing but the devil's work. Suppose the Lord would come and catch you at any such place. We try to raise you right, and you turn around and try to tear down all the things we teach you."

"Forgit it," the "old man" says. "I don't want to hear no more about it."

All this is expected, and the girls just leave things as they are. But they are persistent, and at the table or on the front porch, the subject is brought up again. "Miss Alice is letting her girls go to the dance," one girl will say to her sister, knowing the old folks are listening with their ears wide open. And the other girl will add, "and Miss Sadie too."

"I don't care who is going," the old man says. "You girls ain't going to go to no such place."

Nothing else is said for a day or two, but a girl that has been given permission from her parents to attend the dance comes by and chats with the sisters. That may have been prearranged, for all I know. The girl asks whether the sisters are also going, and there is a quick reply, "No, Ma and Pa say it's sinful and no place for a nice girl."

"I didn't say that," the "old lady" replies, knowing that if the girl told her parents they would think hard of her for implying their girl wasn't nice. "I said it was a place of the devil."

"Ma and Pa just don't trust us," one daughter says. "They think we're common and mean and worse than other girls."

Things begin to weigh on the parents' conscience (as the girls knew it would do).

Talk continues, and in the final analysis the mother flings her hands and tells the girls to go. They ain't no worse than other girls and if you can't never trust them out of your sight you might as well put a rope around them and tie them to the "bedstid."

Almost every girl in the community is there on the big night, all bright-eyed and bushy-tailed, and there are more boys than you can shake a stick at.

And the string music is supplied by anybody in the area that can play a fiddle or a banjo or a guitar. They don't have to be good, either. And a figure-caller is always available.

Things get to rocking and the girls are looking good in their starched dresses and in a crowded room the sweat gets to rolling. And we weren't fortunate enough to have deodorants in those days, so you know what else happened. Body odors filled the room and it was a time in those old packhouses. We brushed our teeth with baking soda and took it for heartburn, but somehow we hadn't been told that if would prevent body odor too.

And if this sounds a little gross, it was a part of our lives. Most girls didn't shave under their arms in those days, nor did they shave their legs way back there. I've seen girls with dark hairs sticking through their stockings. But all those things were acceptable during that period and considered a normal part of our lives.

There might be a little halitosis around too, since there were no breath fresheners. Some people washed out their mouths with peroxide. I remember how that mess would fizz in the mouth and leave a bland taste.

I have mentioned brilliantine in other columns, and it is fitting, for that was one indulgence by the male gender that made us feel modern. We'd pour that mess over our heads and it must have been 99 percent grease, for it made the hair shine and we thought that sweet smell made us sexy and macho, even if it was strictly a 10-cent-store product. Come to think of it, I'd love to have one of those brilliantine bottles from 50 years ago. I don't know how our mothers ever got the pillow cases clean from that greasy kid stuff.

And there was courting and petting on the outside, naturally. It was only on occasions such as a neighborhood dance or party that young people had the chance to really be themselves for the "front room" was not a place for such indulgences in those days. In the first place, the door was left open and those mamas and papas didn't trust those ripsnorting boys, nor their own daughters, apparently.

Anyhow, we danced the nights away in those packhouses and had more fun than you would believe. And yeah, occasionally there was a fight at a packhouse dance. One boy would get mad with another over a girl and on a few occasions switchblade knives were used and somebody would get cut. And this added to the problems of "nice" girls attending dances. But despite such rare occurrences, dances continued to be held and the young people attended and all of us can remember those occasions and see us as we were and laugh at our antics as well as remember the good times we shared in the days when packhouse dances were big events.

Then there was round dancing that young people loved. It brought them closer together and they might get in a little bit of that at the packhouse dances.

But in the 1940s, while a lot of local boys were away fighting in World War II the young doods left back home to farm and work in defense industries got on to other dances, along with the girls, and we were climbing out of the cellar.

Jitterbugging took the country by storm, and anybody thinks we weren't gitting out of the woods then is crazy. The neighborhood girls couldn't go to the stores, but some of the girls from across the tracks in town were brought out to the stores and there was jumping and jiving like you wouldn't believe. And the juke boxes had the music for the lively dancing — Tommy Dorsey's "Boogie Woogie" and the Andrews Sisters "Boogie Woogie Bugle Boy" — and others, and it was a time out in the country.

And the young fellows had begun to shed their overalls in their night capers for pants and a white shirt, and donned their Sunday slippers instead of wearing those old brogans all the time. We were gitting more modern every day.

Look at us closely to see how we were in that long ago that seems only yesterday.   □

Lonely Houses Sat Along Railroad Tracks

Hobos Along Railroad Tracks

T he whistle blowing as the train passed the crossing a couple of miles away in the dead of night was such a lonely sound it made you want to cry. But the sound of the cars crossing over the railroad ties was a lullaby that would put you to sleep.

The train came from the nowhere and penetrated the woods, going to the coast or to all points northward. The tracks led through dismal forests, down lonely cut-out places on the countryside, moving produce and many other products across the state and the nation. There was no truck service in those days, not long-distance anyway.

As the train came from the north and headed for the coastal cities, it meandered through a large pocosin, filled with scrub pines and other bushes and trees that seemed to be lacking proper nourishment, for they didn't look healthy, nor were they nearly as tall as the trees in most woodlands. But the pocosin was a sandy area and perhaps that accounts for the lack of lush growth.

And the houses sitting along the railroad in open places were as lonely looking as the pocosin. They were far apart, with no underpinning, and most of them were bare of trees. On the outside, there would be meager woodpiles, a clothesline and a wash pot and usually there was a raw-boned dog lying around the premises. Even then it made you wonder why people would live in such isolation.

But there was life along the railroad, and there were hobos who rode the trains and sometimes stopped in the local area. A walk along the tracks would reveal where they had stopped, built a fire and used old tin cans to cook a meal. Many hobos rode the trains in those days, some on top of the cars, and it wasn't unusual for those who lived along the railroad tracks to see the grimy-looking men crouching atop the cars as the train sped by.

Hobos were always dirty with the pores of the skin on their faces filled with soot, and they were always ragged. It is a wonder some of them were able to get the rags on themselves, they were so torn and tattered. And their hands were as dirty as their faces.

Once in a great while a hobo would come to the door begging for food. And even if the Bible says be careful of whom you are entertaining, for some of them might be angels, nobody thought of the hobos as being angels, and they weren't asked inside the home. If one came to the door, the women would go to the safes and see what was there and if there were cold biscuits, sausage or meat, or sweet potatoes, they'd fill their hands and the hobos would be on their way, apparently happier than if they had been invited into the home. But we always wondered why they would resort to such a life.

As bad as times were in those days, it is easy to imagine the human suffering experienced by the fly-by-night hobos that had no place to hang their hats, no place to call home, nobody preparing a warm meal for them.

They were outcasts from society, for whatever reason they rode the trains in those dark days of the Depression. Some untenanted old houses along the railroad tracks bore evidence of hobo visits. Fires were lit in fireplaces sometimes and rags and cooking pans left in the rooms.

And in those days there were other visitors in the community, especially in the fall of the year. Everybody was aware that a few dollars were circulating from the sale of tobacco, and everybody wanted to get a share of the spoils. Gypsies would make their rounds sometimes. And they were sly ones.

A woman would be sent to the house to approach the housekeeper. She would get the attention of the woman of the house by showing her scarves or bedspreads or other items of interest to women. And if she found out there were no men around, she would signal to her lieutenants waiting outside to come in for the kill.

While the housekeeper was being entertained, others of the gang would make their rounds in the yard, running down chickens, robbing hen nests, picking up sweet potatoes or anything else edible, for food was scarce, and Gypsies had to eat also. And before the woman of the house knew what was going on, the gang would be off and away and the housekeeper would see them taking their loot to the old automobiles they drove.

But sometimes the scavengers would get fooled, when a man appeared on the premises and began running them down or going into the house and returning with a shotgun. Now talk about a gang of Gypsies sceedaddling, but they took off like a bat out of hell.

And then there were the men who came around repairing stoves in the fall, and everybody that was there remembers that those old stoves were defintely in need of repair. Time and rust had taken their toll and all the men had to do was to shake the firebox a little, or punch around in the ovens, and holes could be spotted everywhere.

If there were a few dollars in the "old ladies'" Golden Grain sacks, they'd tell the men to mend the stoves. And those men knew about as much about fixing those stoves as I did. They'd do the most jackleg jobs you ever saw — put a piece of metal over the holey area with a few bolts — collect the money and be on their way. And the menfolks would get mad with the women for allowing them to "momick" up the stoves. But once the money was collected, there was nothing that could be done about it.

Sometimes men would come around selling oil stoves, and women that had been used to the old wood ranges all their lives thought an oil stove would solve all their problems. They went wild over those oil stoves with four burners for cooking and a two-burner oven. And if there was any way to persuade the "old man" they'd order one of those stoves, and when it came they had to find room in the small kitchen to place the stove, and it often had to go where the sidetable sat.

Let anybody that wants to tell you that those oil stoves beat wood ranges for cooking, but you needn't believe them. There wasn't any comparison between the two. Biscuits weren't nearly as good, and nothing else seemed to be as good as food cooked on the old wood ranges.

Not only that, there was always the smell of kerosene and that's sickening. But despite having the modern oil stoves for cooking, the wood ranges were never removed from the kitchens, and many meals were still cooked on them. The womenfolks just felt that they were cashing in on the more modern things in life with the oil stoves. And of course, the salesmen got their share of "backer" money, as well as the Gypsies and the stove repairmen. After all, they had to eat too.   □

Drunks Caused Problems

H e was a good farmer, loved the land, and seemed to take just a little more interest in his crops than the average farmer. He was a little more meticulous and wanted a field plowed just right. When plowing a young crop, if that fender didn't work just right he'd put on another, or another size sweep if necessary.

Just another old sharecropper, he had nothing to call his own except a good wife and a house full of young'uns. Lord! They were like doorsteps! In fact he told the boys down at the store after the tenth or eleventh baby came along that all he had to do was hang his overalls at the head of the bed and another baby was on the way.

Anyhow he tended a big farm and there was a passel of work to be done, and he led the pack in the fields and had those boys out there by the time they were knee-high to a grasshopper. He'd put them behind a plow and they couldn't even hold the plow up, to say nothing of actually plowing. But he kept at it until those boys knew what they were doing long before most.

Sometimes he had to go to town twice a month for flour and lard and fatback and molasses to feed that crowd, for there was no way to raise enough meat (or anything else) to last from season to season.

He liked to dabble in truck crops and he'd plant an acre or so of string beans, a few Irish potatoes and a few cucumbers. He said that would give him a little cash in the summer when there was no money.

This is the best I can say for the old codger besides being a likeable fellow, for the most part. But he had one failing that took away from the good. He was a drunk. No, not the every-day drunk, but when he pulled one everybody in the neighborhood knew it. He would stay drunk for weeks.

Just let him sell a load of beans or potatoes or cucumbers, and he'd be "lit" up like a Christmas tree by the time he got home. He'd bring in cheese and sausage and fish and stuff for the family to eat, but he also had a jar of stumphole whisky.

Sometimes two drunks would pair up for a day or two and they'd have the best of all worlds for a little spell, but the "old lady" at the house where they congregated would put that fire out right quick.

There was food strewn on the floor, glasses scattered everywhere, greasy fingerprints on the safe and oilcloth, and then there was hell to pay!

I can just see her standing in the doorway propped on an elbow with one leg crossing the other and that finger pointing. "Tell you something," she'd say to the outsider, "I have to put up with that sorry scoundrel over there" pointing to where her drunken sot sat. Then she'd take a hand and clean the snuff from the corners of her mouth, and let back in in almost a yell. "But I hain't got to put up with the likes of you, and you git out of here right now," pointing to the door. And he got.

The whole family would go to pieces for even the younger ones knew it would be bad times around the house before it was all over.

And he forgot about the farm when he got drunk. He only lived to drink and drank to live. He also underwent a personality change. He'd curse at the children and threaten his wife and do all the things a crazed drunk would be expected to do.

After he became "pickled" good he was too sick to be a threat to the family. He'd lie flat on the porch in summer with his beard sticking out like a porcupine's, with bloodshot eyes that saw nothing, and hold his head off the porch and spew and spew until he heaved with spasms and pulled his knees up to his stomach in agony. The vomit would settle on his beard and flies would torment him.

He'd fall into a troubled sleep and fight spastically at the flies. When he sobered up enough that he felt he could make it he'd get up and stagger down the road where there was whisky for sale at a store. The liquor was kept hidden in a woods behind the store.

He'd heave and get a few swallows of the whisky down and head homeward again with his jar of whisky in a paper bag. Sometimes he'd lie down in a side ditch beside the dirt road and completely pass out and lie there for hours, and the children would go looking for him if night was approaching.

They'd drag him out of the ditch and he didn't even know who they were. A boy would get on each side of him and they'd half-drag him home with his head hanging forward and uttering unintelligible phrases. And a younger child would carry his bag of whisky.

They made an effort to clean him up but it did little good. They tried to get him to eat but the very smell of food made him vomit. He'd sleep on a quilt placed on the floor with his jar of whisky beside him and groan and moan and keep the family awake.

He'd soil his clothes and they'd strip him as if he were a baby and clean him up as he fought at them with the little strength he had left.

The good wife would go with the boys to the fields to see that the farming operations were carried on while a sorry drunk lay steeped in liquor at the house. That was the secret of his being able to farm and having a landlord that would tolerate him. She knew how to farm as well as he, and she saw that farming went on as usual.

He finally reached the point that he couldn't tolerate whisky, and by then he was so shaky and weak he couldn't hold himself together. And the good wife would kill a chicken, stew it and add a little meal and got a few spoonfuls of broth in him.

Then he had delirium tremens (DTs). He saw things on the walls and heard sounds. The devil was after him and he'd point him out and scream and dart his head and carry on and it was hell in a crowded poor home. But that was the turning point.

Gradually, slowly the healing process began and in a few days he was beginning to dry out. Today some go to sanatoriums or hospitals to get off drunks, but 50 years ago it was always a family affair and a way of life was disrupted when that happened.

Once sober, he was ashamed to face the family, even the small children, and more ashamed to face the neighbors. He became the model farmer (and father) again. But watch out when the sand lugs were taken to market.   □

Story Of The White Leghorns

P a decided he'd get him some white leghorn biddies and raise layers to bring in some extra money. But you don't take cracked corn and get these hens that lay 365 eggs a year. But Pa didn't take that into account at the time. Neither did he consider other possible consequences. So he sent off an order to the hatchery for a hundred biddies.

In those days the biddies were in transit for a long time, and some were dead on arrival and all the others were half-starved by the time they were taken from the boxes. And Pa bought pullets, for you could buy them by sex, even that far back. However, a few turned out to be roosters anyway.

Well sir, those biddies were Pa's pride and joy and he made them a homemade brooder and provided warmth with the lanterns used at the tobacco barns. And on a cool night they'd pile up and a few would get mashed and they'd flock to the half-gallon-jar waterers and some would get as wet as if they had been put in a tub of water.

I reckon about 50 of the hundred survived and they were rambunctious little devils and ran everywhere when they were turned out.

Ma told Pa those biddies were eating up the garden but Pa paid little attention, like he did about a lot of things. But one day he got out and decided to plow out the garden so he put a fender on the plow to protect the garden peas and cabbage and other stuff that had come up but hadn't grown very much.

Lo and behold! He found out that the rabbits had eaten up a whole row of garden peas on the side next to the ditch, and they had hopped over to the cabbage rows and taken a sizable toll there also. And it made Pa mad. Now Pa didn't fly off the handle at every little thing, but he had his curious ways, and his temper could flare up whenever something struck him wrong.

And about that time those white leghorns decided to invade the garden, and they flew over that fence in droves and began picking at everything in the garden. That made Pa madder. And we boys were out there, naturally, and Pa told us to throw at them with clods of dirt to git them out of the vegetable patch. And it didn't matter what he told me and one or two others, but it did matter where Shine was concerned, for that boy could really "chunk" at anything. He could throw that old homemade ball by us so fast we didn't even see it when it passed the plate. He'd wind up that arm a time or two, and buddy, you'd better watch out.

Anyhow, all of us picked up clods of dirt and threw them at Pa's prized possessions, and of course all of them missed their marks except Shine's. Boy, he hit that little old pound-and-a-half pullet right on the head, and she breathed her last in a hurry. And this infuriated Pa.

He called Shine to him, and Shine said he didn't mean to kill her, but Pa decided it was time to teach that rip-snorter a lesson. He didn't even bother to take the plowline loose from Zeb's bridle, so he started hitting him with the plowline and Zeb would jump with every lick. And it took Shine a pretty good while to cry, or it seemed like it anyway.

Now a plowline is doubled at the end to make it easier in plowing and controlling the mule, and that doubled plowline really hurt Shine's legs and rear end. And we boys hated Pa right then.

He finally quit whipping Shine and Shine strolled off behind the barn and we other boys made a hasty exit from that garden too. We didn't have no business being around an angry father with his face all red and with a funny look in his eyes.

We could hear Shine snubbing behind the barn, and it was like he had the hiccups. He couldn't quit snubbing and we wanted to go where he was and help him share his grief, but we knew it was better to leave him alone until he got it out of his system.

Finally, Shine went to the house and Ma asked him why his eyes were all red and swollen and his face dirtied up from tears. And Shine told Ma Pa had beat him, and why. And you could see fire in Ma's eyes, but she didn't say a crying word to Pa about it before we young'uns. But you'd better believe she laid him low that night after all of us went to bed. And she told him to git down on his knees and ask God to forgive him for taking out his anger on a 15-year-old boy for the things rabbits and chickens did that Shine had no control over.

And we other boys did all the feeding up for Shine that night and he didn't have to turn his hands and we sat close to him and showed a camaraderie that we didn't usually display.

And Shine wasn't really mad, nor did the red lashes on his legs and backside bother him to that extent. Shine was tough. It was hurt that got to him. Genuine hurt. And we didn't go all emotional about things, but we let Shine know that we were behind him, and against Pa in what he did.

Pa's favorite weapon on we young'uns was his big old brogans. It seemed like he loved to come up behind us if we had done something wrong, aim that shoe just right and plant it right on our butts, sending us about four feet forward and jolting us back to reality as well as letting us know who was boss.

Pa didn't resort to plowlines or razor straps often, and I never remember him using a switch on us. That was Ma's favorite weapon — the small ones that could literally burn your legs to pieces when she took us down a notch.

It was sometime later, maybe a week or so, that Pa finally got around to telling Shine that he ought not to have whipped him. He reminded Shine that there had been times when he should have used the whip on all of us when he didn't, but that was no reason to jump on him on that particular day. And a week or so later, he found an extra quarter for Shine when Saturday rolled around. And all of us soon forgot about Pa beating up Shine.

And then there were the beatings at school. Sometimes a bully would get out of hand and the teacher would have to recommend a whipping. And the principal was a man that wanted to present a macho image anyway, although we didn't know what macho meant in those days, and I doubt the word was in the dictionary at that time. He appeared to love to lash those big boys that got bully and sassed the teacher or talked ugly in class, as if it gave him a personal pleasure. So he'd pour the switches to them and talking about a row! There was trouble in the neighborhood then. Those Mas and Pas would march out to the schoolhouse ready for a fight because their boy had been "beat up." They'd say they were going to court and would threaten to fist-fight the principal. But they were reminded that their boy could be expelled for the year and would be anyway for a period of time. And the old folks would quieten down until another beating took place.

The best part about the white leghorns on the day Pa whipped Shine was that Ma said the biddy was half big enough to eat, and that we could take one of the young roosters and dress it too and make a chicken pie. And she did that and put the whole pieces of chicken in that deep pan and a little thin pastry in the liquor with sliced up boiled eggs and cooked those never-to-be-forgotten crusts and we had chicken pie, in the middle of the week!

What was done in those days to control unruly children would be considered child abuse today, but in those days it was considered a Bible principle to use the rod rather than spoiling the child.   □

TB Scared Us To Death

I f there was one thing we were scared to death of when I was a young'un, it was TB. And no wonder. It was a death sentence. They didn't have drugs to treat tuberculosis with in those days, and the victim was placed in isolation in the home and every dish and sheet, pillow case and everything else washed separately. And I never heard tell of any kind of surgery on TB patients. Once they contracted the disease, they just went downhill until the end came, and were shunned by society as well.

Now there were two kinds of TB — the lingering kind and the galloping kind — and when they said so and so had galloping consumption, they might as well get the spade and shovel ready for time was short for the victim.

The person with TB would start falling off so fast they became shells of themselves in a short time. They'd get that sallow complexion and it would look like the skin on their cheeks was stretched tight so it showed the cheek bones and the mouth would be sunk in, showing protruding jaws. And their eyes were so sad looking. They knew they were doomed and they just resigned themselves and sank lower and lower until death relieved them of their burdens.

And the public shied away from them as if it were the plague. Where there was a house with TB inside people were afraid to breathe the air around the premises for fear they'd get the death bug. Young'uns would hold their breath and dash by those houses like wild horses.

The old folks would visit the TB victims, but they never really felt at ease on such visits. There was the hacking cough and the spit cup that held all those germs and although the mouth was covered when coughing and the spit cup closed up when not in use, the bugs were still there.

When the victims died, they'd burn the mattresses and other bedding, scald the springs and slats, sun the bedstead for days and do away with everything associated with the TB patient. It was sad for the victims, the families and the general public. People were very compassionate in those days, but they were aware that TB posed a threat to everyone that came in contact with it.

The best expression I remember from those days is the word "consumption" which very adequately described the disease. It consumed its victims, and I can still hear people saying "so and so's got the "consumption.'"

Medical science has made so much progress since those days there is no way to compare treatment for diseases that were killers then to treatment today. Tuberculosis is no longer considered the scourge it used to be and relatively few people even have to be hospitalized.

But there are some diseases today that we didn't hear much about in the old days. When people died suddenly, people said they "fell dead" and the blame was placed on "acute" indigestion. Today we know that they were apparently heart attacks. But you very seldom heard of "acute" indigestion — maybe once or twice a year — among thousands of people in the area.

We didn't hear a lot about cancer in those days either. I remember very few people who were diagnosed as having cancer, although there must have been many who had it and died that were never diagnosed.

Emphysema was not even heard of in my community. I guess it took the accumulation of smoking over many years to bring the disease to the major status it has today among modern-day killers. But you know they encouraged us to smoke and it was the "in" thing back then. But there was a lot of asthma.

Many people must have had diabetes, although people didn't go to doctors for many ailments in those days and we didn't hear much about the disease. However, I am sure many people died from diabetes 50 years ago.

There was a lot of "heart dropsy" in the olden days. I believe that is called congestive heart failure today. And back then people would swell terribly and the fluid would eventually take over and "drown" the victims so to speak and they would expire. They'd be propped up in bed for weeks or months before death in order to breathe.

There were also a lot of strokes. But remember that there were no anti-depressants or whatever they use today to control high blood pressure. Blood pressure was seldom checked, and many people never had theirs checked. There was much paralysis and some victims were left in terrible shape. But of course, that remains a problem and strokes continue today, although on a smaller scale than then.

We heard tell of a lot of side pleurisy in those days, and pneumonia was another killer. But then again, there was no miracle drug for pneumococcus bacteria and many people died from the disease. It hit especially hard among the very young and the very old.

Before a young'un started to school, he or she had to have a smallpox vaccination. This resulted in terrible sores on the arm sometimes where the vaccine was put into a scratch made with a needle. There were shields made to attach to the arms in severe cases. And now the disease has been eradicated.

There was vaccine for typhoid fever, and county nurses came by neighborhoods and usually congregated at a country store and shoved those needles into people's arms. This was a summertime ritual and they came three weeks in a row. The shots made some people sick.

There was anti-toxin for victims of diphtheria back then, and that's about it as far as protection from the diseases, and in the case of anti-toxin, a help in overcoming the disease.

Other remembrances are of a woman walking remarkably well on a peg leg with the metal surrounding the stiff prosthesis and the leg swinging outward with each step as a result. And a man with an empty sleeve that is folded and fastened at the back with a safety pin.

Yes sir, there were a lot of births and a lot of deaths 50 years ago, but there was also a lot or living and we oldsters today were in our seventh heaven then and death was the farthest thing from our thoughts. Many have gone, but a lot of us remain, and life is still beautiful and we're satisfied to just keep on going.   □

Rolled Down, Ragged Socks: Signs Of An Era

Those 10-Cent 'Seconds'

Weren't we something, we poor folks of the 1930s? In one sense, I look upon us with something akin to pity. Yet, on the other hand I don't know why pity should be associated with that part of our lives. We certainly didn't pity ourselves then.

Anybody remember those "seconds" men's socks we used to get at Woolworth's? They were cotton with no elastic in the tops, of various colors with arrows on each side and you could pick a color to match your "wardrobe" (pardon me).

Now the thing about those "seconds" was that they were sewn up (usually in the toe) and that caused a ridge either at the end of the toes or over them, and they weren't worth toting home. But we bought them all right, for they were 10 cents a pair, and that was right down our alley.

Another thing about those socks was that they didn't fit very well, and it seemed that they were always tight at the top part of the foot where it joins the leg. Well sir, we'd pull those things on (and we bought the biggest ones we could find) and when we got them on the top had stretched all out of proportion.

But fortunately, there was style even in those days, and rolled socks were in vogue. So we'd twist the top of the socks into a ball and then roll them down to just above our shoetops. Still that cramped feeling was at the end of the toes. And you know what soon happened. Those tough toenails went right through that thin cotton, especially the big toe, and talking about uncomfortable!

So we'd take off the shoes and pull the sock up and crimp it together and stick the crimp between the big toe and the next one, but after a little walking that big toe was right back in that hole.

Before long a hole came in the heel and sometimes that caused blisters on our heels and we'd slide our heels above the blisters and walk more on our toes for a while. But that didn't last long either and those 10-cent socks never lasted long enough to get to the washtub.

Then rayon socks came along and boy, we thought they were something else. And they were in patterns also and had sort of a shimmer to them and they were thin, almost see-through some of them. And they felt like they might have been sweated in. But we loved them and it was a pleasure to roll those babies down low and stick our legs out so they could be seen.

Before the roll-down socks era, the menfolks used supporters to hold up their socks. But the socks came up almost to the knee and were made of cotton lisle, which was much more practical than the rayon jobs.

And sleeveholders were a common sight around men's arms. They were almost stylish. I reckon the men didn't pay much attention to sleeve lengths when they bought shirts, and men with short arms always had a problem with the cuffs hanging down their hands, so they'd take those round elastic sleeveholders and slip them on beyond the elbow and pull the shirtsleeve up and have a part of the sleeve blousing out above the holders.

And there were the everyday cotton stockings the womenfolks wore, and the only word to describe them is "ugly." They were even uglier when you saw a woman with a loose stocking dangling around her leg below the string tied around the leg to hold them up.

But remember that this was before the age of nylon. There were also rayon stockings for women but they were funny looking on the leg, and some kind of shimmer was there that didn't look right. The real McCoy in women's hose in those days was "pure silk" from Japan. So the women folks had something to boast about even then when they really "diked out."

And when the girls started getting permanent waves that transformed their lives. They had worn straight hair for so long every girl had a fit to get a permanent wave. They went for years using bobby pins to make imitation waves on the sides of their faces with the hair hanging straight down and they welcomed those curls (or kinks).

They'd go to those beauty parlors in town with all that hair and come out with most of it left in the beauty parlor and they'd have the most curls you ever saw. I mean hundreds of them, rolled as tight as Dick's hat band and even the skin of their heads showed where those ringlets were so tight.

And stink! That solution they used on their heads must have been a lot stronger than they use today. At any rate, I never get that smell anymore.

As to the older men, their hair was either shaggy and oily or cut short so that the skin of the head showed on the sides and no temples were left for they'd grow out too quickly. A man with a fresh haircut then looked pure "skint."

Of course some older men's wives cut their hair and you never saw such gashes as some of those men had in those thick heads of hair. It was easy to tell whose "old lady" had cut his hair. And if the hair was gashed up and there was a layer of dandruff around the collar of his overalls jacket, you got a true picture of a lot of older farmers in those days.

But listen folks. I've gone a lot further back than those houses along the road where there might be some signs of affluence not evident in most homes. Maybe everybody wasn't aware of a lot of the crude ways of life in those days that I describe, such as landowners who might have a few family heirlooms in their homes and maybe didn't have to skimp as much as most of us.

I talk about the masses, the poorer class, rather than the exceptions and those houses way back in the fields gave the truest picture of the way we really were in those days.

I will say this: If there are those from that era who really don't know about a lot of the things I tell, it was because they were not observant of their neighbors. Heck, I didn't ever see much difference between us in those days and it came a lot nearer being a classless society then than today.

Anyhow, I still remember how those "seconds" socks felt and I don't want no more of them.   □

Long Ago Family Washings

I t's wash day in the country, and the busiest day of the week around the house. Somebody has filled up the washpot and raked chips around it and gotten a fire going. Other young'uns have toted water from the well and filled tubs for rinsing the clothes and another is reserved for the "boiling suds" plus the tub for scrubbing the clothes.

Young'uns tote clothes out of the house by the armful and sometimes a sleeve or a sash trips them as they go down the steps and they fall broadsided and the clothes go every which way. It is unbelievable the size of the pile of clothes to be washed until it is realized that there may be a dozen people to wash for. And this is a once-a-week chore, not counting the baby diapers.

Women with small babies put the diapers in soak every day and wash them every couple of days or so. And if a woman wanted to be marked, let her hang out a wet diaper and use it again before washing it, and she got marked good. Whenever a baby wore such a diaper the smell was there all the time and it was evident the diaper had been used without being laundered.

The clothes were sorted by color, with the sheets, bolster cases and pillow cases in one group, the white wearing clothes in another, colored wearing clothes in another, and overalls and jackets and pants and socks in the fourth pile. They usually washed the bed clothing first, and believe it or not, many of those women even starched the sheets in those days, and every pillow case and bolster case was starched.

There were commercial starches then, and I remember Argo and Celulloid starch being used at my house, but sometimes it gave out before a trip to town, and starch was made from flour. Imagine the modern woman making half-a-tub full of flour starch! I can just see the lumpy mess. But they knew how to use boiling water and flour to form the consistency starch they needed, and they'd pour it through the sifter to get out any remaining lumps.

The Red Devil lye was brought out, the lye soap, and the old washing board. And that meant elbow grease, for you had to put some pressure on those clothes on that washboard, and it's a tiring job. And the clothes were rinsed before they were put in the washpot, where plenty of potash was added and a hunk of lye soap cut up fine to form plenty of suds.

As the clothes boiled, somebody went to the pot ever so often and punched them down with the heavy wooden stick that was also used to dip them up with. And when they had boiled the length of time wanted, a woman or girl would tuck the skirt between the legs and get up close to the pot and dip out the clothes and put them in a tub. They were then taken to the wash bench and cold water added and they were punched and twisted and looked over for any dingy places, and then wrung out and placed in the rinsing water.

But it didn't necessarily mean that only two rinsing waters would be used. If there were a lot of suds in that water after two rinsings, they had to go through the third tub. (We called rinsing "wrenching"). They intended for those clothes to be clean. And they were. When they finally hung those dozen or so sheets and other bedclothing on the lines, they were the whitest white I have ever seen, and I've tried to remember something whiter.

Wringing all those clothes was something else, and I don't know why every wrist wasn't sprained. They were wrung out of every tub and then starched and wrung again. And the wash pot had to be refilled two or three times to boil all of those clothes, and before it was all over, every available place to hang a piece was used. The sheets would dry and they'd separate them for they had stuck together on the line from the starch, take them in and hang Sunday shirts and other white clothes on the regular clothesline.

There weren't nearly as many towels to be washed as might be supposed, for everybody dried in the same towel that hung on the back porch. And they were all made either from flour sacks or salt sacks. And there were no washcloths, for they were made of rags, and once they became dirty I doubt that even box lye would have whitened them.

Those colored dresses and other non-white clothes were hung on garden fences and sometimes the lines of clothes would extend down toward the hog pen. Last to be washed and hung out were the men's overalls and jackets and socks and young'uns stockings and they were closest to the hog pen. If the men had been working in tobacco, gum was all over the work clothes and kerosene would be added to the water to help get it out, and more potash added. I've seen that water almost ropey after all that washing.

After all the clothes were hung out and the water dumped in the yard, the women would sigh and put their hands to the lower part of their backs and they were almost completely exhausted. It was actually impossible for them to stand erect after all the scrubbing and toting water and carrying the clothes to be hung out.

And a lot of the clothes didn't dry on the day they were washed and had to be left on the lines overnight. If a bird soiled a piece of clothing, it was taken out and gone over to remove the stain.

Finding a place to put all the dried clothes was a problem sometimes for if all the beds were in use, there was little space to lay them down. If there was an extra bed, they were dumped there. If someone had to have a piece of clothing that had been washed before the next day when the ironing was done, they found it and put an iron on the stove and ironed it themselves.

And ironing was another enormous chore. Sometimes they sprinkled the clothes from a pan, using their hands to get the water on them, but some people had these gizmos that you put on the end of a bottle with a sprinkler on it.

Anybody think we had it easy 50 years ago? ☐

'Arning' Before A Hot 'Far'

I can just picture the modern woman doing a family ironing of half-a-century ago. It seems that in general, the iron has been delegated to a shelf in the utility room or hidden somewhere on a lower cabinet shelf. And why not? We are a wash-and-wear generation today. Even if the material isn't really wrinkle-free it doesn't matter all that much anymore. And who has the time to spend the greater part of a day at the ironing board?

But they did just that long ago, and I remember it just as it was.

The "old lady" is speaking: "Anybody ask me what I got to do the day after all that pile of clothes is washed is crazy. I can answer 'em in one word. 'Arn.' God pity the woman with a house full of young'uns. 'Arnin's' not so bad in the winter time, but when it's as hot as all "gitout" that's another story.

"Here I was planning to "arn" with the cookstove and there's no wood split up. Now the "far" has got to be lit and the "arns" heated in front of the "far" with all them coals piling up around them and making it easy to smudge up something. But just git a speck of something on one of them starched white shirts and them boys will be yelling their heads off. Well I'll do some yelling too for if they had split up some wood I could have "het" the "arns" on the stove.

"Here are two pillow cases stuffed full of sprinkled-down starched clothes to be "arned" and it pure stifling in this room with a big "far" going. Windows raised to the top but a fly would fan more air than's coming in them windows. Already sweating. What will it be like 'fore I git through? Face all red-pited and hair damp around the neck.

"Let me git the "arning" board and see if I can git it propped up anywhere so I can git to "arning." Putting it flat on the washstand is too low to go with the top slat in the "chur." Let me find a catalog and see if that will make it even. No. I might have known it. I'll find two or three Farmers Home Journals and maybe that'll do it. Yep, it works.

"Now I'll spittle-test them "arns" to see if they're frying good. They're hot, but not much hotter'n I am. I'll "arn" these sheets first. Might be crazy to starch sheets, but they feel so good when you lie down on them. On the other hand, sweat soon dampens them and they don't have that starched feel long.

"Here I go piling on more wood when it's already so hot I can't hardly stand it. I'm glad that pile of sheets is "arned" but here comes the worst of all — them white shirts starched as stiff as a board. I'll bet them collars would break if they was bent hard. But they shore are pretty when they are as slick as glass and as white as pure snow. But I better hush that chat, for I'm liable to end up with smut on one. Let me wipe off these "arns" good for I don't want no extra work.

"Got to cut a piece from that old quilt and put a new cushion on this "arning" board one of these days. Got to put a new top on too. This top is as brown as a dead leaf and pure burnt in some places. Got reason to be though with all them clothes "arned" over it.

"Here comes a young'un trying to sneak in the safe for a tater and biscuit. Git out of there, young'un, ain't going to be no cooking at this house tonight! We'll eat what's left from dinner. You think I'm going to git over a hot stove after all this "arning," you're crazy boy. Git back to that field 'fore your daddy finds out you've slipped away and tears your hide all to pieces!

"Anybody's coming to this house let it be one of them girls. One of them slips in I'd put them to pushing this "arn" 'fore you could turn around, and dare the "old man" to say anything about it as hot as I am.

"Let me pull off these old tennis shoes and git splinter barefooted. This bunion on my foot is killing me and my back's a hurting and I'm sweating all over. I can't stand it no longer. I've got to have a dip of snuff or I'll be pulling this straggly hair out. I know my head smells pure sour from all this sweating.

"Don't seem like these girls had this many dresses, but I ought to know, for I made every one of them, with the help of God. Time. What is it? I'm running here and yonder from light til bedtime. Never have a free minute. But ain't no need of dwelling on that.

"What on earth's the need of "arning" these boys' BVD's? Won't make a mite of difference, but no, I've done it all these years and no need to quit now. Crazy me, I even "arn" their overhalls, and their socks, and them sleeveless knit undershirts.

"I've just got to sit down and rest my bones a minute. I'll find a toothbrush and swill me a good-size mouth full of snuff. Might as well go to the front porch for I'll be spitting my head off. I know there ain't no air out there, but maybe I will see somebody pass and won't feel so all-alone.

"Let me rub this bunion with my other foot and maybe that'll take out a little of the sting and soreness. I can't hardly stand to touch that thing. Lord! This snuff's good and here I have gone and spit on a chicken running by. Them corn silks shore smell good out there and if I weren't so "tard" I'd pull a mess of corn and have some "rosenears" for supper. But it'll never happen this day.

"Now comes all the boys' blue work shirts and the "old man's" hickory-striped ones. But at least the "old man's" ain't got collars to "arn." He likes his shirts without collars and that makes 'em easier to make as well as "arn." But since he don't want a collar, I wonder why he buttons that top button all the time. Men are the craziest things. There he is with a buttoned collar in the heat of summer but he can't stand nothing around his waist so he buys them light-colored pincheck britches three or four sizes too big and puts on a pair of galluces and walks around like he's the king of the walk. Men! Walk around with a thumb stuck under them galluces.

"He's worked hard, but no harder'n me, and now all he does is go around bossing the young'uns and telling them what to do in the fields while I'm up here busting my gut to git this work done. He's good though, and I could have done a lot worse. I ought not to even think such a thing. Forgive me, Lord.

"It's all done, and now all these piles of clothes to be put up. But I'll just let them girls do that and put the something to eat on the table too. I've had all I can take for one day. □

The Taylor Clan (Except For Me) And Everyone Gone

Those Old Photographs

O
ld family albums are treasures stuck away in some drawer that are pulled out periodically when someone mentions a grandparent or great-grandparent and the faded pictures are scrutinized, laughed at and promptly put back to rest in their niches and out of public view. But those old albums provided us with a pictorial record of our ancestry and although they are seldom referred to, they are still considered an important part of our past.

And we oldsters today remember our participation in those "pixture takings" when we were fair of skin, wrinkle-free, and dressed in those "funny" clothes.

Now if there was a way to say a word correctly and a way to say it incorrectly, we young'uns out in the sticks ALWAYS said it the wrong way. We didn't say "picture." Instead we said "pixture." And if anyone thinks we said words incorrectly, they should have heard our parents and grandparents! And use of the language in this column is in keeping with our vocabulary in those days, and to say it correctly would be a distortion of the way we were.

Anyhow, every family had to have a group picture, whether the family was still growing or whether part of the family was away. But credit for a lot of that can be given to the "picture takers" in those days who managed to come up some Sunday afternoon soon after dinner. They had their "Kodaks" with them which is what we called all cameras in those days. I'll bet you 99 out of any 100 persons would have said that the correct name for a camera was "Kodak."

As a matter of fact, an appointment might have already been made to get the family picture after dinner, for we young'uns got out of that Sunday garb as soon as we hit the house after church, and to have everybody "dressed up" would almost require that they know about the picture taking. On the other hand, they may have made us go back and put on that mess again.

And background was of no consideration in those days. What background? An old, weathered, unpainted, dull gray house with a front porch and two-by-four posts holding up the roof with the ends of the porch floor rotted by the weather was as good a background as there was. And the front porch is where most families had the picture taken.

The picture taken of my family was a dilly. (Look at it!) There they were, diked out to kill for a summer day; the girls in white dresses and black stockings and some kind of ribbon in the hair of the younger ones and the older girls with hats; Ma in a light dress holding the breast baby and Pa holding the lap baby, dressed in black (or blue serge) with his mustache that would be the pride of mustache fans today and a white shirt buttoned at the collar, but with no tie; the boys with their legs sort of spread apart wearing knickers (they were from about age 9 through 13) and looking as if they were bored to death.

I hadn't come along at that time, so I was never photographed as a part of a "family" picture, but you should have seen some shots of me with a little old box "Kodak." I'm glad I wasn't in the family album!

Today most old pictures of that type are either stored in attics or have disappeared over the years. For many years, our family picture hung on a wall somewhere in the house, but as time passed something happened to the oval frame and the picture got broken into several pieces (it had a cardboard backing.) But I still have all the sections and sometimes I put them together to see what "they" were really like in the days when even my parents had a youthful appearance (and I thought they were old as far back as I can remember).

Also in those old family albums are snapshots of uncles, aunts, cousins, family acquaintances and others that bring laughs to today's generation. But nothing reveals change more than photographs viewed a few years after they are taken. It seems an individual has totally changed from what he or she is at present and what they were such a short time ago.

Although I wasn't a part of a family "pixture taking" I recall seeing the photographers at other places during my childhood with their big "Kodaks" mounted on a tripod with that black cloth they placed over their heads and the use of their hands in getting the family closer together and calling to them to look into the camera and how everybody would straighen their clothes and rub their hands over their hair to be sure it was in place. As a child, I was always fascinated by the big "Kodak" and the black cloth that surrounded it. I thought of it as something magical.

When we look back upon the field of photography and how far it has come since those days, we know that it isn't the same world of 50 or more years ago.

And if the young people of today feel that they will escape that "funny" look that all old photographs have, they have a big surprise in store for them. All they will need to do 25 or 30 years from now is to go back to the old albums and they'll find the same "freaks" as we are today. The worst part about us is that

The Horace Raper Family Picture

we looked like freaks then, and we look like freaks today. Oh well, just wait for time to pass (and it will go by faster than they can keep up with) and they can look back and see when they too were ''freaks.'' □

Getting Saturday Baths

One Meal From Long Ago

I t all comes back like a song, drifting across the woodlands, the hills and streams and the rolling farmlands from many yesterdays; like a poem set to music with the beautiful language of the southland oversimplified but with an eloquence that gives it distinction.

It speaks of the very poor, of life as it was with the greatest reality of family of any one thing I can remember from all those years. It says something about unity and togetherness and imparts the feeling, as it did then, that there is an all-seeing eye watching and protective wings hovering over the places.

Those long tables and benches filled over half of the rooms. They were so close to the end walls you had to stand on tiptoe and draw in your stomach to get by the chairs when the "old man" and "old lady" were seated.

With eight or ten young'uns in a family, it was a pile of folks around those old eating tables. And there may be those of you who didn't do "exactly" as we did. But heck, I'll bet more than half of you did.

Anyway, crawl on that bench and take a place around the table and see if you can remember how it went during the course of a meal.

"Ask the blessing, Little Bud."

"Thank you for this food, Lord, amen."

Plates that are turned bottom upward are turned over at once.

"All the ice is in the glasses. So drink tea according to the ice you have. Little Bud, did you mess around with that ice the reason there won't more'n two fistfuls of it? And quit sticking that fork in the hole in the oilcloth. You done made it bigger than it was."

"Pass the biscuits."

"Collards may not be good. Seemed like they were hard, and I picked just the top leaves. Are they tough?"

"I can eat corn like a mule. Look at me Fuzz."

"You eat corn like a mule and you'll be eatin' it in the yard, boy, and quit pickin' at your nose. You've got it pure red."

"I want some Ish taters. And some cucumbers."

"Pass the meat."

"Little Bud, you be careful with that warmed-over piece of fish. They's bones in there and if you gobble it down somebody'll be poking a finger down your throat or feeding you gobs of cornbread to force it down."

"My tea's gone and I ain't got no ice hardly."

"Ma, Miss Effie's got a little baby. I heard them talking about it at the store."

"If something ain't done to them peas down by the pasture we won't make a quart. Grass has took 'em over and we need them peas for late summer."

"Fuzz, you and Little Bud's snickering down there. What on earth is so funny?"

"We smell something," they say almost hysterically.

"Git from this table til you learn how to act. Stay away long enough and there won't be a mouthful left for you. You know better'n that, boys."

"Shine, how is the cotton doing? Did you see a lot of blossoms when you were cultivating it this morning?"

"Sis, you and Lizzie Mae's acting up over there. Quieten down."

"Pass the cornbread."

"Looks like there could be enough ice for tea. These little young'uns around the house ain't no good for nothing else. Ought to be able to walk to the store and back without a nickel's worth of ice melting. This tea ain't even cold."

"I want another biscuit!"

"Can I drink the vinegar in the cucumber dish Ma?"

"Them collards taste better'n I thought. 'Specially with this good side meat."

"Move that pot liquor to the other side of the plate. The baby could git burned with that mess. Lordy mercy! That baby's got a meat skin in his mouth. Let me git that thing out baby boy or you might git choked."

"Sit up straight, Sis. Look at you stooped over the table."

"Fuzz, you and Little Bud ready to come back in here and act like you ought to 'fore all this something to eat is gone?"

"What holds up the world?"

"Crazy fool questions. This pack of young'uns would drive anybody on earth crazy. I know I won't that crazy when I was their age."

"Hush up. You were the one that asked the most God-awful questions of the whole pack."

"Any more ish taters? And another biscuit?"

"Anything sweet, Ma?"

"Yes, there's biscuit pudding. I don't know how it come about that biscuits was left over. Flavored with vanilla. Go git the pan, Lizzie Mae."

"I'd rather have 'lasses."

"Shut your mouth, girl, talking about 'lasses at dinner time."

"Biscuit pudding sticks to the top of my mouth."

"Something shore must stick to it, the way you cram it down. And just look at that young'un pure sopping that ish tater gravy!"

"Little Bud, did you finish that piece of fish? I'm scared to death you'll git a bone in your throat if you didn't. Just look, he even chewed up the bones. That young'un loves fish the best of anybody I ever seen."

"Pass the maters."

"I thought everybody was ready for pudding."

"I want some more string beans."

"And I want some more meat."

"Fuzz, take this dishrag and wipe your mouth. You've got grease smeared all over your face. And your hands too. And pass it around."

"I heard about a killing last night at the store but I didn't know who it was. Happened in town."

"You young'uns look pure nasty. Shore glad tomorrow's bathing day. Got to git tubs of water out in the sun in the morning so all of you can wash all over."

"Pass the pudding."

"I'm going to drink my tea without any ice. It's better'n just water."

"I heard there was going to be a baptizing Sunday from a church down the road."

"Pass the pudding."

"I want the vinegar from the mater dish. It's got a lot of black pepper in it and a little bit of sugar. I love it."

"It's a pure shame not to feed any of this good stuff to the baby. But it just wouldn't do. Might hurt his little stomach, and they'd put soda to the garden if they knowed it would kill every single one of us. Still, it does make a garden grow and we need all the garden we can have."

"Lizzie Mae, you and Sis wash the dishes. I'm jaded after gitting all this meal together. And wash all the grease from them pots and pans, and all the other dishes too. I just can't stand that greasy feeling."

One meal around a long family table from a bygone era.   □

A Dog Story; A Backer Story

I f the contents of this column couldn't be substantiated, I wouldn't even attempt it, since I am directly involved. But I have been ribbed long enough about the first story, so vindication is in order.

Anyway, I was a "backer-looping" fool in my young days, and everyone who knew me then is aware of that. And I made the mistake one day long ago of telling some of my buddies with whom I have worked for many years about what was accomplished one Saturday morning, and you never heard so much ranting and raving and carrying on about one thing. So I'm going public and telling it like it was.

On that Saturday morning, my brother had a field of tobacco that had to be put in, and you know that us country folks wanted to go to town on Saturday evening. So we decided to get that tobacco in the barn in half a day. At the looping shelter we lacked one hand having enough to run three looping horses. So a neighborhood woman and I took three handers apiece, and we lay down the ground rules. Each stick of tobacco had to have 40 bundles. And I'll call this woman Ruth, since that was her name. And I knew that she could loop equally as many sticks of tobacco in a day as I could. So we got things rolling.

There was a hand to take away the sticks of looped tobacco, another to get the empty sticks and place them on the looping horse, and all that we had to do was tie the string and get to looping. And man! We looped tobacco. Each of us looped 300 sticks in that half-a-day, hung it up and were home by 1 o'clock.

There was a quick splash in the washtub, fresh clothes, and off we were to see the "pixture show."

So now if those loud-mouths want this confirmed, my brother's wife can attest to that fact. And so can Ruth. If anybody wants to check it, I'll tell them how to get in touch with either or both of them. And the ironic part about those that let off so much steam is that they came from as far back in the sticks as I did. They just worked slower than me.

Next comes a dog story.

When I was about 14 years old, I picked me a puppy from a litter of six pure mongrels. The mother was part-fice perhaps, with some hound mixed. And there's no telling who the fathers were. There was certainly more than one father. That was easily detected just by looking at the difference in the puppies. Some even looked like an old birddog that roamed around the community.

This puppy was the smallest in the group and the only one of a black-and-tan color. I chose her, and named her "Boots." She never had a shot in her life and I don't ever remember even deworming her. When she was young she had some running fits but eventually outgrew them.

Boots grew up to weigh perhaps 12 or 13 pounds. She was low of leg and had a thick coat. Not a bad-looking little dog for a mutt. And when she was some six months old, she started going out in the thicket by the house and running rabbits. She took it up entirely on her own. Then when the hunting season came we took Boots with us, and she'd run through those briar patches like a breeze while the short-haired hounds who were higher on leg had trouble. Boots would bring a rabbit out almost in front of you.

In time, Boots' hunting record became known all over the neighborhood, and she loved to hunt so much anybody could cup their hands around their mouth, yell "Boots" and she'd be on her way. And that went on for years.

The only other pastime Boots was as interested in was raising a family. That dog must have had 50 puppies during her lifetime, and not a one worth a damn. A lot of those puppies were "dunked" on their birthday, but a few were kept over the years, and when those puppies got three or four months old, Boots ran those rabbits from the thickets right in front of them and they didn't pay those hares one bit of attention. And if anybody thinks they could keep Boots shut up during her season, they've got another thought coming.

I've known that dog to hunt all day after she got along in years, and head for home and get as far as the garden and lie down, and I've been out and brought her to the house. And she was a fixture at the neighborhood store. She'd go in and take her a place by the heater and just lay there until somebody wanted to go hunting.

There was this fellow that I will call Wayne, because that's what his name is, who loved to rabbit hunt. And he knew all about Boots' credentials. So one day in the fall Wayne called up Boots and they set out on the bunny trail. Well sir! He brought back more rabbits than he knew what to do with. And do you know what he did to show Boots his appreciation? He called Boots and placed her on his eating table where there was a variety of food, and if I remember correctly there was country ham on the table. I don't know where Wayne's wife was. He was a young man in those days and full of life anyway. So Boots feasted from Wayne's table.

So if anybody wants to verify this one, Wayne is still alive and well and his telephone number is available if anyone wants to check with him.

As to Boots, after such a productive life, it was a sad ending for her. After people became a little more knowledgable and began putting insecticides on sweet potatoes before they bedded them for sprouts for the potato patches, Boots got hold of one of the poisoned potatoes and finally went into convulsions and unconsciousness and it fell my lot to use the ax to get her out of her suffering.

And those poisoned potatoes stopped Ma from getting them after the beds were pulled and making those delicious sliced-potato pies with all the spices and the delicious crusts with that butter and stuff smeared over them.

So much for a slight look at my personal life.   □

Radios Put Us In Touch

N o, not even television had the impact on the masses that radio had when we began to receive programs in my area in the early 1930s. Before radio, we had to go to movie theaters to get Lowell Thomas' news programs as a part of the theatre program. We were almost ecstatic when a few people in the neighborhood bought sets. And you'd better believe they had plenty of company.

At first all of them were small table models and people went to the woods and cut down the highest pine saplings they could find to use as antennas. And even then there was so much static on them when the weather was inclement there was little pleasure in listening. Sometimes they just had to be cut off.

But when the weather was good, those radios were turned on when anybody was around the house and that volume was turned as high as it would go so it could be heard when people were a good distance from the radios.

At dinner time, everybody rushed to the house and ate as fast as they could so they could congregate in the front room and listen to the "Tobacco Tags" that originated in Raleigh. And it seems like the "Sons of the Pioneers" also came on at the noon hour. If it was string music, everybody listened no matter who it was.

"Mustard and Gravy" that originated from Wilson was also a very popular show that the masses listened to. And nobody wanted to miss any of the programs if they could help it. And getting the news regularly seemed almost unreal. Even weather forecasts! It seemed almost unbelievable.

Everything went fine during the daylight hours when the weather was good. But stations crowded in on one another at night to the extent that only a few very strong stations came through without a lot of interference, such as WJJD in Chicago, KDKA, Pittsburgh, WOR, New York, and a few others. And there was a great amount of fading out when the entire program would be lost and in many cases Mexican stations, or stations in Texas near the Mexican border would come in loud and clear in the Spanish language, and there was always the Spanish guitar dominating the program.

But Saturday night was the greatest of all, for that's when the Grand Ole Opry was broadcast, and the young and old alike gathered in a circle around the radio and listened and stomped their feet and dipped and smoked and fussed when the drowning-out periods came. And this was the pure "hillbilly" period.

People almost had fits when Roy Acuff sang "The Great Speckled Bird" and Minnie Pearl came on with her jokes and played the piano and sang. And Little Jimmy Dickens drew praise from the crowd. Everybody even loved the "solemn old judge."

Then there were Lum and Abner and their "Jottemdown Store" that came on in the week and Amos and Andy, and Jack Benny on Sunday nights and we looked forward to those programs as much as we look forward to TV programs or specials today. Boy, we were really getting out of the woods then.

But young upstarts that had radios in their cars were beginning to listen to other sounds that came on around 10 p.m. It was the beginning of the Big Band era and there was a new dimension to music. We loved it! Tommy Dorsey, Jimmy Dorsey, Glenn Miller, Vaughn Monroe, Harry James, Kay Kyser, Guy Lombardo, and others. And popular songs were becoming hits across the country. The performances were live in ball rooms in large cities and we knew that things on the farm would never be the same again. If we hadn't seen, we'd heard about the world beyond the backer patches and modernity was creeping in despite all our country background.

I remember "Ma Perkins" as one of the early soap operas, although I never listened. And there was the Andy Hardy series that everybody loved.

And the "Hit Parade" on Saturday nights was a tremendous hit on radio, and even followed on television. L.A. "Speed" Riggs of Goldsboro was the auctioneer for Lucky Strikes and the top ten popular songs of the day were featured, and it made "hep cats" out of farm boys and girls. We were moving on up the ladder then, man.

And "The Shadow" brought chills down the spines of even the stout-hearted, and gangly young'uns would run out of the room or pull the cover over their heads if they were in bed. "The Shadow" had a laugh that we associated with the grave.

And when the World Series came on in early fall we were just about always in the packhouse grading backer and the radio was unhooked from the antenna and toted to the packhouse along with the battery, for we could pick up local stations that carried the game over a network. We thought that was the finest thing there was and we began sprouting wings along about then in anticipation of flying high one day. What a time in our history! □

Miss Mag

Dr. Heck

Life Along The Roads

T he drama of life unfolded daily along the rut-filled dirt roads and arteries that led into the fields and behind the woods where many of the rural population lived.

Our lives touched. We might not be closely associated, but some facts about our personal lives were known by the community.

Miss Lillie was an old maid and two of her brothers were bachelors. They lived together at the home place and were among the upper echelon of society in the community. They visited the sick, attended church regularly, and were the salt-of-the earth kind of people. But what I remember best about them was something they told about Miss Lillie. People said she wore a wig (and that was during the days when wigs were unheard of almost).

Young'uns at church would sit behind her and get a good look at that heavy head of hair with many horn hairpins holding it up and combs with jewels on them, to see whether they could find any evidence of it being a wig. But nobody ever came up with an answer. Anyway, it never became gray, and looked the same the last time I saw her as it had during the years when she taught my Sunday school class.

I can still see Miss Mag with her half-poodle-half-just-dog Boss by her side as she walked along the road on her way to visit a neighbor. She must not have weighed more than 85 or 90 pounds, and her dress was down to her ankles and that hair done up tight on her head.

Miss Mag had a gang of young'uns, and they said when she had a baby she stayed in bed for a full month. She said that was one time she was going to get a little rest, and according to what everybody said, she did. She had 12 young'uns so she spent a year in the "child bed."

Miss Mag had to cook a whole peck of "ish taters" every day to feed her brood and hired hands that she was always cooking for, and she didn't have a pot large enough to hold the taters, so one day she was in a furniture store and saw what she thought was a pot just like she needed. It was really a "slop jar" and something new on the market. Those old porcelain chamber pots were wearing out and a lot of the tops broken and they were filled with veins where tiny cracks were showing through the glazy finish. Anyhow, Miss Mag made good use of that "slop jar" and had plenty of room in the pot to cook that peck of "ish taters."

And Dr. Heck was a miracle worker out in the sticks. He lived in town, but made the rounds out in the country on his dilapidated old car regularly and had two Pomeranian dogs that dominated the car when Doc wasn't in it. He was considered a giant in the medical profession, but hard times during the Depression had their impact on him also. He was becoming an old man by then, and had married one of the girls in the community, and she was a beauty in those days, and quite a bit younger than he. And they called her "Emma Heck," although the Doc's last name was Person.

He wore a baggy old suit and a string tie and an old black hat that drooped around his face, and was a walking drugstore with his coat pockets full of pills. And there were others in his satchel. And the poor man did all this for nothing except for farm products, for nobody had a dime to pay him. So he doctored out of the generosity of his heart. But he healed many who would have received no medical aid without his care about people.

And Miss Pashey could talk out fire. Her real name was Patience. I reckon there was one person like that in every community. But many a person visited Miss Pashey at her house down a long lane from the main road. Many a young'un got burned by climbing up beside a stove with hot grease or boiling foods on it that were overturned, scalding a part of the body. Also, people dumped ashes out on the edges of the yards and sometimes there were live coals in them and a young'un would step into the ashes and suffer a burned foot. And they landed up at Miss Pashey's. They said she really did talk the fire out in many cases.

And it seems like folks back then had a lot more nose-bleeds than we have today. Sometimes the flow was so profuse they had to go to the doctor and get the nostrils packed and they had a heck of a time stopping the blood. But there was a woman in the community who said her piece over them also, and sometimes the blood stopped. I think she used the Bible or quoted scripture in that ritual.

Incidentally, Miss Pashey's brother, Mr. Bob, courted Miss Lillie, and Mr.Bob and Miss Pashey never married either. So Mr. Bob and Miss Lillie never made it to the altar, and if Miss Pashey ever courted anybody I never hear about it.

There goes Sarah Dail down the road with a fishing pole and a can of worms. She's a fisherwoman if there ever was one and she'll spend the day on a creek

Aunt Sene   **Mr. Emmett**

bank and before the sun sets she'll be back with a string of fish on a forked limb and a smile on her face as well as fresh-water fish for supper.

Where looping shelters were situated alongside the road, it wasn't unusual to see a woman ironing at the tobacco barn while curing the tobacco. She'd put the ironing board between the racks that held the sticks of tobacco and iron away with the little young'uns busy playing under the shelter.

Yonder comes Mr. Ed Parks in his five-passenger Model T. Git out of the road, young'uns. Git!

And in the fall, people would pick cotton and empty it on the front porch and that was the best place in the world for young'uns to play. They'd dig them out a hole in the cotton and snuggle down among the lint and fill hours playing on the front porch. And when there was a slow rain, it was all the more appealing for it gave the young'uns warmth as well as the pleasure of romping in the cotton. But they'd better pick up any that got pushed off the porch during their play, or they wouldn't want to return to the porch after the "old man" got through with them.

Just listen to John Smith picking the pure strings off that dilapidated guitar in that old shanty. Making the strings talk picking out the blues and stomping his feet to keep time.

It was a sight to see all the people meandering about their places on walks along the road. They were doing a hundred different things and carrying on everyday life.

Up a field path about a quarter of a mile from the road lived a family with a popular teen-ager named George. But George mistakenly used gasoline on a stove fire and was burned unmercifully. He lingered at home for several days, or maybe weeks, and they built a screen to place over him to keep the flies away.

They said great hunks of skin and flesh would come off when they turned him on sheets placed under his body, and he finally lost his battle for life. Such events were rude awakenings for young people of that time. At such an age, we thought of life as being eternal, but a hunting accident, a car fatality, or tragedies such as George's made us aware that it wasn't just the old that were vulnerable to death.

A turn to the right from the main road led you to Aunt Sene's, the community midwife. Aunt Sene was as bow-legged as anybody you ever saw, and because of that fact she was low of stature. But she was one of the most popular people in the community, for many a baby was born among us poor folks of that era. And going to a hospital to have a baby was unheard of way back there. They'd pack up the young'uns and send them to a neighbor's house, get a kettle of water boiling, gather up ragged sheets to use at the birth, and run off for Aunt Sene.

They carried out sanitation as far as was possible, but it certainly wasn't a germ-free atmosphere. And there ain't no telling how many hundred cords Aunt Sene cut during her long career.

Howdy Miss Bertie.

And a left turn took you to Mr. Emmett's. Mr. Emmett was a landowner and enjoyed a somewhat better life than sharecroppers. And they ate country ham when most of us were on fatback diets. But Mr. Emmett worked equally as hard as any sharecropper. And Mr. Emmett boasted one expertise that was appreciated by area farmers. He was adept at castrating hogs.

When a farmer had several young boars to be castrated, he usually called upon Mr. Emmett to accomplish the job. So on the appointed day, we'd round up the hogs and place one at a time on their sides for Mr. Emmett's sharp razor.

Those hogs would squeal and try to jump up and flee, and we had to hold them by main strength as Mr. Emmett wielded the knife, depriving them of their masculinity as well as inflicting pain. Then the openings were saturated with coal tar and the hogs would run and seek relief in the nearest mudhole.

I knew of one or two people in the community that they said considered the gonads a delicacy.

Out at the fairgrounds on the outskirts of town is where cattle from the Dust Bowl had been shipped in in an effort to prevent them from starving. But it was too late for many who were emaciated and already on wobbly feet. With grazing lands parched by drought, they were skeletons almost with hip bones protruding over skinny bodies. They died and their bodies were burned, leaving a stench over the community of cooked hides, bones and meat, a reminder not only of the Depression, but of natural disasters as well that exacted a heavy toll on top of all the other upheaval in a world gone haywire.

All these things happened along the roads that I traveled as a boy. □

(N.C. Dept. Archives and History)

Wallace Strawberry Festival

Headlines From The Past

W e didn't lack for headlines in the 1930s. Plenty was happening in the world and of course Herbert Hoover was a daily topic from 1929 through 1932, since he was president during the Great Depression. But even before his presidency, he was in the news. His opponent was Alfred E. "Al" Smith, then governor of New York. And Smith was a Roman Catholic, and man, they really played that up out in the sticks. Many ignorant folks said if he were elected we would be forced into Catholocism, and there was a lot of talk about that.

Then Franklin Delano Roosevelt was elected president and in 1933 he got his New Deal started and every day there were big headlines about his National Recovery Act and what he was doing to get the nation turned around and on solid footing again. That went on for years.

And Eleanor (Roosevelt) was a big figure in the news too. She really made herself known while FDR was in the White House and fought for many causes. She was loved and talked about too.

Once she came to Wallace to the Strawberry Festival and that made big headlines in North Carolina. But the thing that I remember best about her visit was the way people poked fun at her cotton stockings. Yeah, she was wearing pure old cotton stockings, and even poor women in the sticks were wearing silk stockings when they dressed up in those days. The cotton stockings and the fact that she was a "plain Jane" dominated the topic of conversation. But we were flattered to have her visit the eastern section of the state.

Some other big headlines from the '20s and '30s:

Charles A. Lindbergh made the first solo flight across the Atlantic in his Spirit of St. Louis plane nonstop. He left on May 20, 1927 and landed at Le Bourge Air Field in Paris on May 21 and logged 3,610 miles in 33½ hours. That was really big news then.

The Empire State Building opened on May 1, 1931 in New York City.

Another real big news item occurred in 1932. Charles A. Lindbergh Jr. was kidnapped on March 1 and his body was found on May 12. It was news every day on the front page from the time of the kidnapping until the body was found. Then Bruno Hauptmann was charged with the kidnapping and subsequently paid with his life. Every detail about the kidnapping, the finding of the body, and the trial of Hauptmann was read avidly by the public.

Beloved Will Rogers was killed in an Alaskan plane crash on Aug. 15, 1935. By then many people had radios and were hearing news flashes via the airwaves as well as reading about them. And a nation mourned for Will Rogers.

An act was passed in 1935 that has more impact on us today than in the early years after its enactment. On Aug. 14, the Social Security Act was passed by Congress.

Another biggie came along in 1936. Britain's King Edward abdicated his throne for the woman he loved, Wallace Warfield Simpson, a beautiful Baltimore divorcee who was unacceptable to the Royal Family. That made everybody mad to think that an American wasn't good enough for British royalty. Of course we realized that in that hoity-toity society it had to be that way and we were just glad a king gave up his throne, and we thought that was the farthest you could go to prove your love. Come to think of it, I guess it's still that way today.

Anybody remember Orson Wells' dramatization of the war of worlds on radio? That was on Oct. 30, 1938 and scared thousands of people half to death.

It was on July 2, 1937 that the famous aviatrix, Amelia Earhart was lost near the Howland Islands in the Pacific.

And on May 24, 1934, something happened in Canada that made headlines around the world and became a continuing story for years. That was the day the Dionne quintuplets were born. They were delivered by Dr. Allan Defoe. They were Cecile, Yvonne, Annette, Emile and Marie. Emile died in 1954 and Marie died in 1970.

The quintuplets captured the imagination of the public, and everybody wanted to read everything about them. As far as we know, they were the first set of quintuplets to survive and it was considered a modern miracle. National magazines would run features and pictures on the quints, and we couldn't get enough of their story. I recall that they were shown to the public through glass panels that showed them at play while they could not see the crowds watching.

It was stories like the quintuplets and the Lindbergh kidnapping that kept us waiting for the daily paper. And the comics. The Katzenjammer Kids was one that we loved, along with Lil' Abner. Now Lil' Anber was right down our alley and we identified with him and Daisy Mae and Dogpatch and every other character in that Al Capp masterpiece. We loved all the comics as a matter of fact. Anybody remember the Willises? That was a single feature, perhaps two columns. It was called "Out Our Way" and if the boy was named Willis, he always had a leg hanging over an armchair and his tongue hanging out of his mouth and he was some character and in some kind of pickle.

These were among many remembrances of major news items that helped to fill our lives and our thoughts in the 1920s and 1930s. But in this case, I had to look up the dates, although I remember all the stories.   □

A Sharecropper's Lament

The laments of a sharecropper as he observes a ruined crop during the Depression era, resulting in another shattered dream:

Terrapin bugs eatin' up the collards. Might as well crap 'em off to the buds and feed the leaves to the hogs and put some Paris Green on 'em and hope for rain to bring new growth. The hogs need something extra anyhow since corn's scace and mostly nubbins to feed 'em.

Mightly lanky looking, them shoats. They'll need a lot of fattening later on. Hate to even go near the feeding trough for they squeal like they've never been fed and they almost take the slop bucket away from you when you try to pour the slops into their trough. Longest-nosed shoats you almost ever saw, 'specially being so thin and all. No wonder they can come under the wire so easy. Put down stobs to hold 'em in and they can git them noses under the wire and be out before you can git back to the house.

Tater vines are mighty thin. Ought to be thick and vines everywhere, but the ground's showing between the rows. Dry. Dry. Dry. Lord, it's hot. Hot and dry and a lean harvest coming up. Too late for corn. Already dried up and ears half filled out. Won't be enough to last til spring hardly, but we'll cross that bridge when we git to it.

Backer will be a failure too. Been a drought all year. Never was able to git a stand. Replanted over and over and toted plants up and down the rows no telling how many times and the plants just stood there and dried up under the hot sun.

Then what lived buttoned out knee-high and even after topping it out at the very top leaves, it just managed to git thigh-high and the leaves little and spindly and feeling like paper and burning up half-way up the stalk.

The same with cotton, even with it being a dry-weather crop with its long tap root, seems like it's too dry for that too.

Pea-vine hay fields showing effects of the drought too. Turning a yellowish color too early. But maybe with the fodder there'll be enough to tide us over. Might not be much left for fodder, though. But we got to feed the mules somehow for we can't git along without them. Got to tend a crop. Got to do our best for that's the only way we know.

Lord, Lord, what next? Chickens' got the limeberneck. Pigs' got scours.

Cow's going dry. Garden's growing up with grass waist high. Plowed out the collards late, the only reason they ain't taken over with grass. But the dry, hot dirt burned the leaves and left the buds for the bugs.

Must be a dead chicken or a pig out in the weeds somewhere with all the stink in the air and if it ain't found all the chickens will die, for if they git to them live things it'll kill them as sure as the world.

Cockleburrs taking over the corn fields and cotton patches. Strange how they can be so rank and green when it's so dry.

Never asked for much, just enough to git by on. Looks a little doubtful about this year though. But we'll make it. We always have. We'll have a big turnip patch, come fall. Rain will come and the collards will grow and be just right for winter. They'll need "turning down" to put them on the south side of the row 'fore winter comes. Have to run a deep furrow beside the rows and just push the collards over so they'll git some protection from the winter freezes, then turn a furrow over the stalks.

Fatten them shoats and git some meat in the smokehouse and if there's enough taters to winter us over, things will be OK agin. Depression or whatever, life's got to go on and there ain't no soup kitchens out here in the country so we got to make it on our own.

Woodpile's looking thin too. Cut enough stove wood in the winter it ought to have lasted two families. Where in the world has all that pile of wood gone? Well, when it's used up they'll have to start sawing left-over backer wood. Pretty good pile of wood at the backer barns. Won't be as easy to saw though for that wood is bone dry and a saw's teeth don't sink into dry wood like when it's green.

The big ditch is what you might say dried up. Just a little trickle of water and it's thigh-deep when the rains are plentiful. On the edges the black mud has dried and cracks are showing. Lord, it's dry.

Bad enough to be dry any year, but worse this time with all the problems everywhere. Money system gone haywire. Talk about Depression and all that. Papers telling about people jumping out of buildings and killing themselves after losing their money when the banks closed. All that mess just adds to farmers' miseries for if the landowner's got a dollar he shore as hell is going to hang on to it and you can't hardly blame him for that. But it ain't solving no sharecroppers' problems.

Never heard nobody cussed like Herbert Hoover. He's catching it from all sides, according to the papers. People carrying on in the streets of the big towns and pictures of all the mess. They say a lot of folks is hungry and that they're dishing out soup to them in pure lines.

Would make little difference to us folks here if we could just make a good crop. Never been used to much. Never asked for much — just a chance to feed and clothe us and maybe have a few dollars for hard times. Like now. It's enough to make a man scratch his head and just look into the distance and ponder nothing in his mind, just wondering what it's all about.

A man's supposed to marry a good woman and raise a family. That's what the Good Book says. And it says to be fruitful and multiply, and you need them young'uns if you're to raise big crops. Course that's not saying what they might want to do when they're grown up. Somebody might want to leave the farm some day.

"Old man and old woman" is what they say behind the back. Good names for we farmers that git old before our time. Wrinkled and reddened by the sun, why even our eyes look faded. Wore down to a frazzle. Sunrise comes early and dark late and there is no time to dream and plan. Only time to doze.

Day was when we looked good with clear skin and heads of hair that glistened in the light. A right handsome man and woman when we started out. But Lord! Look at us now. Man of 40 ought to be still considered young, and woman too. It's not been all that long but the load's just been too heavy. Same way with others too. But it hurts still when we hear 'em say "old man and old woman" to our backs.

Old lady trims up my hair and sometimes leaves gaps. And she just balls up hers at the back of her head and with her tired-looking eyes she does look old. Don't seem quite fair. Old before our time. Must be the hard life on the farm. Could be a lot worse though. Could be a lot worse. We're mighty blessed people out here on the farm.   □

Roy Taylor — The Huckleberrier

The Huckleberriers

I f they only knew! I'm now thinking about these great big blue huckleberries people buy in summer, grown domestically in back yards that are as large as the end of the thumb. Of course they're called blueberries, and that still sounds a little hifalutin for a berry that went through most of its history as the humble huckleberry. Whatever it is or ain't, as far as name goes, it's good.

But we used to have to go up in the woods in late June and July to find and pick them and the only way it seemed worthwhile is to remember the taste of those pies and dumplings after they were cooked. And people had to "huckleberry" when there wasn't anything pressing to do in the fields.

You'd often see a woman and two or three young'uns walking along the roads toward the woods with pails in their hands and you knew where they were headed. But a lot of those huckleberries weren't eaten at home. Some people didn't have the sugar to sweeten them with. They'd sell those berries for a dime a quart to anyone wanting to buy them.

Now Ma was a huckleberrier. She just loved to get up in those woods and find them. And Ma was deaf. And Ma wouldn't stay with anybody else after she got in those woods. She rambled until she found a bush that hadn't been picked, be they blue or the smaller black berries. You never heard a crying word out of her and she didn't hear your cries. You could holler to the top of your voice but the only thing you received was an echo.

That would worry you half to death, and not being able to pick enough berries to make a dumpling with unless you took into account all the green ones in the bucket anyhow, it was a lost cause for anybody accompanying Ma up in those woods. So the only thing to do was to begin searching for her. Ever tried finding somebody in a thick woods where a bush was available to hide behind every foot or so? Ma could hide behind a big bush and you'd never know it, for she wasn't but about five feet tall.

It wasn't long until the skeeters got to biting you and there was no getting rid of them. They'd bite and a whelp would rise and they'd pop you again and then the gnats got to plaguing you and you were constantly trying to get them out of your eyes. And a snake would slither by and nothing to kill it with.

And anybody who ever went into the woods in summer knows what else you get. Red bugs! You don't know it at first, for it takes a little while for them to get under the skin. But you'll find out. Lord have mercy! Those things will itch you to death. I can still hear people saying to us young'uns, "quit diggin'." Were they kidding? How do you stop digging when something is eating you up? Those red bugs would drive you crazy.

And that's saying nothing about getting tangled up with poison ivy or poison oak. Try that along with red bugs and skeeter bites and you'll go as crazy as a loon.

Now back to searching for Ma. You'd think she would have been in a nearby area from which she started, but not so. You had to ramble and look hither and yonder and cuss (cause you knew she wouldn't hear you) and fight skeeters and gnats, and by then if it wasn't hot when you entered the woods, it got hot. And it's about as sticky a hot as it can get when you're up in a woods and no wind stirring and the sweat starts popping out and you begin to itch all over.

You swear you'll never go huckleberrying again, but as long as there's a loving mama and she says "go huckleberrying," you'll go. So you keep on searching and if there's a thundercloud somewhere around (that you can't see in the woods) and you hear it thunder one time, you almost panic, for Ma's in there and she's got to be found and gotten out of those woods before it rains.

By now you've gone far enough in the woods you wonder whether you'll find the way out, particularly if it's where you aren't used to going. And something stinks that has been dragged in the woods for the buzzards, and not far away is a skeleton of a mule or a cow that has been picked clean by the vultures. You want to vomit and you hurry to get away from that area.

Then you backtrack and start walking all the way around every huckleberry bush you see and just keep doing that, and after a while, there she is, as happy as a lark, still picking those berries with a peck pail practically full and only a few green berries to be seen, and no trash and tiny limbs from the bush.

There's no way to describe the relief you feel when you actualy see Ma in the flesh, doing her thing with the least concern you ever saw. Away from the house, from a schedule, from the routine of housekeeping, it is pure diversion for her.

All the cuss words are gone then, and all the irritation of having to accompany her way up in a piney woods to pick berries. The miracle is that you have found her, and it's only a repetition of the last time you went with her on a huckleberry expedition. And you'll do the same thing again on another day this very year, and maybe more than one time. You did the same thing last year. It's a ritual and will be performed again next year.

Not one word is said to Ma about wandering off. It has been said in the past and it did no good. It is her pleasure at our expense, and now those red bugs have started up and we'll be "diggin' and diggin' and diggin'" for days and there's a red place on a hand or the face that's beginning to itch (bad) and the more you scratch it the more it itches. Uh oh! Poison ivy. And we're as bad as a dog scratching fleas and never getting relief.

But the next day for dinner there'll be huckleberry pies with that purple juice oozing out the holes sliced in the top and that syrupy filling will cover the tender crust and we'll eat with one hand and "dig" with the other and either Pa or a grown young'un will say "stop that diggin'," but we pay them no attention, for we couldn't stop if we wanted to. □

Cleaning The Church Grounds

The Community Church

I t was a warm night. I was curing a barn of tobacco and lying on my bunk between firing the furance, eating a slice of watermelon. I would take a mouthful and spit the seeds straight into the air while trying to catch lightning bugs between my toes just to pass the time away. A slight breeze was stirring and I heard the strains of a sad song coming from the church a little way down the road. There was the deep bass voice of Mr. Bob distinguishable above the others, and Miss Myrt coming in on the alto.

We are going down the valley, going down the valley, going down the valley one by one

We are going down the valley, going down the valley, going toward the setting of the sun

My first thought was of the graveyard on the church grounds that was ever-widening to accommodate the bodies of those who had gone through the deepest valley of all — death. It seemed unfair to think of the babies who hadn't been given a chance at life — those who died from pneumonia and colitis mostly; the mother who gave her life for a new life; the 12-year-old boy who ran into the path of a car on his bicycle and paid the supreme sacrifice.

I felt differently about the aged and the infirm whom I thought of as being victorious in death over the relentness hand of time, that took away their dignity and left them as babies again. Those with quivering limbs and eyes that peered unknowingly with withered bodies and minds that no longer functioned. They were the ones who had outlived their time and usefulness and who represented a burden on society. Everything about them spoke of the scourge of living too long, of becoming obnoxious in the eyes of the world, even to the odor of the very old. They were the victors in death, leaving behind the masses who would some day follow in their footsteps.

I observed the bright lights at the church, brighter than other lights in the area for there was a Delco engine in a little house behind the church that generated the power to light the church. There were the plain bulbs that hung from the ceiling in a straight line down the length of the sanctuary. I also thought of the small engine that supplied the electricity, for I sometimes primed the engine, poured gasoline into it from a gallon jug, and watched the engine as it came to life. I could hear the purr of the engine after the singing ended.

I visualized the oil lamps that hung from the ceiling before the Delco engine was installed. That was the first sign of progress at the old church with its hard pews and dim amen corners.

Then I thought of the carbide lights at Mr. Fenn's and Mr. Jim's houses, the only homes in the community that had brightly-lighted interiors. I didn't know by what chemical process the lights glowed so brightly, but I did take note of the covered area built beside the house where the process was carried out.

I only fully realized at that time the true role the church played in our lives. It was the very fiber of community life and it had an impact on all of us. Not everyone attended church by any means — the backsliders, the drunks, the bootleggers and others who had no interest in religious activities. But from almost every home, someone was involved with the church.

There were the colored cards picturing scenes from the Bible for the beginners with the word text that was studied each Sunday and the cards were collectors' items for some of the young children; the higher grades when Sunday school books were more detailed; the little parties given by the various classes occasionally; the singings in which area churches participated; Recitation Day when children diked out in their Sunday best curtsied and said their recitations before a full house; the hand-dipped Hines ice cream on the grounds later, along with lemonade.

I think I realized at that moment the full goal of the community church. So many of the rituals were boring to the younger generation, especially the long-winded sermons and a lot we didn't fully understand about religious practices. But I saw clearly that the church was fertile ground for planting seeds in the minds of the young. I knew that a lot more of what was said was absorbed by those young minds than we believed at the time. And those seeds sprouted later and bore fruit, even if some fell on barren ground. They would have their impact in the future.

The church, along with our neighborhood schools, represented the moral, spiritual and educational values we placed on life. They were our lives outside the home, which came first, even before church or school. That is where the entire process began. The greatest value of all was home, the very foundation on which our lives depended. I knew that without teaching that began at home there was little value in other facets of life.

I had to replenish the fire in the tobacco barn furnace, but I returned to the bunk and concentrated on the little church set among a grove of trees with overgrown ditches on its perimeter and the leaves that had to be raked after the first frost and before quarterly meeting, or the annual conference if it was at our church that year. A simple, ordinary building that spoke of reverence and even empty gave a feeling of being a hallowed place.

I looked again at the bright lights from the church and they represented a symbol to me of what the church really was in the community. It was the light that shone above all others, lighting the pathway for all the community by offering hope to those who would participate in its activities. It wasn't a promise. It was a reality to those who believed in a life beyond the trials and disappointments encountered in life.

Then they were singing "Just As I Am" and at the end of the song the lights were extinguished, but I gained a new perception of what the church meant to my community on that night. It was the light and the hope of better things. And I appreciated that little church that has had its impact on my life through the years.   □

Pulling Fodder Is Hell

In late summer when ears of corn hang heavy on the stalks and the blades of corn are getting a faint yellow hue, it's time to pull that fodder.

Even as a child I never understood why we couldn't grow enough hay to feed our livestock through the winter. I still don't understand. I figure that Pa felt that to give us a well-rounded lesson in life, we had to "do it all" which included pulling fodder. And when I say Pa I mean hundreds of pa's. And in retrospect, he did a pretty darn good job in giving us lessons in life that have proven invaluable. But of course we couldn't know it at that time.

August is hot and sticky and a cornfield ain't no place to be. It's late enough that the sky has taken on a different hue — bluer than in earlier summer months — but not as blue as it will get in early fall. Watermelon patches are getting bare and only "knots" are left in the fields, but they taste all right if you get to them before the sun has heated them up. They need to still have dew on them if they are to appeal to the taste buds.

Anyhow, like it or not, we have to start pulling fodder. For the millions who know nothing about such a heathen practice, it's stripping the corn stalks of the blades and tying them into bundles and breaking down a part of the stalk and hanging the fodder on the stalk to cure.

And how is it all accomplished? Well, you pull enough blades to fit in the hands, and then you take about three blades and use them for the tie. They are wrapped around the blades three or four inches from the top and then run under the tie-around and tucked so the bundle of corn will hold together. This is done over and over until a field is filled with green fodder that has to dry several days before it is ready to be stacked.

But as hot as it is in the fields, rest spells are taken several times during the day. There are always trees on a ridge nearby or on hedgerows in the field. So we plunk down on the ground and rest on our elbows and wait for a young'un to bring us water in a gallon jug that is as warm as tap water by the time it reaches the field. The only thing that can be said for that water is that it quenches thirst and gets the dryness out of the throat for a little while.

If anybody brought any meat and biscuits to the field they retrieve them and gobble them down, that is unless the ants have taken them over, and that happens many times. Anyhow, everybody cools off and the grown boys roll their cigarettes and savor that Golden Grain for all it's worth. Then it's back to the field.

The sun's shining down and everybody is sweating and blades of corn hit the neck and cause it to sting and everybody's madder'n a junkyard dog. One of the grown young'uns can't take it no more. "I'm going to git under that shade tree and just sit there til sunset," he says. "Ain't no reason why fodder has to be pulled every year when we could grow enough hay to feed the team and the cow too. But no, that fodder's got to be pulled come hell or high water."

"If you quit I'm going to quit too," a smaller young'un says.

"Me too," a third voice says.

The grown one cusses and stomps a hill of corn to the ground and slings a handful of corn blades to the ground. "It's the "old man's fault," he says. "Anybody knows we don't have to have fodder to feed through the winter unless it's what he wants. That old man's like every other one in these parts. He's a fodder-pulling fool. His "old man" made him do it and it has been handed down from generation to generation and some kind of quirk in his mind makes him think there ain't no way to go through a winter without fodder to throw in them stables."

"Let's quit," a younger voice says.

"Pa would half-kill us," another says.

"Old man" ain't going to git on my back no more," the oldest says. "I could git by if I quit, but you young'uns would catch it. Like it or not, we got to pull this fodder. And just look at me. My face is burning up and I'll bet it looks like the blood is about to pop out. And hot! God almighty! How can it git this hot? And it's just as bad when we go to git it up. May be worse. And I'll be the one that has to stack it around that pole. Tell you what. When I git out on my own, fodder-pulling will be over for this Buddy Roe. If I have 15 young'uns I'll never put them in a corn field pulling fodder. You can count on that."

"Ain't no worse than suckering backer," a young'un says.

"But there's some reason for suckering backer," the older boys says. "You have to git out the suckers or the backer won't do nothing. With fodder, all you have to do is grow enough hay and fodder ain't necessary. It's just one of the old man's "isms" and you couldn't talk him out of it no matter what you said."

"How long will it take the fodder to dry?" a young'un asks.

"Three, four days," the oldest answers. "This is Tuesday. You know what young'uns, we'll probably be out in this field toting this mess to the stackpole

Saturday night at sunset. I think I'll just go to town and forget to come home."

"How come Pa fixes it so it will be Saturday when the fodder's got to be got up?" one asks.

"Cause that's the way the "old man's mind works," the oldest says. "He wouldn't be happy about it if it was a Monday that the fodder had to be got up. If there ain't some kind of sacrifice in it for us young'uns, the old man wouldn't git that special charge for him out of it. I don't understand it, but then nobody understands "old men's" thoughts."

"We've been doing so much talking and belly-aching, we're almost through this field," a youngster observes. "We ought to have started complaining a long time ago. Look, the sun will soon be setting too. Look at that old bullbat up there, flying and flying and then taking a straight dive and almost hitting the ground. I ain't so tard after all and I'll be ready to do something after supper."

□

The Years Of Our Youth

I n the years of our youth, we walked through the tall grass of summer and explored all our world about us. In our spare time we were as free as the wind that blew over our domain. Like wild horses, we scampered over all the places that we knew and our world was filled with happiness.

We took the minute things and shaped them into something beautiful. Where the water in the big ditches was shaded by the tall trees that grew beside the banks, we waded and caught minnow bugs that darted across the water and placed them to our nostrils, and they really did smell like vanilla. We climbed the tallest trees and ate the wild grapes that grew there.

We found the guinea nests in the lush foliage beside the streams and removed the eggs with spoons so the human scent wouldn't send them to other nesting places. We took the prized eggs home for they were yellower than hen eggs and were used in cakes.

Where the geese nested among the reed beds, we were attacked by angry ganders as we approached. We observed the Indian hens that habitated the marshlands and found rabbit nests in the ground, uncovered them to see the tiny babies wriggling in the nest, then replaced the hair the mother rabbit had pulled from her fur to keep the babies warm. There were partridge nests under large tobacco leaves and we watched as the frustrated mother fled with her brood of brown-striped chicks to safety out of the reach of human hands.

We ate the wild strawberries that grew on hillsides, and where briers grew thick we picked the black berries they bore in profusion and took them home to be made into jelly.

We climbed the tiers in the tobacco barns and scraped off the turpentine that ran from the fat wood when high heat was applied to cure tobacco. We also took rosin that flowed from pine trees when notches were cut and chewed that, as well as sweet gum.

Over the ridges and down in the little valleys, we roamed all the way back to the marshes and the lowgrounds that were black soil near the canal that took the water on to the rivers.

The cows chewing their cuds under the shade of the trees and swishing the flies with their tails intrigued us. We observed the rabbit paths and kept them in mind when the frosts came and we set rabbit boxes. Out in the wide open places, the air was clean and exhilarating, and when the skies were clear it seemed that we could see to heaven.

At the zenith of our special little hill — actually more a mound than a hill — we sometimes watched a day end and twilight appear. As the sun dropped behind the pines if clouds were floating about the horizon they reflected hues of purple, pink and red and for a little while the western sky would glow red and we would pick out objects created by the trees that became a silhouette on the horizon.

Then there would be a few moments before twilight merged into night when the birds performed their rituals in the skies around us.

Suddenly the day was ended and the stars appeared in the heavens, millions of them. We would lie down flat on our backs and try to count them. They appeared so near it seemed we could reach up and almost touch them. And out there where we had a clear view of the heavens, we often saw shooting stars that made long, red gashes in the sky as they sped through the vastness of space millions of miles away.

There wasn't a care in the world in those glorious days and we didn't envy anyone. We dreamed the dreams of youth and concocted all manner of mischievious things to do. We were not little angels and we came up with some pretty wild tricks.

We were also at that awkward stage when we were neither boys nor men and sometimes we felt we were sort of misfits. We knew that boys matured into men, but nobody had told us of the bodily process.

Our voices sounded like a gander's squawk sometimes and we were embarrassed when we talked. We became ashamed of our own bodies and fuzz began to appear on our faces, especially the upper lip, and they laughed at us when we got out the straight razor to get rid of the fuzz.

And nobody bothered to sit us down and get us straight about the growing-up process. The "old man" never mentioned anything about sex. Not one word. And it wasn't that we didn't know. Boys growing up way out in the sticks learned it all just by observing nature in the raw. We didn't need any sexology courses like they teach today. All that we needed to know was whether those "funny" feelings we had when we were around girls were natural. But we had to find that out for ourselves.

But we knew that that phase would pass and we would emerge as young men and that our boys' world would come to an end. We didn't like that thought, but we were beginning to entertain other ideas and all of it was a little confusing.

So we savored all the joys of childhood during those last years of our youth. Our stomping grounds were prettier, more cherished. We knew it was ending and that the younger boys would follow in our ways and that those special years would all too soon become a memory.

How tall, how green the grass as we began to see a world fall apart. How great had been the carefree years. Now we'd have to fill a man's place in the fields — crop two rows of tobacco at a time, learn how to get on the haystack and handle the hay, climb the tiers and hang green tobacco — and perform all the duties on the farm that grown-ups did.

So we had our last fling at boyhood, romping in the hayloft, taking smelly fish boxes and mounting them on abandoned tobacco truck wheels, made mules of ourselves and did all kinds of shags and tore up the soil in the yards. We even rolled wheels with tobacco sticks again and swam naked in the pond. We'd run our hands in the holes at the edge of the pond and pull out catfish, and even eels. And sometimes a snake would glide by us in the water.

We ate watermelons from everybody's patch and pulled up turnips just for meanness and when the apples turned red we took to the trees like birds after wild cherries. But we were sly. We did this when nobody was in sight. We knocked the apples from the very top of the tree with brick bats and pieces of stove wood. What we didn't eat we left to rot. We stole tobacco from the "old men's" tobacco sacks and smoked behind the barns. We even smoked rabbit tobacco, corn silks, and grape vine.

They were years of beauty, years of wonder, years of seeing the world as we wanted it to be rather than as it was. But we accepted the challenge of life and put away childish things and assumed our roles as adults in society.   □

A Look Into Yesterday

I f I could pierce the curtain of yesterday and actually be there again for a few fleeting hours, I think I'd choose a mid-afternoon in summer when the tobacco barns are running at high heat and the smell of curing tobacco hangs in the air.

Children are playing in the yards. Little girls' dresses are raveled at the waist and part of the hems ripped out with splotches of pope berry juice coloring the faded garments red in some places. Their hair is in strings and their faces mottled with dirt.

Little boys are running around in their tattered overalls with some legs split up to the knees and the fabric dangling around their legs as they play and their eyes squint as they run in the afternoon sunshine. "Tater ridges" are evident around their necks where dirt has accumulated.

The tops of cotton stalks are thick with pink and white blossoms and the lower part of the plants are filled with green bolls awaiting maturation in the fall.

Cape jasmine blossoms in the yards send their sweet fragrance over the area as the flowers reach full maturity and acquire a tan color at the outer edges from the relentless heat of the sun.

Cockleburrs are thigh-high at the end of corn rows and some of the fruit on low, bunchy briar bushes is turning yellow. Soybeans are rank and green in the middles of the corn rows.

Cows staked out on hillsides are chewing their cuds in the shade of the trees, regurgitating the grass gathered in the cool of the morning and swishing their tails at the ever-present flies that plague them.

It is a tranquil scene with thick foliage on the trees shading the housetops, butterbeans thick on the vines awaiting picking, watermelons weathering the heat of the day on the crawling vines in the fields; cantaloupes giving off their odor as they near the rotting point; peas drying up in the patches but with half-grown fruit at the top of the vines and blossoms still evident.

The oaks, the pines, the gums and walnut trees stand as tall as ever and one look around the horizon places everything in its proper place. The church looks lonely in its grove of trees and the tombstones in the cemetery add to the loneliness of the scene.

In the distance people are working in the fields and a tobacco truck going down a road filled with ripe tobacco sends up dust as it makes its way to the looping shelter. But there is a calmness everywhere and about the only noise is that of the children at play in the yards and the occasional bark of a dog. The quietness is actually disquieting. No large machinery. No planes flying overhead. No large trucks and few cars dashing along the roads. Only children laughing and playing and a silence over the land.

And it seems that you can see to eternity. The mid-summer sky is the kind of blue usually seen in October on a sunshiny day when the air is dry and the humidity low. Things are a deep green and the amount of woodsland is amazing. It appears as a giant forest with communities located between the wooded areas.

Standing on the banks of the old mill pond, the sun cuts a bright streak across the water and the water lilies sway gently as the miniature tides come to shore. A fish occasionally jumps out of the water and creates a ripple over the surface for a moment.

The sand along the roads looks washed white by gentle rains and the clay hills are even redder than in childhood. The bridge over the little creek is the same and the construction still solid. The dead tree across the road from the bridge still stands and the summer weeds grow at its feet.

It is a land of simple beauty for it lacks the adornments created by man to give it a more modern look. But order is evident everywhere, in the weed-free lanes leading up to the houses, in the swept yards and the tidiness of the surroundings. Trees are filled with ripening fruit and there is a feeling of being in a millenium where everything is in its right place and all is well with the world.

A mockingbird mocks everything in its repertoire and a jaybird does its silly gawks as the afternoon wanes.

The sun begins to take on a reddish hue, and soon the day will end. People begin returning to the houses and traffic along the roads increases. The cows and mules are brought to the watering troughs where they swill the cool water and boys are dragging up armfuls of green corn to feed the livestock. Guineas and turkeys return from their foraging and fly to their perches on high tree limbs. Chickens make their way to their roosting places in the henhouses except the wild ones that habitate the trees.

The lamps are lit and the glow shines in every kitchen window and the fireflies are everywhere. And the children have to leave the yards to get cleaned up for the night.

The afternoon has passed swiftly and the curtain will be closed shortly. It has been a rewarding visit. There is no desire to linger on nor is there a desire to bring the people back to the world of today. Everything is as it should be in the land of my visit and there is no reason to wish to change it.

The curtain is closed and that look into the past sealed. But it was beauty and a serenity that cannot be fitted into today's society. Too much has changed since those days to associate them with today's world. It would only add unnecessary burdens to the people of yesterday to expect that. Let them rest in their unenlightened world. They're better off than us.   □

Pearl Harbor Day

I t was a warm, overcast Sunday, too warm for the approaching Christmas season when we always thought of snow, even if it never came. It was usually more seasonal in December than in 1941. And it was my birthday! But that meant little in those days. There was no money to spend on gifts, and if the honoree got a cake to mark the occasion, he was lucky.

But there was a certain loneliness about that day that you couldn't put your finger on. The setting was dismal for the landscape had been stripped of the autumn colors that had beautified the community. Leaves lay dead around the towering trees and acorns were thick on the ground. Small coveys of birds would fly overhead occasionally.

With an overcast sky and a barren landscape, the buildings seemed to take on a grayer hue.

Hogs that had been on floored pens for weeks were fat, with their jowls hanging down and the rapid addition of weight from all the shelled corn they could eat making their tails appear receded in their bodies. But it was too warm for hog-killing. It would be risking the loss of the meat and farmers were hoping for some cold weather to get the pork salted down before Christmas.

There was no way of knowing on that fateful Sunday morning what effect the events of that day would have on our lives and all the generations afterward. When we look back upon our history, we can say without question that that day began the change that has carried to the present. Just 42 years ago the world had never heard of an atomic bomb!

That was the day the Japanese bombed Pearl Harbor in Hawaii, Dec. 7, 1941. And we were a nation unprepared. And if the nation as a whole was unprepared, the farming class people in eastern North Carolina were more unprepared. We had gone on in the same pattern for so long we couldn't comprehend the impact this event would have on our lives.

It was Sunday afternoon when I walked into the house and everybody was hovering around the radio. We had an old Philco battery-powered model and the batteries were beginning to get weak. Everybody was talking at once and trying to tell me that the Japs had attacked Pearl Harbor and that many of our ships had been sunk and a lot of our boys killed in the attack. As they talked someone was holding an ear to the radio to try to get every word of information possible.

All of us sat around in a state of shock. It was unbelieveable that another nation would attack the United States of America. And the radio was saying they feared attacks on the west coast of the United States of America. And we could visualize Japanese planes filling the skies around us and blowing us into bits and pieces.

Pa reminded us that we had sold all our scrap metal to Japan when we wanted a little extra spending money, and now they were throwing it back at us in bombs. And God knows we did haul up every bit of scrap metal we could find and put it in piles and trucks would come by occasionally, weigh it and pay us by the pound.

Everybody knew this was war, and something my generation hadn't known, although our parents knew all too well about World War I. Everybody knew it would mean conscription for many healthy, draft-age young men, and might affect married men also, which certainly did happen as the war progressed. Many young men felt that married men with children would stand a better chance of being deferred, and after the attack on Pearl Harbor and the year following, many flocked to the altar and got families started as soon as possible.

We knew somehow that our lives would forever be changed by this day. President Franklin D. Roosevelt came on the radio and said "This day of infamy will live forever." And no truer words were ever spoken.

We knew so little about the world in that dark day of our history, we poor farmers in eastern North Carolina. We were not ignorant, but time and circumstances had not worked in our favor for real progress. We were just plodding along, hoping but not really expecting, very much from life. The battle had been too hard, had lasted too long to be optimistic. There was nothing we could really do about our circumstances.

One of my best buddies lost his life at Pearl Harbor, and a few others whom I knew.

Poor and with the masses of the rural population relatively uneducated, and having lived our lives in a farm environment, we were aware that momentous changes would come immediately. The United States had to have fighting forces as early as possible. We also had to have a strong agricultural base. A lot of young men would have to remain on the farm to raise the food and fiber needed to fight a war. But we knew that a great many men would be called into service, and that deferral would only mean postponment until it became necessary to draft them.

The fields looked so lonely after the news of the attack on Pearl Harbor — less protective — as if I were viewing a strange place that to me had been hallowed ground. Great droves of birds flew over the dead corn fields and blackened the sky before pitching and searching for meager pickings in the bare fields. Much later I remembered that scene and associated it somehow with the endless bombings by hundreds of planes over the war zones in the years that followed.

It was too much to comprehend at the outset, and a pall was over the community. People seemed to be in a stupor and something akin to fear was evident in their faces as well as in their talk. Everyone seemed to be aware that it was the end of a way of life as we had known it; that no longer would our world be bounded by the pine trees that formed our horizon.

War had been talked for a long time and Hitler had made great headway in his march in Europe. And Japanese officials were holding talks with bigwigs in Washington even as Pearl Harbor was bombed. The world was suddenly in an uproar and the United States had to gear up hurriedly to fight a war it didn't want, and wasn't prepared to fight.

That was a black day in our history, and we country folks were afraid to project our thoughts into tomorrow, for we feared the worst.   □

World War II Years

We need some sugar, but all the coupons' been used up," Ma was saying. "We can't git no more til the first of the month. May have to go a week or two without sweets. May even have to go without tea for a day or two." She spoke as she gazed out on a world that didn't appear as bright as before the war started.

There was a good bit of traffic on the highway for hundreds of men were traveling to and from New River, Camp Lejeune, Cherry Point and Fort Bragg where a lot of government building was going on.

"All the young'uns will need shoes for fall, but there ought to be enough coupons for them," Ma said.

Many young boys from the area were already in service and others were being examined at regular intervals. Fifty or sixty young men would stand around a large room as naked as a picked bird and the examiners would go around and do (very little) examining and most were classed 1-A, but there were also a few 4-F's.

There was a lot of work to be done in the fields and if a young farmer complained he was reminded that he'd been deferred because he was considered essential to the war effort.

"The allies have suffered substantial losses in the European theater," the radio announcer was saying. "And Hitler continues his march."

"I'll be needing sugar for preserving later on," Ma said. "Ain't they got coupons for sugar to be used in canning and preserving? They shore ought to let us have sugar for canning when we hear tell of them bootleggers hauling hundreds of pounds up in the woods to make whisky with."

Ma watches that mailbox like a hawk, and rushes out to the road as soon as the mailman passes, hoping for a letter from Bud. And one arrives and she opens it right there.

Dear Ma,

I'm somewhere in Europe, but I can't tell you where. All of you just write me at the APO address above.

It sure ain't like home here, Ma, and I miss all of you and I'm homesick. I won't never want to leave home again when I get back.

I didn't know how good your home cooking was. I don't know nobody here but I did see one fellow that was examined when I was, but I didn't know him.

Hey Ma, pray for me. It means more to me now. I may be dodging bullets, you know.

All of you write, and I love you.

      Bud

The drone of planes is heard in the distance, and almost instantly it becomes a roar as Air Force aircraft fly over the countryside in V-formation and head toward Seymour Johnson Air Field. And a war song breaks the monotony of the afternoon on the battery-powered radio.

"There's a lot of work to be done," the "old man" said. "Shore could have used Bud, but I know somebody's got to fight."

"Ain't right nohow," Ma replied. "Look across the field over there where there's three boys and every one of 'em still at home. I hear tell some folks is buying off the draft board. I reckon if you've got a little money you can buy anything."

"Right smart of traffic out there," the "old man" says. "Shore has been a lot of difference on the roads since the war started. And all of them womenfolks working in factories and welding and riveting and the like and gitting into God only knows what."

"It's gitting night now and supper to fix and I want to be out of this kitchen 'fore Gabriel Heatter comes on," Ma says. "If we didn't have him to cheer us up I don't know what we'd do. No matter how bad things sound he can always calm us down somehow. Go see that nobody hain't turned that radio knob from where it's marked or we'll be gitting that town in Texas. What is it they call it? Loreda? Laredo? Whatever. If we git that we'll be hearing a lot of foreign talk we don't know nothing about. With all them thunderheads around may not be gitting nothing but static nohow."

There'll be bluebirds over, the white cliffs of Dover

Tomorrow just you wait and see

There'll be love and laughter, and peace ever after, tomorrow when the world is free.

Time to think about finding a deep cigar box, brown wrapping paper and twine to fix some kind of package to send to Bud for Christmas. Have to mail it while it's still hot weather, hoping it'll git there by Christmas. Got to find that old ink pen and the bottle of ink if it ain't dried up and scratch his name and all that Army stuff on it. Then the ink gits splotched on the wrapping paper. But a pencil writes too light on that brown paper.

"Rationing is having some effect on 'mobile' travel too," Pa said. "These boys left at home shore can't do all the running around like they used to no more. They got this thing figured out so a man can git just enough gas coupons to git by with. And gitting new 'mobile' tires is out of the question."

"Unless he gits them through the black market," Ma replied. "Just look around the community. Whose 'mobiles' do you see flying by all day long, and at night too I hear? You know who as good as me. It's all right for us to sacrifice. It's what we're supposed to do. But it ain't right for some to git off so light while other folks'es young'uns go off and fight, and it's folks like us who are the most willing to sacrifice at home.

"Did you fix that radio? It's time for Mr. Heatter. He ought to of been a preacher. Talks just like one and he's bound to be a good man."

He died in battle, the paper stated. Only 18 years old. First time he had ever been away from the cotton fields and backer patches of North Carolina. They sent him to Fort Bragg and from there he was put on a troop train and taken to Amarillo, Texas, and from there to the battlefields of Europe. Not even dry behind the ears.

"The allies have suffered a crushing defeat," the voice says on the radio, followed by a long period of static, and Ma takes the hem of her apron and wipes her eyes. "---------- 500 casualties and the loss of (static) planes."

"I believe a cloud's coming up," Pa says, and Ma's thoughts are thousands of miles away. "I wonder where my boy is tonight?" she asks herself. In her mind she thinks the baby years were the best — the years when they trampled on your feet. They were there, touchable, under your protection. But when they grew up in one way or another, they trampled on your heart. If not of their own doing, then at times like this when the call of duty comes before motherly love, even.

"It's beginning to thunder," Pa says. "Better pull down the windows for the rain will be here in a minute. And cut off that radio for you can't hear yourself think with all that scratching."

"Reckon will they call Shine too?" Ma asks.

"I don't know, but if they do we can call it quits as far as farming goes."

"I pray all day that God will protect our boys, not only mine but everybody's," Ma says. "I pray til I fall asleep that He's looking after them, but I know that when you're facing the enemy when them guns go off some mama's son is going to fall on the battlefield. And just a cross will mark the graves of the ones that die somewhere across the sea and we'll never even see where they're buried.

"It ain't fair and I know we can't allow the Japs or the Germans or nobody to take over our country. But when it gits close to home, you sure see things so differently."

A slow rain falls and the thunder fades away and all is quiet, while planes roar overhead in the war zones, bombs fall incessantly, people die and sirens scream in the night. A world is caught up in all-out war and a world suffers. □

More On War Years

T he skies were no longer silent over eastern North Carolina. Everywhere one looked, planes were darting across the skies, leaving white trails of smoke in their paths. And no wonder. Training exercises were carried out from Cherry Point, Camp Lejeune, Seymour Johnson Air Force Base, and Fort Bragg, all in the eastern region.

The pace of life quickened as the war progressed. Soldiers, Marines and sailors were everywhere, thousands of them. Some appeared as boys in their uniforms and on weekends, they flooded area towns, filling up all the hotels and any place rooms were available. They were on weekend passes and had no desire to remain on base.

It was a common sight to see MP's with their arm bands, pistols in slings on their waists, billy clubs in their hands, patrolling the towns to keep order among the servicemen. And the streets were filled with military personnel.

Hotels were the favorite gathering places of GIs and they assured full houses every weekend, in contrast to empty rooms and falling revenues before the war, when traveling men were at home with their families. And on weekends after pay day, it was bedlam. Rooms would be rented early in the day, and then other GIs would join the group, get in with the bell hops, purchase liquor and find out where the prostitutes were located, and begin a weekend of fun and devastation.

They'd rip rooms apart, splash ink on walls, burn mattresses, make a pigsty out of the rooms, and line up outside the prostitutes' doors in a sex-for-pay ritual. And to them it was all in fun. It was a don't-care time when servicemen knew they were preparing for their overseas tours and would no doubt end up in battle. They were far away from home, family and friends, thrust from a sheltered world as a bird would be thrust from the nest.

But not all military personnel were like that. They were just as people are in everyday life with all manner of lifestyles and morals. But as is a perfectly natural thing, their main interest was girls. They would flock out through the countryside because there were too many servicemen and too few girls to date. If they saw girls working in fields, they would stop by to talk, and although they might be amazed at the simple lifestyles of rural girls and have a feeling of pity for them in doing menial tasks, they were overcome by the girls' smiles, their simple beauty and their good-naturedness. Many found them enchanting and as a consequence fell in love with them.

They might help a girl pick a row of cotton just to get to talk with her, or go to the packhouse and make some effort to help in grading and tying tobacco, although the process was totally foreign to them. They'd even hand tobacco at the looping shelters.

As the GIs and the girls became better acquainted, they would be invited to eat with the family on Sunday sometimes, and although some of them couldn't stomach Southern cooking, they'd go through the motion just to be a part of the gathering. But many others latched on to collards, baked sweet potatoes, fried chicken and potato pudding like it was better than any delicacy they had had at home. Many liked the bill of fare and the girls well enough that they stayed on in the South, and many others took their girls with them after the war and transplanted them on foreign ground, but with enough of Southern tradition in them to ensure that a certain part of Dixie was carried on in their families.

The people accepted the influx of military personnel in a generally positive way, for many of our local boys were training in camps across the nation and many were serving overseas as well. The GIs from other places could make it as they desired. If they accepted our Southern ways and were congenial, they were welcomed. However, there were a few who wanted nothing to do with this God-forsaken area of the world, who poked fun at everything about eastern North Carolina and considered us less than human, and it's easy to imagine the treatment they received.

Quite a few people who were too old for military service went to Norfolk to work in the shipyards. Others classified 4-F did the same. And many women went into office work at the military bases, while others went for big money in the defense industries by becoming welders and mechanics and other jobs that hadn't been customary among the female gender. And building was carried out on a large scale at all the military bases in the area and carpenters flocked to those places to work. So change was evident, even before the war ended.

Farming was geared to the war effort, and those left behind to tend the land had their hands full, with fewer family members to carry on the work in many cases. It wasn't an easy life at home during the war years until all those who were on the firing line were remembered. Then those at home counted their blessings.

And the newspapers gave a periodic list of local fighting forces who lost their lives in battle, and that brought a sadness to the home front.

But the world didn't stop because a war was going on. We danced and sang and made love and worked hard and played equally as hard. Some of the girls went to the officers' dances on the posts. Some worked in canteens on weekends. Some volunteered to help make bandages to be sent overseas, and many young wives traveled long distances for the first time to be with their GI husbands when they felt they might be stationed at a base for several months. They'd take their frayed suitcases, board buses and leave on a journey into an unsure world.

So the planes flew endlessly over North Carolina skies, their sound becoming a part of life that no longer commanded attention. Convoys of military vehicles would sometimes pass along the highways and they were several miles long. The realities of war mingled with the rural setting and it was a different eastern North Carolina. Something new had been added to the old and there was a new perception of life as the war unfolded. Everyone was aware of the change and that it would have an impact on our lives for the rest of time.

Dilapidated old automobiles sat with blocks of wood holding them up and others with flat worn-out tires as bushes and weeds grew up around them. There were many do-it-yourself mechanics who searched the old cars for water pumps, fan belts, and even engines to install in other cars. Parts were hard to come by during those years.

And train service was stepped up dramatically. War equipment and supplies for the military as well as the civilian population resulted in long trains moving across North Carolina tracks. The whistles blew loudly at crossings and the rumble of cars over the tracks lulled many to sleep during those years. The relative quiet of former days was gone from the rural area, never to return. An era was starting to come to an end.   □

The War Years End

A mother with graying hair sits at the side table in the kitchen with an oil lamp before her and a ruled tablet and lead pencil at hand to write to her soldier boy somewhere overseas. Wind coming in from cracks in the window causes the lamp to flicker, sending shadows across the walls that move, resulting in a buildup of soot on the chimney.

Touching the pencil to her tongue, she begins:

Dear son,

I'm sitting here with the lamp looking dim in the kitchen, and it's hard to see. I know I need glasses for I just don't see things clear like I used to. One of these days when there is enough money, I'm going to the eye doctor. And we still have not found the money to have lights put in. Your daddy says if we got them in, we probably couldn't pay the bill every month.

I wish I could tell you about everything that's happening everywhere around this part of the country, but you know me. The only thing I can tell is just about the things close to home, and it don't seem like nothing I say is important.

We graded tobacco today, and it was pretty outside with the sun shining bright and butterflies were flapping about in front of the packhouse door. We've had to put up the scaffold over the door for you know how the sun comes in the packhouse door after dinner. It looked so peaceful outside it was hard to think about a war being fought.

The weather has been pretty and it's not been cold yet, just cool, and there's a growing moon and I step out on the porch at night and it does me good to see the things about me in sort of a shadow. And I think about you and know that you can see the same moon wherever you are.

Your daddy's reumatism is acting up. His hands swell up and he complains with his knees hurting and that stuff he rubs on him smells as strong as ever. And your aunt Sis has took to her bed and nobody has said what's wrong, but it wouldn't suprise me if it's not TB. She has that sallow complexion and it looks like her face is flushed with fever to me and she coughs a lot. And Mr. Sill had a stroke a few weeks ago and they're still sitting up with him. He seems to be paralized (I can't spell it right) all over. Janice has a baby girl and she's at her ma's for Bill is over there somewhere, too.

The apple tree in the field beside the house was loaded this year and I've had me a time peeling and cutting and drying apples lately. With the sun shining bright, they've cured out so pretty on top of the shelter and they are a rich, golden brown. I wish I could make you a plate full of apple jacks and get them to you still warm, for I know how dearly you love them. And the pears are ready to preserve and I may have to do that Saturday evening.

Old Sooky had nine little pigs and I wish you could see them. Didn't lay on a one and they're fat and really growing. Your pa has four shoats he will run in the fields after corn is got up and he'll put them on a floored pen maybe by Thanksgiving.

I look around me and see all the things you remember as well as me. The wooden waterbucket at the back edge of the table, the same dipper, the towel hanging on the nail beside the door. The same old oilcloth, and you know it was faded when you left and all the covering is wore off on the corners and the cloth looks dark and grease-filled. Even the slop bucket is over there, and your Pa didn't take the slops to the hogs tonight. I reckon he felt like it would hurt his sore hands too bad to lug it to the hog pen. Ha. There's even two or three biskits at the top, swelled up with slops, and apple peelings where I peeled them and made dumplings today. The wood box is not as full as it used to be when you young'uns were little. But the reservoir is full of hot water and we can get a bath without freezing to death, even without a fire.

Tobacco's right pretty this year. It cured up bright and there's not as much in the trash grade. The second grade is the biggest with not too much going in the first grade. But you know your daddy wants that first grade to be what he calls "wrappers." There's quite a bit with yellow leaves but with veins of green running through it. I sure hope we can clear a few hundred dollars this year, for we need so many things. And we're not farming next year, son. Your pa just ain't able to do it all. But we'll manage, so don't you worry. Mr. Jim said we could stay on here and someone else would tend the land. I'm glad of that, for we've been here so long it wouldn't seem right nowhere else. When spring comes I'll help people pick tobacco beds, pull plants, chop cotton and put in tobacco. And your pa will too when he's able. And we ought to do right good grading tobacco in the fall. With all the things I've got canned and dried we won't suffer for food. And I've got a few late biddies and they'll come in good.

I nearly forgot to tell you that little Shep has three puppies, and they're a pretty sight. One is pure white and looks like a ball of fuzz. One is white with black spots, and one is solid black. I remember how you used to walk across the yard and holler to Shep and she'd come up and jump two or three feet to try to get you to take her.

We've got a pretty turnip patch and the turnip salad is so good! And we have cured out some sweet taters on top of the shelter and they just set the salad off. And shucks are thick on corn, and you know what they say about it being a cold winter when that's the case. I hope not, for I dread real cold weather and my feet stay cold all the time.

Everybody asks about you at church and I tell them you're doing fine and all that, but still there's an uneasiness that I can't get rid of. But I think about all the others going through the same thing. And I love you son.

Well, it's getting late and I still have to wash off and your pa too. He just passed through and I asked him what he wanted to tell you and he said to say he was doing all right and that he missed you and would be glad when you got back home. The lamp shade has become so black with smut I don't know how I see the paper and I know I've run off of the lines. But you know I'm not a writer nohow and a poor speller. I got hungry while writing so I've been to the safe and forked me out a couple of ish taters and got me a piece of boiled meat and I wish you could be here to eat with me. Here I am getting grease all over the paper. And it's getting chilly in here and I've told you everything that I know. It's not much, for you know as well as anybody that I don't know much. I'm just doing the best I can, trying to stay busy and keep things going and waiting for the day when this war ends and all the boys get back home. That will be a happy day in this old world and somehow I feel like that after the war is over everything will change. It scares me to think about it all.

Be a good boy now, and let me hear from you whenever you can. In my heart I am with you always and I hope that means something to you.

    With all my love,
    Mother

The war dragged on for three years and eight months, but Germany finally surrendered on May 7, 1945. Then on Aug. 6, the United States dropped an atom bomb on Hiroshima, Japan and another on Nagasaki, Japan on Aug. 9. This was the final blow, and Japan surrendered on Aug. 15, 1945, and World War II came to an end. □

No More, No More, No More

P ickins' are slim for the old turkey buzzards that soar above the pines today. A lot fewer of 'em too. We ain't hauling our dead animals up in the woods anymore to feed those old buzzards. Matter of fact, we ain't got the animals no more. A lot of rural America is as animal-free as the city streets today.

And if we had dead animals it would never do to drag 'em up in the woods. The health factor would kill us I reckon. I expect they'd say germs would git up in the polluted air and settle on all of us, and they might have something there. What we did 50 years ago would no doubt kill us today. I reckon we were just healthier then, for we didn't git sick like they do today. And if we did, home treatment cured us.

No more cardboard fillers in those old shoes. No more. No more. No more.

We've got good shoes to wear today. One pair of good shoes costs more than a whole family's 50 to 60 years ago. No more nails sticking through a new heel or half sole that dig into the foot. The old shoe last was thrown away or lost many years ago.

The mills that ground our wheat and corn have rotted away with time and most of the dams broken. Very few mills remain as reminders of the past.

The churches don't look the same. Practically all of them have been completely renovated and bear little resemblance to the former structures. There are stained-glass windows and padded benches and plush carpeting, and additions as well as omissions. Don't seem to be any Amen Corners anymore. But I reckon few would "amen" if there were. And most churches have buildings where feasts are spread inside today. The old-style long wooden tables or tightly-stretched wire tables were long-since outdated.

The chamber pot under the bed is as obsolete as the oil lamp and would provoke laughter unless they were shown in settings such as Williamsburg that are recreations of our past.

No more overalls made from Smith-Douglass fertilizer bags. No more dresses made from print hog-feed bags. No more BVD's made from flour sacks. No more towels made from salt and flour sacks. No more tin or wooden tub baths. No more water buckets sitting on the back porch shelves along with the wash pans and the aluminum or gourd dippers. No more. No more. No more.

No more toting ice from the store and beating it with the wooden mallet or the ax. No more chicken fries at the tobacco barns or neighborhood parties under moonlit skies. No more ironing with flat irons. No more toting a soda bucket. No more rides on tobacco trucks and hauling or toting up green corn for the mules or hauling watermelons from the patch. No more cooking in a hot kitchen on an old wood stove.

No more washings behind the smokehouse and boiling the clothes in the iron pot on the edge of the woodpile. No more scrubbing on a washboard. No more lye-eaten hands. No more patching young'uns clothes over and over and darning socks and starching everything. No more. No more. No more.

Don't look for the "something to eat" on the back of the stove anymore. There ain't none there. Go to a fast-food place today. Our mamas ain't cooking like they used to. Many of our mamas are away from home, helping to make a living, remember.

Don't try to star-gaze through a knothole in the weatherboarding anymore. The rooms have interior walls today. Don't wish for the snow to drift in under the eaves of the house during a night snowfall and light on the patchwork quilts. Don't wish for any of these things for they are from another way of life in another time in our history.

Don't expect the trill of the mockingbird to sound as it did in the past. The song was enchanted then because of youth. Maybe it sounds as beautiful to the young of today.

Let the old beds with their high headboards and fancy designs live in the memory, for they are no more. Let the feather beds remain fluffy and padded out until not a wrinkle shows under the counterpanes.

The old houses are either redone, rotted down or sitting forlornly in back fields overgrown with vines and weeds, or burned down with only old chimneys standing amid the rubble of yesterday. The wells are gone, the hand pumps, the watering troughs.

Where there are hogs today, most of them get their start in "pig parlors" where the large producers raise them for market. The "hog pen" as we knew it is gone. The chicken house is gone. One once in a while, but very rare.

The "slop bucket" beside the stove is only a memory. The mule lot, and even the mule are gone. As far away as that ancient past. No more. No more. No more. The wagons, the carts, the buggies and surries, the cultivators, hay rakes, mowing machines, old-fashioned hay balers, all the implements of old-timey farming left somewhere in the rubble to rust away, to rot with time, to return to the earth.

No more long, homemade tables in modern dining rooms. The long benches are delegated to memories. Reproductions, maybe, but not those we remember. They were ancient in our childhood and we were happy to discard them. Who wanted anything of that past?

Drag out that old foot-pedaled organ with all that fancy woodwork and oval mirror, and if you can't find anybody to give it to, chop it up and burn it. And a modern world can't stand those old center tables with all that crocheted stuff on top.

Throw 'em away. Git rid of that old-timey tin-door safe and the one with the glass front. Throw out that horrible old kitchen cabinet. The old trunks ain't worth a dime. What good is that old pitcher and bowl except to clutter up something? It sat there all those years just an eyesore. And that old washstand too. Git it out of the way and we'll git new, modern furniture to go with a modern world.

And so we did. We left behind much of the old, the outdated, the "junk" that we grew up with and reached for the utopia of the new world. We found a lot of the things our hearts longed for. Many of us were able to have modern homes of our own with all the conveniences — cars, boats and a lot more.

Some acquired wealth. Others were able to live comfortably and a lot have remained poor but are able to live on a higher plane than during that era.

We found that new world and we loved it. It has done all many of us could ask of it except, somehow, it hasn't brought that inner peace that we longed for. It would have been paradise 50 years ago, but we don't think of it in that light at all today.

Somehow, it failed to bring that happiness, that feeling of security we had hoped for. Somehow, there is a nagging feeling that the world ain't right. Amidst all the prosperity there is a loneliness, and something held over our heads that we can't define. We're more selfish today, busier, more unsure of ourselves or our world. Better times, but that utopia is as elusive as ever. □

Memories Of Yesterday

I looked for the mist over the meadow, but there was no fog and the meadow wasn't there. I was on strange ground. I sought directions as to where I was. I needed a landmark. The "big ditch" would put me on the right course. I searched in vain for the ditch, only to find it had long-since been filled with a pipeline and covered over. The trees along the banks were gone, leaving a solid mass of land for cultivation.

The graveyard in the back field would give me proper orientation, and the stones were still there, standing stark in the open field but without the protection of the tall walnut and gum trees that had stood for a century over the burying place, but it wasn't the same. The graveyard had lost its identity.

The old dirt road that once carried traffic to town would be a place to visit that would still hold reminders of my land of the past. It was about all woodsland and few people even traveled the road after the highway was built some distance from the old road. But it was now a paved highway and homes were everywhere. The only reminder of the past was an old oak tree that had acquired its full stature half-a-century ago and still appeared the same, but with the shanty beside it that it had shaded and protected no longer there. The old mill pond was gone. There was not even a path leading to where it had been. There was no sign of the house that had stood on the hill where the miller lived.

There were no overhanging bushes on the sides of the highway; no turtles slowly crossing the road; no cowbells ringing in the distance; no reminders of the past.

Surely on the back roads there would still be a few homesteads where people carried on the tradition of country living, with chickens in the yards, hogs in the pastures, tree-shaded lanes leading to the homes, rabbit paths among the growth on the edges of the forests. But some of the forests had been cleared, most all the old houses gone, all evidence of the past wiped off the map. Brick homes and green lawns were everywhere. Was there even a place for huckleberries to grow anymore?

There were thoughts of days when children walked the roads to school, sometimes with snowflakes striking their faces and the fields becoming white as they hurried home before the storm grew worse; familiar paths and mailboxes along the roads with red flags showing when people had letters to mail; rabbits darting across the road; children laughing and singing; slingshots showing from boys' hip pockets; grape arbors in back yards; houses with the kitchens separated from the living quarters by piazzas.

I looked for mules plowing the fields, but only tractors were there. I thought of the brilliant sunsets, the sunrises, the big dews when spider webs gathered the moisture and showed all the intricate patterns of the web dominating a weed-covered area; the picturesque scenes of autumn; the greenness of summer; the drabness of a rainy day; the joy of nights by an open fire.

I sought desperately for something of a life that had been, still evident in the modern world. It was a sobering experience. The kitchen in the old homes of the past had been the main part of the home where hungry children were filled with home-grown foods and the dining room tables around which much of life centered. Instead, there were restaurants and fast-food places everywhere. Didn't anybody cook anymore? Were all the old recipes buried in the rubble? Then I realized that most of what I refer to as recipes were in the minds of the cooks rather than written down as a guide to good cooking.

I looked for vultures soaring over woodlands in the distance, but then I realized that they had no place, nor little purpose, in the modern world. I listened for the call of the whippoorwill when day faded into night, but there was only silence.

I thought of the untold thousands who never crossed the dividing line that separates the old from the new, and wondered whether those who lost their fight for life were better off than we who have seen it all.

I searched for the warmth and the smugness of yesterday, but it wasn't there. Everything was prettier, in better order, modern and indicative of the trends of the day, but beyond the highways it appeared so lonely. There were no signs of animal life or barnyard scenes. It was as if everything from a long-ago era had been wiped off the face of the earth.

I expected to see children at play in the yards, but none were there. Then I realized that they had all the things to play with in a modern world inside the homes — video games, electronic trains, home computers, television, stereos — all the things to make modern children happy as compared to our homemade contraptions and games that had made our childhoods happy.

I turned in all directions, trying to find the odor of home cooking as it had spread over the area during childhood, only to find disappointment there also. I wanted to feel a cool breeze that I remembered from that world blowing on my face as I surveyed my little kingdom of the past, but it was on a windless day. I wanted to see neighborhood life, but it was only along the highways when cars sped by. I looked for bales of cotton in the yards and piles of loose lint on front porches and corn at corn cribs, but none were there. Some homes of the past still stood, but the surroundings were changed to the extent they bore little resemblance to the way they had been.

Only then did I realize that none of that world could be re-created or duplicated. It had outlived its time and had become a victim of change. There had been no attempt at preservation of a way of life most of the older people of today remember. It could never again live except in the hearts of those who had been a part of that past. Time waits for no man and it takes its toll as days turn into months, then years, then decades as the new overtakes the old, always changing in an endless pattern. □

The Questions Of Youth

We asked: "How will it be and what will we be like?"

That was in the days after we reached young manhood in body with a child's intellect. In our serious moments we stopped to ponder what life would be like, say 25 years hence when we had become middle-aged men. We dared not think in terms of 50 years, for that was an eternity.

There were seven or eight young fellows who were closely associated and we almost knew each other's thoughts. Of course, we carried on and told all about our conquests and how the girls were crazy about us and all of us always wondered whether the speaker was lying. That was a part of being young men, and there were a few "conquests" of a sort that couldn't be ignored. Such conversations took up a good part of our free time, but there were occasions when we talked in a more serious vein. That was usually between only two or three of the gang.

We were boys with almost identical backgrounds who knew nothing of a life beyond the farm except what we had read about, seen in movies, or our observations of city life. But some of us were more aware of our circumstances and the odds stacked against us than others.

There were usually settings for such conversations, like a rainy day when we were under a shelter whittling away on a piece of wood with our pocket knives or walking through a field and observing coveys of birds flying overhead or walking through the snow when the flakes were falling on our faces and clothing. And we never looked into each others' eyes when we talked about the future. Somehow, we couldn't face each other with such intimate thoughts.

One would say, "I don't want this. Look at us. Where can we go from here? What is there to hope for?" Then there would be silence while the mind pondered the prospects.

One might say, "If anybody died we wouldn't even have a suit of clothes to wear to the funeral." This would sink in while we tried to fashion some way of changing our present situation. That is when we ran up against a brick wall. Life was passing. We were teen-agers, ready to enter a world on our own. We weren't prepared.

"I wonder what I will be like and what the world will be like when I'm a 40-year-old man?" one would ask. Then there were visions in which we had lived to be middle age, but with no general idea of what to expect.

We fashioned dreams in those days and they separated two worlds — the world of reality and the world of make-believe. The world of our dreams made the real world more bearable, for time would pass and fortune would favor us and we would have the good life.

We dreamed childish dreams and reveled in our fantasies. That is doné in all societies. We never really expected all our dreams to come true, but we did have the hope that some of our visions of grandeur would some day become a reality.

The years passed. The dreams faded. Teen-agers became men and the real battle of life began. Separate paths, separate ways, each trudging down the path toward his own destiny. We lost the closeness of boyhood. The world changed.

Until death do us part. Marriage. Responsibility. Unto you this day a child is born. Spring. Summer. Fall. Winter. The seasons change. The responsibility grows. Mortgages. Tears. Wisps of blue skies. Despair. Longing. Deprivation. Moving. Seeking the better life.

Hope. Eternal hope. Fear. Prayer. Elusive goals. Sorrow. Sleepless nights. Starless skies. Brilliant sunshine and crops. Renewed strength. Babies, Sickness. Grim rewards. Success. A flash of starlight. Laughter. Songs. Cheer. Christmas.

A house divided. Broken dreams. Divorce. Lost identity. Misplaced children. Lost commitments. Challenge. New determination. Renewed vigor. Gray days. Boredom. More babies. More responsibilities. Quarrels, reconciliations. A bluebird and spring. Lost horizons. Lost youth. Lost years.

War. Terror. The bomb.

Laughing in the rain. Crying in the sunshine. Pent-up emotions. Unfulfillment. Doom. Shock. New beginnings. Faith in God. Faith in country. Faith in fellowman. True blue. American! The "Star Spangled Banner." Sundays. Apple pie. New perceptions.

Disillusionment. Following the web of desinity, predetermined. The all-seeing eye...

Time marches on. Five, ten, fifteen, twenty, twenty five years. Middle age. Gloom. Hippies. Long hair. Ponytails. Sandals. Braless women. An end to tradition. Disbelief. Regrets. Change.

The grim reaper. Death. The circle is broken. So long, old buddy. May you rest beside the still waters. May every beautiful dream now be lived in perfect peace. They were noble dreams. God understands. You tried hard. Now you're the winner.

Shades of gray. Mirrors don't lie. Downhill. Passions cooled. Going to pot. Aging. Remembering "when." What happened? Time — what is it? Relentless, taking its toll. Forgetfulness. Aches. Pains. Stature changing. The good life. Home, car, affluence. Grandchildren. Indulgences. Looking for the man and the woman behind the mask of childhood. The highest mountains. The deepest valleys.

Missing chapters. Loneliness. Pondering. Plodding along. Glasses. Hearing aids. Arteriosclerosis. Drugs. Changing values. A closer walk —. Heart attacks. Hospitalizations. "Patched-up" oldsters. Supplication. Prayers.

Tiny, golden nuggets. Remnants of life after the filtering process. So much lost. So little retained. Shimmering highlights — special moments, special events, happy hours — the drudgery, the mundane forever buried in all the yesterdays.

We squint through the maze of time, searching for those golden nuggets. Something to hold on to. Something to remember.

Time marches on. Thirty, thirty five, forty, forty five, fifty years —.

And we asked: "How will it be and what will we be like?" So many years ago.   □

Judge The Sharecroppers

T oday we stand for final inspection, representing the older segment of our population, which is growing larger daily. We stand proudly, but no more so than when we stood in our gingham dresses and overalls in that ancient past.

We stand for so many who have fallen by the wayside along that long trail.

They were the ones who played the major roles in that world of yesterday and many of them never reaped the rich rewards of affluence. So many of them would have been the most appreciative of the good life. They fought gallant fights, yet lost the battle for their lives.

We climbed toward the mountaintop, inch by inch, along a treacherous path. We ignored the precipices, the deep valleys left behind, and holding on to a toehold, started an ascent that has taken us to the present. And we may not remember what happened yesterday, but events that happened along the way are still fresh in our memories.

We seek no accolades for our accomplishments. They came about through a series of circumstances that worked in our favor. After World War II when things settled down, our entire way of life changed. Even during the war, change was everywhere. People left the farm in flocks, finding employment in defense industries and departing the only way of life they had ever known. Some achieved a higher level of living than had been possible on the farm. Others continued to live in poverty, although most work was less strenuous than farm chores.

Government farm programs were implemented that helped farmers to reap greater yields from their crops. The tobacco program that began in 1933 proved a great help to the farmer. As the economy began to pick up, many who had been tenant farmers and sharecroppers were able to buy their own farms. And even sharecroppers were able to realize a profit from farming.

It wasn't easy, but people who had been used to sacrifices all their lives were willing to sacrifice further to own their own farms.

Veterans returning home from the war were able to get a college education through the GI bill, and many who were educated after serving their time in service today hold positions in high places.

As the economy expanded, the face of rural life began to change. New homes dotted the scene, often in front of old homesteads that were delegated to outbuildings. Old houses were renovated and changed to the extent they were not recognizable as the structures they had been. Rural businesses sprang up along the highways. Customs changed. The rural area was becoming modern. The old ways were cast aside and the ways of the modern world adopted.

Many people did away with all the things that were reminders of deprivation and hardship, much to their regret later. But at that time there was no beauty associated with that era. It was too close to them and had not acquired the mellow glow it radiated later.

Many high schools had been built, and rural children were given the advantages the children in cities had enjoyed for years. Education became all-important, to the rural community as well as the cities. Modern machinery took over in the fields and the mule faded from the scene, along with the lots and the picturesque barnyard scenes, with all the farm implements hauled away to some lonely hillside or up a woods path.

Affluence became a key word in our society. And nowhere was it more appreciated than in the rural areas. The changing face of America merged the rural dweller with the city slicker and they became indistinguishable. Country boys and girls drove the latest model cars, wore the latest styles, and indulged in all the activities of their city cousins.

A few of those who lived the identical lifestyles I have described became millionaires along the way. Others involved in other endeavors became wealthy, while many have lived a poor-person's life, although on a much higher level than in the '20s and '30s.

It has been a long time since the days about which I have written. Most of the momentous pages of history have been written since then, and we are now in another world. Only in the memory does it live today.

We can't go back, nor do we want to. But it is well to look backward to the serenity of those days sometimes and to recall pleasant events that warm our hearts. Many people from that era have to make momentous decisions today, often in crowded dining rooms or around corporate tables. There is no doubt but that it would be easier if they could meet under the shade of a towering tree with a cool breeze swaying the corn and a rural landscape setting the mood. Even a cool drink of well water would be an asset.

But all this would open a floodgate of memories about a life we have almost forgotten. The two worlds are separated by time and they could never merge.

Today we stand to be judged by society. Our life story has been told. We were so very poor, so ignorant of the ways of the world, so isolated from the mainstream. We don't apologize for that. Those circumstances were not of our own making. We held on by a thread, and it became a lifeline that brought us through those days and into greener pastures and the affluence of a modern world.

We are proud of our accomplishments. We forged the way for our children and their children to have a good way of life and most of the things to enjoy during youth as well as adulthood that we never had until late in life. We remain a proud people and proud of our heritage.

Nothing remains to be said as to who we are, how we were and the simple lifestyles of our past. We can say it all with banners waving high and with pride in our hearts. We are the generations of the past who stand today as symbols of what can be accomplished in America.

And now the curtain is being pulled and this is the final glimpse of a close-up look at us in a period now glorified by time. The halo is still bright as the yesterdays become a closed chapter. We can always look backward to what was, but we can't ever tell about tomorrow, for tomorrow never comes. Judge us as you will.   □